Forging Ahead

Recollections of the Life and Times of Esther Dartigue

by

ESTHER DARTIGUE
and John Dartigue

ISBN-10: 1490970851

EAN-13: 9781490970851

Library of Congress Control Number: 2012915660
CreateSpace Independent Publishing Platform
North Charleston, South Carolina

Dedicated to the late Stanley Brossette,
the first to introduce me to genealogy

Foreword

Soon after my father died in 1983, my mother, at the age of 74, embarked on what became a ten-year project of researching, writing, and publishing two accounts of my father's career. The first was in French, Un Haitien exception- nel Maurice Dartigue, *and appeared in 1992. The second,* An Outstanding Haitian, Maurice Dartigue, *she translated from the first (after making a number of revisions) and had it issued in 1994. The undertaking was a labor of love—her two great passions being my father and Haiti—and it allowed her, I believe, to stay more closely connected to him in the years following his death.*

Then in 1995, she turned her energy—and she'd always had lots of that—to writing about my first fifteen years and, as a further gift, began a narrative of her own life. Unfortunately, she stopped at 1947, leaving a good many years undocumented, except for certain passages included in the books about my father, her text about me, published articles, talks at educational conferences, and notations she made on her monthly calendar from 1962 on. I and others encouraged her to pick up where she'd left off, even sug- gesting she speak into a small tape recorder so as not to tire herself. But she never progressed further. It may have been that the pain she experienced daily in her back and shoulders prevented her from properly concentrating, and/ or she had grown weary of writing. Or, possibly, she felt the struggle and drive of her early years and the adventure of Haiti could never be matched and thus viewed the second half of her life as comparatively routine.

There were sources of great happiness for her: my father, Haiti, me, education, literature and the other arts, travel, nature, good food, the books she produced, and a huge circle of close friends and acquaintances from all over the world.

But she encountered challenges as well: growing up poor, childhood beatings, surviving on her own from age 11 to 23, pursuing an education, years of ill health in Haiti, the trials of a sickly child, a revolution, starting over in a bigoted America, caring for my father in his decline, soldiering on after his death, championing my father's work, knee replacements, a brush with breast cancer, and coping with severe pain. But like her astrological sign, Capricorn, she overcame almost all her obstacles. She set out on life's path and kept going, working through one potential roadblock after another—just as when, in the face of a traffic jam, she would say to my father, who was a respectful man behind the wheel of a car as he was in the day-to-day, "Forge ahead!"

It occurred to me, therefore, that my mother deserved a published chronicle of her own, a sort of companion piece to her books about my father, destined for family and friends, drawn from her various writings, in addition to my recollections and those of others, notably my uncle John Reithoffer; my cousins Marie-José Dartigue NZengou-Tayo, David Reithoffer, David Knesper, Lorenz Schwegler, Susan Reithoffer, Carol Hawley Perry, Nancy Knesper Frantz, and Jehan Henri Dartigue; Ghislaine Grant Stecher; Ghislaine Rouzier Ruas; Jacqueline (Godefroy) and Robert Delannoy; Simone Gardère Godefroy; and Chantalle Verna, as well as Noha Akiki, Austin Atherley, Sylvia Washington Bâ, Drew Boatner, Patricia Gould Booth, Sibylle Brandt, Bianca Brandt-Rousseau, Nieves Claxton, Rev. Lorand Csiki-Makszem, Barbara Barron DiPierre, Maria del Rosario Etayo, Carolyn Fick, Hal Fuller, Annette Metis Gallagher, Markku Järvinen, Dr. H. Lee Kagan, Fred Kroll Jr., Ségolène Lavaud, Claude-Hervé Liautaud, Ginette Rouzier Mangonès, Muriel Merceron, Robert Nadal, Jacqueline Pereira, Melissa Pereira, Charles Pierre-Jacques, Adrienne Dufour Seiler, Anne-Marlène Stecher, Meg Benjamin Taylor, Patricia K. Tsien and her daughter Ying-Ying Yuan, Frantz Voltaire, Barbara Wilkins, and Brooke Wooldridge, plus the help of Karolyn Ali, Jim Blume, Fedo Boyer (Creole Translations), Vivian Boyer, John Eakin (Film Solutions), Bette Einbinder, Eda Einbinder, Joan Farber, Jack Golan, Patti Hawn, Bogdan Hladiuc, Claude and Lindsey Jones, Charlotte Kandel, Josiane Mangin, Sabrina Merceron, Alain Morgat (of France's naval archives), Joan Nagler, Marilyn Nelson, OMEP-Haïti, Robert Schwartz, Ida Subaran, and especially Carl Samrock.

*I am extremely grateful to everyone. I was also very for-
tunate in having on either side of the family a cousin interested in genealogy: Marie-José NZengou-Tayo and David
Reithoffer, who are excellent detectives and helped me
immeasurably in this area.*

*The book is a combination of my mother's voice and mine.
It does not claim to be comprehensive; it is a collection of
remembrances, big and small, and more than a touch or two
of the times. It serves as a record of things that had meaning
for my mother, and thus I pruned very little from what she
wrote. Too, it assembles in one place for family members
certain information as presently known about Reithoffer and
Dartigue antecedents. A number of quite different audiences
are being addressed all at once—our American, Haitian, and
German relatives; her Haitian, American, French, UNESCO,
and UN friends; and people who knew her slightly or not at
all. Therefore, certain passages may be boring to some, and
a reader may choose to skim. These may include various lists
whose inclusion, I think, provides a flavor that merely saying "she traveled a great deal" and "she read a lot of books"
doesn't. Also, I have taken the liberty of not using footnotes
because most people don't bother with them, and I wanted
these bits of information seen; consequently, they've been
incorporated into the text, usually parenthetically. One further indulgence: my captivation with Haitian nicknames and
family relationships.*

Some have asked if my mother knew a book would one day be written about her, and the answer is no. When she chronicled her first forty years and my first fifteen, it was to leave me a legacy. I myself didn't start thinking about a book until after her death when, in going through her effects some months later, I said to myself, "Don't be so quick to throw files away. Take them to Los Angeles; you can decide later what to do with them."

The reader may encounter here and there what may appear to be slightly odd phrasing. It is the result of my mother's then-forty years of living in Paris unconsciously seeping into her written English (but, curiously, not her spoken).

I have chosen a somewhat-larger-than-usual typeface to make it easier for those whose eyes (like mine) may be less nimble than they once were.

Chapter One

Vizakna (1908-1914)

(This chapter and the next seven were written by my mother in 1995 and appear largely in normal vertical typeface. Occasionally, I'll interpose something and that will be in italics. [Foreign words and book, play, opera, and magazine titles also appear in italics.])

In the foothills of Hungary's Transylvanian Alps was the town of Vizakna *(pronounced Vee-zäk-na, accent on the first syllable, 'zäk' pronounced like Mach 1, and 'na' like in the final syllable of banana)*. It is still there today, but its name was changed to Ocna-Sibiului after Transylvania was given to the Romanians in 1920 as part of the spoils of the First World War under the Treaty of Trianon, which followed on the heels of the Treaty of Versailles and which Hungary was

1

forced to sign. Just like that, two million Hungarians were deprived of their homeland, culture, and identity!

I was born in Vizakna on December 30, 1908, and named Eszter. Our father János Reithoffer declared the birth on January 4, 1909. Why could he not have had the birth registered as happening on January 1, 1909? I would have been a year younger and could have profited from a whole year, rather than the two days of 1908!

Now in my 86th year, I still smolder over these two facts, but they in no way hindered me in making my way in the world. This is due to a third fact, this time a most happy, wise, decisive act by our father. He sensed that some kind of trouble—an uprising? war?—was coming and wanted to spare his family the terrible consequences. So he decided that we would join his younger (by a year) brother Sándor, who had left Hungary eight years earlier, in the United States.

We owned two houses. One was sold—as was the livestock—for our passage to America, while the other was kept to give us a modest rental income in the U.S. We left in late March 1914. The war began in August with the assassination of the Archduke, and because of the war, we never saw a penny of income from that house, which was taken over by cousins on our mother's side.

* * *

Vizakna (1908-1914)

My first five years, in Vizakna, were quite happy as I remember them. I was a vivacious and sometimes mischievous child. Our house seemed spacious. It was on two floors built against a hill, the upper floor giving on to the street, with windows in the front and the rear, which had an open, narrow porch. In the winter, we slept upstairs. In the summer, the rooms were let to visitors coming for the mud baths for which the town was well known. The Hungarian word for water is 'viz'; hence, Vizakna (water town). I resented giving up the room I shared with my older sister Katalin and having to sleep downstairs. In the summer before my fifth birthday, I climbed a tree, one of whose large branches reached the porch, determined to go back to our room. I had already climbed up and was perched on the branch when I heard our father's strong voice down below saying, "Eszti, come right down." Of course I scrambled back to the trunk and slid down the tree. The wonder was that I had not been afraid nor was I badly bruised. But I did feel the spanking I received.

The back of the house gave on to a large yard, the grounds sloping toward a brook that seemed to be the end of the property on that side. The brook served to water the various animals—several cows, horses, dogs, chickens, and ducks. It was also where our clothes were washed. It was placid and gentle. However, once, I remember, there were heavy rains. We were sent upstairs. Looking out of the back window, we saw the brook become a torrent, carrying down barrels, a squealing pig, a chair, and other objects. I was awed by the power of the rushing waters.

Our drinking water was brought from a well down behind the brook. A girl helper carried it in a bucket on her head. In that same summer of my fourth year, I wanted to go with her. Our mother Katalin (whose name was the same as my sister's) gave me a small pottery pitcher. We arrived at the well. My pitcher was filled and placed on my head. I held on to it with one hand. We had started up the hill when we were attacked by a flock of angry geese. Down fell the pitcher, and away fled I. I suppose the helper chased the birds off and came home later with bucket and water. I got a spanking for the broken pitcher and never went back to the well.

Our paternal grandmother lived above us on the hill. I do not remember ever seeing her, but we had a photo of her: a buxom, white-haired woman dressed in black and wearing a gold watch as a brooch. She seemed austere. I later learned that she would have nothing to do with us because our father had married "beneath his station"—he was of the middle class, while our mother had been a peasant—and as a result had been disinherited. Our maternal grandmother lived down the hill, far down. Once a week or so, we three older children—Katalin, our brother Attila, and I—were sent to spend the day with her. She was usually sitting outside her small house waiting for us, dressed in black with a black kerchief tied under her chin. I did not like going to see her because little was happening there, whereas in our home many things went on in the backyard—the clothes-washing, the dogs, the cleaning of the stables and coops, the grooming, the running in and out of the house. Moreover, we must have eaten well at home because that is what I missed most at our grandmother's. We had only soup and black bread when we visited her. To me it was punishment to have to go there.

By 1913, we were five children: Katalin (born July 1906), Attila (October 1907) and I, who often played together or fought one another; our sister Rózsi (*short for Róza,* July 1910), who was too young to join us; and the baby Arpád *(October 1911)*, who would die in *May 1913, just shy of 19 months,* because of an eye infection *(probably staphylococcus, it has been suggested)*. The day after his death, we were taken into our parents' bedroom, and there was Arpád very quiet, not moving. What interested me was the coin he had on his eye. Evidently I knew about coins because I made a grab for it before I was shunted out of the room.

The following afternoon, our mother went into town. By chance I looked into the bedroom and saw two straw hats with lovely artificial flowers as hat bands. To me they were beautiful. I could not resist putting one on, parading around our part of town without permission, and then sneaking back to leave it where I had found it. On waking up the next morning, there were the hats but with black bands. No more beautiful flowers. I was convinced that the flowers had been removed to punish me for having worn the hat.

I remember nothing of the funeral. Later in the year, on November 1, our mother took me with her to the cemetery in the evening to light candles at the four corners of a grave. I did not know whose it was but enjoyed being with her and solemnly watching candles being lit on many other graves as well.

Since we lived in a mountainous area, our father went hunting. One day in the fall, a terrible noise arose in the stable. I raced over and saw a small pack of bleeding hunting dogs whose tails and parts of their ears had just been cut off. I found this a monstrous act and would not go near our father for days. Another horrible act was the fall killing of pigs. The screams and the butchering were dreadful for me. I hid away until the pig was cut up and the tripe was being cleaned. At that point, it was a different matter, and I looked forward to eating the chitterlings and the delicious sausages our father made.

Santa Claus was unknown to us. It was an angel who brought the Christmas tree and gifts. Although we lived upstairs in winter, on the evening of December 24, we children were sent downstairs. Later, we were taken back upstairs, and when the door was opened, there was a most beautiful tree. "Who brought it?" we asked. "The angel, of course," replied our mother. "Don't you feel the cold air from the open window by which she flew in?" We did have a wide window, which was open at that moment, and I really believed it at the time.

Our father must have been a notable. The reason I think so is that one cold, wintery day, when ice had formed on the windows giving onto the street, our mother hurried to de-ice them by heating water in an open kettle to put on the ledge so we could look out. We kept jumping up and down crying, "Hurry, hurry"—we were so afraid we would miss him. But just in time, we saw him pass by in the first rows of the parade. Later in America, my relationship with him became so strained that I never thought to ask him about this or other occurrences I had not understood.

My sister Katalin and I had a gibberish language we had made up. A visitor and our mother popped in once when we were already in bed. We continued our conversation. I recall our mother remarking, "They must have picked up some English." I did not know what English meant but did think to myself, "How silly! We made it up ourselves."

Our parents spoke to each other in German when they didn't want us children to understand. Was that one of the reasons I later took German in college—so that I could better communicate with them?

It is probable that my grandparents were ethnic Germans whose predecessors had immigrated to Hungary. The first such settlers were imported as far back as 1150 CE when Hungary's then-king established seven Saxon (i.e., German) settlements in the southeastern part of Transylvania to protect and defend the area from foreign incursion. One of those settlements became Hermannstadt (renamed Sibiu more than six centuries later, after 1920), just a short distance from Vizakna, which had once been known as Salzburg. Over time and during the various political configurations, German immigration continued, especially under the Hapsburgs. By 1880, the year my grandfather was born, some 12% of the Hungarian population consisted of ethnic Germans, and as late as 1903, German was still the language of the Hungarian military. Many of the settlers assimilated, which would likely explain why my grandparents spoke both Hungarian and German and why they had Hungarian first names and Germanic last names.

(There is in Vienna a Reithofferplatz [Reithoffer Square], and at one time one could also find a Reithoffer haberdashery, a chain of Reithoffer hardware stores, and a Reithoffer rubber factory, whose former owner was living in New York when Uncle John Reithoffer happened upon him in 1944 after John's arrival on Staten Island to continue his Navy service. None of these were related to us, it turned out, nor were the German Reithoffers with whom Uncle John made contact in the U.S., including a bakery in upstate New York and the Reithoffer Shows in Florida, founded in 1896 [and still active today] to service carnivals and fairgrounds.)

(That kind of information is, unfortunately, not available for my grandmother's maiden name, although the internet does show a German composer and an Austrian trauma surgeon bearing the same name.)

The orthography of my grandmother's maiden name had for years been a point of dispute. Aunt Katherine maintained it was Hasler, Uncle Art and the Cleveland birth certificate for Uncle John stated it was Hassler, and Uncle John believed it to be Haszler.

Confirmation of the correct spelling came only recently from my second cousin David Reithoffer. A Chicago realtor whom in October 2012 France declared a Chevalier de l'Ordre National de Mérite (Knight of the National Order of Merit), he had for some time considered a trip to the "old country" to see what he might unearth to supplement the bits and pieces known to us. During a week's stay in November 2012, David managed to find (in the town of Ocna-Sibiului, formerly Vizakna) the little church in which my grandparents were married in 1905, the official church records for that event and for my mother's birth three years later, and my grandmother's surname, Haszler.

In that same church, David uncovered in some cases (and clarified in others) names from the previous generation: our paternal great-grandfather János Reithoffer (same first name as my grandfather, perhaps a family tradition), his wife/our great-grandmother, the former Zsuzsa Preiner (she of the austere visage and gold-watch brooch), and his brother/our great-grand-uncle József Reithoffer, married to the former Róza Szombati, our great-grand-aunt. Turning to the other side of the family, my maternal great-grandparents were Sára (Papolczi) and András Haszler, and my grandmother had eight siblings: my grand-uncles Imre, Ferenc, Pál, Lajos and two named Károly, both of whom died young, as did a grand-aunt Zsuzsa. (I am using here and elsewhere the less common but more descriptive terms of grand-uncle and grand-aunt rather than great-uncle and great-aunt. With grand-uncle, for example, one can immediately tell that the generational level is the same as grandmother. And the same can be said for great-grandfather and great-grand-uncle.)

David also located the property (now an empty lot) where my mother and the family had lived until 1914, as well as the street's original Hungarian name, Fürdök utca (No. 2), or 'baths street' (which is what the current Bailor strada means in Romanian, or as the French would put it, rue des Bains), since it leads directly to the mud baths and curative waters of the town's huge spa.

(The little church was the Reformed Church of Vizakna, which, its young pastor, the Reverend Lorand Cziki-Makszem, told me in an e-mail, "was built between 1240 and 1280" [Tatar invasions would interrupt its progress] and "dedicated to the Virgin Mary" [without the word 'reformed,' of course]. "During the Reformation, after a short spell as Lutheran, the congregation in 1596 designated itself as Reformed" [part of the movement that swept through various European countries and included, for example, the Dutch Reformed Church]. The building was restored in 1767 and again in 1882, with a helping hand [in the latter case] from a pos- sible relative, Sándor Haszler. The Reverend added that despite communist dictates that Hungarian names be purged from buildings, street signs, and so on, communities have

sometimes been able to hang on to their local identities, as the Reformed Church of Vizakna has. I say a resounding cheer for those who kept and are keeping a part of Vizakna's memory alive!)

Some two months after his trip, David was key to unlocking the biggest Reithoffer family mystery of all: the birth and death dates of the baby Arpád. In his efforts to discover information about his grandparents, David found himself in touch with Bogdan Hladiuc, an archivist with the Roman Catholic Church in Romania, who then dug back one hundred years and miraculously found Arpád's dates. (In "mixed" marriages—my grandmother was Protestant; my grandfather, Catholic—the wedding took place in the bride's house of worship, as did the registration of daughters' births, while sons' births were recorded in the father's church.)

* * *

Because our town was near the border with Romania, Hungarian soldiers were once billeted in our home. The only bicycle ride I ever had was offered by one of these soldiers. I sat on the handlebars. It was very exciting until, on going downhill, the soldier could not swerve away from a rock ahead of us and I fell off and landed on the stony road. I was badly bruised and refused ever to ride again.

I am sure the Romanians had as much disdain for Hungarians going over the border to them as we had for them coming over the border to us. We were warned not to go near any of them. They had a distinctive dress so were easily identified. But we must have had some contact since I knew several Romanian songs and sang them without knowing their meaning. However, Romanians were more welcome than Gypsies, about whom we were told dreadful tales. When we were naughty, we were threatened with being given away to them. Their music was often played or heard and was liked; but when they camped nearby or passed by, we were kept indoors. When I thought I was being punished unfairly or too harshly, I would shout, "You can't be my mother. I have been stolen by the Gypsies and sold to you. A real mother would not treat her child this way."

* * *

Something was happening. This I realized from the hustle and bustle of visitors, transfers, new clothes, and whisperings. Katalin and I were already in bed when our mother opened our door and came in with a visitor. We were so surprised that we used our special language. It was still night. We children were bundled up in heavy coats and taken to the train.

Vizakna (1908-1914)

Years later, my Aunt Katherine (known in Hungary as Katalin) recalled to her younger son/my first cousin David Knesper that this leg of the journey was particularly "difficult, because we were piled into a sort of wagon and obliged to go over the mountains to escape detection. Secrecy was paramount. Other families were leaving town as well"—rumors of impending disturbances or of actual war had been circulating—and "local officials were trying to stem the exodus. Had the family taken the main exit routes, they would have been stopped."

I do not remember the journey, but I shall never forget the lights, the many lights of the great city of Budapest. I now know it was the bridge across the Danube. I had never before seen a real bridge, or a city. To me it was a fairyland, and the bridge was not a bridge but a road in the sky, and the flashing lights of the vehicles were like stars. I have forgotten where we stayed, for how long, and about the train ride from Budapest to Fiume *(then essentially a free city-state within the Austro-Hungarian Empire, today part of Croatia)* to take the boat for America, but not the voyage on the ship *Franconia*. That seemed to go on forever.

We went down the Adriatic, into the Mediterranean, and through the Strait of Gibraltar. Once we were on the Atlantic, the ocean became rough. We were in steerage. I can still see the huge room where we sat to eat bread and soup that slopped over the long, green-oilcloth-covered tables. We sat in rows on backless benches hanging on to our bowls, trying to get a spoonful of soup between the boat's lurches.

In our cabin were three bunk beds. Since I didn't want to sleep alone in a top bunk, I joined our mother in her bed. During a part of the day, everyone was shooed out to the steerage deck. We sat on rolled heavy cordage. The boat heaved up and down. I threw up. After several tries at staying above deck, I was hidden in our cabin on a top bunk with pillows to conceal my presence and was told to keep quiet. Otherwise, I would have been sent outside as all the others were. Fortunately, the sailor who inspected barely opened the cabin door. Once he was gone, I could free myself to stay quietly until the family returned.

Evidently, warned by Uncle Sándor of the awful nature of the food onboard, our father had brought along several smoked salamis, which hung from hooks in our cabin, as well as sugar and jams. Since we had the sausages, we had to have bread. But there was not enough bread at the table to bring back to the cabin. Attila, Katalin, and I found a bread barrel, probably put there to hold what was left over from the upper deck. It was decided that Attila and Katalin would lift me up and hold me while I bent over headfirst into the barrel to reach for the bread. One of my hands held on to the barrel edge, while I grasped the bread with the other and handed it to them. One day, they let go of my legs and ran away. My head went down into the barrel, my legs beating the air. Luckily, I was lifted out by a deckhand, roundly scolded, and made to understand not to do it again. My brother and sister had seen the deckhand and, frightened, had run to hide. I refused to go back after that.

Chapter Two

Cleveland (1914-1926)

The last image I have of the *Franconia* is of its stopping in New York Harbor. It was April 5, 1914. We were ready to get off and were watching the maneuvers. I held my favorite stuffed animal, a gray-and-white rabbit. Well, I let go of it, and it fell into the harbor. What a great loss that was to me!

Like thousands of others, we waited for clearance at Ellis Island, and the wait was interminable. We were told to sit on one of our two huge trunks since there were no chairs. The one I sat on was of reed or bamboo and contained the bedding and linens; the other, made of wood, with a rounded top, contained dishes, pots and pans, and other household articles. The trunks were at least a yard high, a yard-and-a-half long, and almost a yard wide. Until recently, the wooden trunk was kept throughout the many moves the family made over the years.

Our first names were Anglicized: our parents became John and Katherine, while we children were henceforth known as Katherine, Otto, Esther, and Rose.

When we finally were on the New York City wharf, Uncle Alex or Al (as Uncle Sándor was now called) was there to meet us. I only recall that we were taken on a train to Cleveland—the ride, like the *Franconia*, seemed never ending—and we stayed in our uncle's home for a while. There I became, temporarily, a somnambulist. I walked in my sleep or crawled or slithered along the floor. Once, I found myself out in the street in the middle of the night. This happened even when we came to live by ourselves. I grew out of it when I was eight years old.

My cousins David Reithoffer and Susan Reithoffer had heard, as part of family lore, that their grandmother Agnes and my grandmother Katalin/Katherine did not get along. (Agnes still thought of her in-law as a peasant and didn't hide it.) Their grandfather Sándor/Alex didn't like the way his brother treated his kids. (For example, in a variation on the notion of droit du seigneur *[the rights of the lord of the manor], János/John was in the habit of taking for himself all the meat prepared for the family's dinner, leaving the children only potatoes and vegetables.) And "when Sándor and Agnes discovered that we had brought no money with us, we were thrown out," Aunt Katherine recounted. (She suspected that her father had had to pay a bribe to get on the* Franconia.*) The family was for a while "homeless and lived in a lean-to."*

We moved many times. Uncle Al lived on the East Side in the Collinwood area. We moved for a time to the West Side but returned to the East, where our father joined Uncle Al as a barber.

The brothers had been barbers in Hungary, and, Agnes Reithoffer told Susan and David, their clientele included Carol I, the king of Romania (born a German prince, Karl, of the powerful house of Hohenzollern), who came to the throne as ruler in 1866. (He was not proclaimed king until the defeat of the Ottomans in 1881.) Never mastering Romanian, he seemed to prefer being tended to by German-speaking barbers. Agnes said she was once invited to the royal palace (Peles Castle, in Sinaia), after which she told her husband, "We're crazy to leave this and go to America" (which they nonetheless did in 1906). But, like anything else, royal appointments need not be lifetime guarantees. In October 1914, at the age of 75, Carol suddenly died, and it is possible his successor, his nephew Ferdinand, though German-born and -raised like his uncle, might not have retained the royal barbers.

* * *

We were quite poor. I remember staying home because I had no shoes and a truant officer coming to ask why I was not in school. Since among the three eldest children there was only one decent pair of footwear, we took turns going to school. The truant officer, out of great kindness, took me that day to buy shoes.

We received food tickets *(perhaps the forerunner of food stamps, which actually didn't come into use until 1939).* We had a wagon and had to go on foot to the Fisher grocery store (for us children it was at a great distance) in rain and snow, over a bridge, below which were the railroad repair shops of the New York Central. That Fisher store was the only one that honored the tickets.

I also recall going to get milk in a pail for our evening meal, which often consisted of cornmeal mush and milk. (There were other times when we might have soup with either veg-etables alone or sometimes with bits of meat added.) Winter evenings were dreadful. I had to be so careful not to spill the milk, for if I did, I was punished despite the fact there was ice on the sidewalks or I had to run from a barking dog. The milk was sold by pint and quart dippers. We had it fresh for supper and the rest boiled for breakfast, along with chicory and bread.

Fat for cooking and spreading on bread was made from beef or pork suet cut into cubes and cooked down. The cubes became translucent and crisp as they gave up the fat. These, called cracklings, were scooped up with a sieve and salted, and we who had been eagerly awaiting them quickly wolfed them down. Another pleasure for me was permission to eat bread that had been toasted, rubbed copiously with a clove of garlic, spread with fat, and salted. In fact, I ate so much garlic that Katherine and Otto refused to walk with me to school. I probably reeked of it.

In the spring, we collected elderberry blossoms. They were dried and used for tea, into which was put a teaspoon of rum and a teaspoon of sugar for fevers or colds. We also picked elderberries, from which a sweet wine was made that was offered to the few visitors we had. No regular wine was ever served. Neither our mother nor our father drank or smoked.

Our brother Arthur was born on a cold, dark day in February 1915. (*He was actually first known as Arpod, in remembrance, I imagine, of the baby who died in Vizakna, though one vowel was changed, perhaps superstitiously.*) We were living on the West Side, in two small rooms and a kitchen of sorts, with a privy in the yard. Katherine, Otto, Rose, and I slept in one large bed; our parents, in another. At the time of Arthur's birth, we were all at home, huddled in a corner of the kitchen with our father at the door to the other room where our mother was in bed. We were angry and anxious because we could not see her. A woman was with her, and our mother was moaning. Finally, we were allowed into the room, and there was our new brother.

Sister Elsie (thereafter known as Betty) was born in June 1918. We were living on Hale Avenue, not far from the main street that led over the bridge to Nottingham. It was there that we learned about the end of the First World War. A great noise of drums, kettles, and tin barrels made us run out into the street to see at a distance an impromptu parade by the railroad workers, some black-faced from soot, beating with anything on anything they had found to celebrate the war's conclusion.

Then we had the flu—*the world pandemic known as The Spanish Flu that is said to have killed between 20 million and 40 million people worldwide in just two years.* The house had an upstairs, but as more of the family became ill, beds were brought down and filled the living room. Everyone was sick except my sister Katherine. She took care of all of us. I was in bed with my father because I had awful nosebleeds with high fever. It was he who watched for them, staunched the blood, and put cold compresses on my head and neck. We had no doctor. The public nurse came in only when we were all better and Katherine finally had come down with the flu.

It was also in that house that I had the measles. I was placed on the dining-room table, which had been made into a bed so I would not be alone upstairs and it would be easier to take care of me. Later, I spilled two quarts of boiling milk over my right arm when the dishcloth I was using to remove the pan from the stove caught on the gas tap. Huge blisters formed, and my first reaction, luckily, was to run to the sink and let cold water splash over the arm to cool it.

We moved to Grovewood Avenue, where sister Susan was born in November 1919. We had four rooms upstairs with a cold-water bathroom and no central heating. A pot-bellied stove was used to heat the sitting room/bedroom, while the wood and coal kitchen stove did whatever it could. The door to our bedroom (with two large beds—one for Rose and me, and the other for Otto and our father) was tightly shut, so it was cold, very cold inside, and our icebox was a shelf in that room. We dressed and undressed quickly to rush into the warm kitchen, where we had our weekly Saturday night bath in the large round washtub set on the floor. Our mother first bathed the little ones before Katherine took her turn, and then I. Otto stayed in the living area. When it was his turn, we were either in the sitting room/bedroom or in bed. Although our mother started with a clean tub, it was only partially emptied to put in more hot water, heated in the large clothes boiler. On Sunday, we put on clean underwear and stockings, which lasted the week. We all wore long-sleeved, long-legged, cotton-knit underwear; the women's had a drop-down with three buttons in the back, while the men's had slits both front and back.

In the kitchen, we ate, we studied, we played, and the weekly laundry was done as well. Many objects were stored on the back porch, among them the baby stroller. During the time we lived there, a pair of robins nested in the stroller. They built their nest in the seat in the spring, and from that point on, we were careful not to make noise going up and down the stairs or in and out. Since our bedroom window gave on to that part of the porch, by lifting the curtain slightly aside we could watch the progress of the three fledglings. When they all flew off, we again took possession of that part of the porch.

While we still lived on Grovewood, our father brought home our first gramophone. I think it was "His Master's Voice," with horn and turn-handle. The first records were Enrico Caruso's "O Sole Mio" and Emilio de Gogorza's "La Paloma." I was enchanted. We were not allowed to touch the machine and were deprived of hearing it whenever our father thought we had not behaved well enough to have the right to listen to the records.

At this house, we had playmates—the three downstairs and others from the neighborhood—because of the play area our father had created by building two swings, a seesaw, and a turnabout (a board the size of a seesaw, rotating on a knee-high pivot so we could go round and round, pushing it or being pushed, until we became dizzy). One day, my dress caught in the pivot. I managed to have the board stopped by screaming just as the last of my dress wound into it and I was tight up against the board. My screams brought out our father who removed me and the shredded dress and gave me a hard beating with the leather strap that often left welts across my back. (As if the accident had been my fault! I resented it.)

I never saw either Katherine or Rose beaten, but Otto and I often were. (*In actuality, Katherine was also beaten, she told her son David "with considerable distress," and "started to run away from home as early as the age of six" because of it. She knew that Rose and my mother were beaten, too, but was under the impression that Otto "got off easy" [which of course was not the case]. My first cousin Carol Perry, Aunt Rose's daughter, said her mother did not talk much about her family life; but every so often a remark would slip out, and one day Rose did say that she had been beaten.)*

The four younger children—Arthur, Betty, Sue, and John— have much happier memories of home life. Evidently, with them, our father was much less severe and demanded much less in the way of proper behavior, playing with them and letting them talk at table.

Halloween was the biggest outdoor event. We were told not to join the group of revelers, but I did, despite the possible beating. We put pins in door bells, displaced the short porch steps, built bonfires in the field, and burned leaves. The fires left a special feeling of freedom and created the fragrance of fall. We had no fear.

We celebrated both Christmas and Easter. Whereas in Hungary it was an angel who brought the gifts, in America we soon knew about Santa Claus. No matter how poor we were, there were always presents and a candle-lit tree. Since my birthday was on December 30, it was too close to Christmas for any separate present, except once when I received a new pair of galoshes. Gifts usually consisted of new underwear or bonnets, and one toy. Breaded pork chops were served, along with a homemade cake. For Easter we were also given presents, and we had colored eggs. We brought the custom from Hungary, for there, too, we had exchanged colored eggs or oranges, which for us at the time were a great luxury. We had very little candy, and chocolates were unheard of.

Most everything we wore was homemade, or remade by hand, hand-me-downs from charity barrels, or gifts from other people. (I got my first new dress, made for me from new material and a bought pattern, when I was 14.) Our clothes were largely washable—no dry cleaning; we did not even know such stores existed. Once, we were given fluffy, white woolen berets. Our father would clean them with white flour, dipping them, rubbing them together, then shaking them outdoors.

Every so often we would go to the movies, and I especially recall Pearl White and her adventures.

One day, I was visiting the owners of the house, who lived downstairs. They were an Italian family. The father worked in a foundry. He seemed far younger than the woman who kept house and looked after the children, three girls our age. Their breakfast consisted mostly of bread and watered-down wine in a soup plate. A large round of cheese was kept under the bed in the couple's room, which was locked; when a piece was needed, the cheese was withdrawn, and a chunk hacked off. They never came upstairs, but we children often went to sit with them. Their customs seemed so interesting, one of which was to catch and squash hair lice. So there I was on a Sunday morning with them, sitting on a chair holding

Betty, when one of their children passing behind me tipped my chair forward. Clutching Betty in my left arm, I thrust out my right arm and hand to cushion my fall. The floor was an old wooden one. As my hand hit the floor at an angle, a splinter was driven under one of my fingernails. Of course Betty cried loudly. A shout from upstairs bade me bring her up. Our mother took Betty, while our father brought out the strap and gave me a beating. Betty had been frightened but not hurt. I had been frightened and hurt. When after an hour I was still crying, our father said, "Why are you still crying? Surely the beating could not have hurt you that much." I answered, "It is not the beating that hurts, but my hand." On looking at it, he realized how serious it was: a splinter from the dirty floor wedged between the nail and my flesh. He immediately took measures. He had me sit on a kitchen chair on the porch. Our mother held one of my arms, Otto the other, and Katherine and Rose grasped a leg each. Our father started and cut out half the nail to extract the splinter. Those holding me were hard put to keep me still enough so he could operate. I screamed and wriggled in desperation, but it had to be done. Neighbors all around were outside or at their windows, wondering at the screaming. The pain was simply dreadful. The signs of the injury to that nail, though much reduced, are still evident today.

(*Aunt Katherine told her son David that her father had "wanted to be a doctor, but his parents thought he should become a priest. At the time, it was possible for children to be taken away involuntarily to join the church. So to avoid this fate, at age 14 he ran away from home and joined the army." My mother, too, was under the impression that her father had done military service, as a medical assistant in the Balkans. Uncle John, who became a barber, as did Uncle Art, doesn't remember his father ever talking about the military but recalls being told that in Hungary, at the time, barbers were required to serve an apprenticeship during which they received medical training [in case that straight razor went awry and no doctor was handy, especially in the hinterlands].* In some way, then, our father had picked up enough medical knowledge to take care of the family for most illnesses and injuries. He brought me through a severe ear infection with his concoctions. We called a doctor or visited one only when our father knew he could not handle the matter, as when Arthur caught diphtheria and we all had to be vaccinated. (A sign was placed on the front door, warning people of the contagious disease inside.)

When Otto and I needed to have our tonsils removed, we were taken to the hospital, but afterward I felt terribly deceived. I'd been told I would have red cheeks once the tonsils were out. Our father did often have pink cheeks. Our mother, who had dark, straight hair, brown eyes, and tannish skin, never did. I was hopeful. After returning home and being allowed to go out, I raced up and down the street, feeling the cold wind on my cheeks. I then hurried upstairs to look in the mirror, only to find my cheeks as sallow as ever.

What I liked about this house on Greenwood was that it had an attic to which I could escape by a ladder in the bathroom. I would pull the ladder out, climb up, lift the attic cover, clamber in, reach down to put the ladder back in place, and shut the cover. There I stayed, hoping no one knew where I was so that I could read without being interrupted by anyone for anything. In winter, it was out of the question. In summer, it was often hot, but it was a haven of peace and quiet.

On the other side of the street, there had been woods, now cut down, except in one corner. This area stretched a few blocks toward the amusement park called Euclid Beach. (Beyond it, just opposite the park, were cornfields for the popcorn supplied to the beach.) The tree roots had been dug up whole and left lying on their sides. During the rains, the holes became small ponds in which tadpoles and frogs thrived. Violets, jack-in-the-pulpits, pussy willows, and so many field flowers grew there. I went often, even though in the summer we were terribly bitten by mosquitoes and sometimes stung by bees. We were careful of snakes. In the trees nearby were squirrels. I spent hours in the field, walking, climbing or sitting still, watching birds or squirrels or contemplating a flower.

In back of our house was a garden with a shed. Our father grew vegetables (which everyone else with a garden did, too) and kept rabbits in the shed. (I watched him skin them, which later served me well in Haiti.) Beyond were other gardens and sheds and the backs of houses whose fronts gave on to the next street. From our rear porch, I often looked at the backs of two houses. In one was a returned soldier who lived with his sister's family. He evidently had not found a job, for he was either on the back porch or sitting under the trees near the cornfields. I sometimes sneaked out to chat with him. To me he was so handsome.

In the other, a small house, there lived a black couple. She had graying hair. They were very quiet. They had a grown son, whom at first we saw only once in a while. Then he came to stay. We learned he had pneumonia. His mother nursed him, but he did not recover. The death was a shock to me, and for days after the funeral—which to my eyes was an extraordinary affair with funeral carriages, flowers, people— I mourned him and felt how unfair it was that the old couple would now be terribly alone.

We lived for a time on Calcutta Avenue, where our father rented a house with a shop in front, and next door was an empty lot where he made a garden. When the tomatoes were ripe, I would slip in and, hidden by the cornstalks, would take a large ripe tomato and bite with delight into the flesh warmed by the sun. I was never caught, or perhaps I was seen but never punished. We worked in the various gardens our father cultivated—on Calcutta, Grovewood, and another street whose name I've forgotten. I did not like the evenings we spent taking the green caterpillars off the tomato plants and throwing them into the bonfire, or hoeing around the corn and bean plants or picking them.

The first time I saw eggs being served for breakfast, my eyes opened wide. It was next door, at my first job of house-cleaning, at the age of 9 or 10. The lady of the house, after explaining to me what there was to be done and before leaving to go shopping, said I could eat whatever was on the breakfast table. I saw eggs. She said I could eat as many as I wanted. I fried two, then three more. I ate five fried eggs and bread generously spread with real butter and jam.

Despite the hardships and the disappointments that befell us in the New World, our father remained who he had been in Vizakna. He was concerned about his looks, especially his mustache, which was cut or kept with ends upturned like that of the Kaiser, using a special net over it at night that was held by thin elastic bands behind his ears. He often played on a rosewood shepherd's flute, which to me sounded beautiful. He also wrote poetry and read a few books. (While he read we dared not move or talk, or else we would be beaten.)

He took up spiritualism. Many Sunday afternoons, he led us a long distance on foot to a meeting at which a preacher talked, then went into a sort of trance, and called out names of loved ones passed away, with individuals in the audience claiming a relationship. People also put objects—watches, earrings, rings, a small personal possession of some kind—on the table in front of him. The preacher would pick one of the objects and describe to whom it might have belonged, as well as events that had occurred or would occur in the future. I liked the singing, and to this day I sing a few of the songs, such as, "To the work, to the work, we are servants of light/Let us follow the teachings of reason and right." We were also taken to séances, where tables were supposed to be lifted or pushed in the dark and voices from the past were going to be heard. But the table never rose in my presence, nor did I ever hear a voice. Our father gave us the freedom to choose our own religion or none. I did shop around and was Catholic for a few weeks, then tried various Protestant denominations, subsequently went to a Presbyterian college, then in New York took a course in comparative religion, later attended Ethical Culture, and now am without any religion.

On a few Sundays in the summer, we went with our father to parks with a picnic lunch. Or he paid visits to friends, often taking us with him either on foot or on the streetcar, which we invariably had to leave quickly because I was prone to motion sickness. When he had a free moment from cutting hair, he sold combs and brushes until the time when he was demonstrating the strong qualities of a comb by throwing it to the ground and to his dismay a tooth broke. When we first arrived in America, he also made sausages, buying the meat, the spices, the casings, and the apparatus. He priced them, and after school two of us, pulling the wagon, tried to sell them from house to house. Often it was very cold, and there were times when we were driven away.

Another chore was to go after school with the wagon and two empty burlap bags to find bits of wood from building sites to feed our stoves. We would first remove our school clothes and put on old ragged ones. Instructions were that we come back with two full bags. We were sometimes chased and occasionally met other children on the same quest, which led to fights as to who had first rights. For a while, this wood was the only fuel we had. Fortunately, houses were being built, leaving odd pieces for the taking.

We were never without a dog. Our father would bring home another when one died or did not return. One I recall was Blacky, a black-and-white dog that followed me everywhere, especially when I went to fetch the milk in the cold and dark of winter (there were few streetlights and lots of dark places), a much longer walk than I had had before. Dogs avoided Blacky, so I did not have to stop for dog fights, though why they gave him a wide berth I never understood.

As we grew older, we were given more and more chores. Apparently I was stronger than Katherine. Most days when I came home from elementary school, diapers were waiting for me. After putting the tub between two chairs, our mother would have bathed the babies and then soaked the diapers. I washed them and then boiled and rinsed them. I did all that scrubbing and lifting. It also fell to me to scour the wooden kitchen floor on Saturdays. It was hard work to get out the grease spots. I hated it, and if it was not done to our father's liking, he used the strap to show his displeasure.

Our father managed with his shop, his hobbies, his friends, and our outings. Our mother managed, but at great personal cost. It is because I witnessed the changes in her over the years that I decided that if I married, I would have only one or two children. I remembered her in Hungary, a handsome woman. There we had help. The main thing I recall her doing was baking, perhaps because the smell of bread in the oven kept me close to her. She would let us have a bit of fresh bread as soon as it was cool enough to eat. I also remember her putting clean sheets on shelves. She took with her to America a dress of purple taffeta, high-necked, long-sleeved, the skirt sweeping the ground. When she had worn it in Vizakna, I thought she was beautiful. She never wore the dress in the New World. In Hungary, she had been the mistress of a household. In America, she became an overworked drudge. Only after the first primitive washing machine came out and enough money had been scraped together to buy one did the task of hand-washing all the sheets and all the clothing of the growing family end. It was backbreaking work to heat pails of water, fill the wash-tub, throw the water out, then boil the sheets and towels, followed by hanging everything outdoors and then ironing. Besides these onerous tasks, our mother had to put together our meals from the little money she had to work with.

In America, our mother made no friends. She stayed at home, barely going to the store. She had no money, except for absolute necessities.

At the age of 35, our mother got her first false upper teeth. We were so happy to see her with new teeth since she had been toothless and eating only soft food for some time.

Cleveland (1914-1926)

In March 1924, in her 38th year, our mother gave birth to her last child, our brother John, her ninth during the course of eighteen years. By this time, she bore little resemblance to the woman who had left Hungary just ten years earlier.

We had moved by then to the Hungarian section of Cleveland in and around Buckeye Road, where the family, though changing houses from time to time, remained until it set down roots in 1934 in Auburn Corners *(a name seemingly straight out of Thornton Wilder's* Our Town*)*.

* * *

School was not pleasant the first year in America. Katherine, Otto, and I were put into a special class to learn English. It was in a prefabricated room, and our coats hung in the cold vestibule. One day, I did not want to go to school because I had a handkerchief tied around my head to protect my swollen cheek which hurt from a toothache. I had to be dragged to school, but I refused to go beyond the vestibule. Finally, the teacher, hearing my sobbing, came to fetch me. Another time, I was humiliated when my underpants fell off as I ran around the classroom while we were playing cat and mouse. I flopped to the floor and refused to budge. I sat there huddled until class was dismissed and the teacher found a safety pin. In the fall, Katherine skipped to third grade, Otto passed into second grade, and I stayed to do the year over again because of my age.

Our father preferred Katherine, and our mother preferred Otto. I was odd man out. In various ways I noticed the difference in the treatment I received, and I resented it. Perhaps this was why I decided to do as well or better in school to prove my worth. There were times when I was discouraged and felt unloved.

Although the family moved seven or more times, we children attended the same elementary school. It was called Memorial School, named for the building that had burned down, killing over 170 children. The grounds on which the old school had stood were turned into a memorial garden through which I often wandered. It had stone seats where I would sit. To me it was paradise. The daffodils, tulips, jonquils, narcissi, and roses lifted my heart.

In the third grade, the teacher was sympathetic and often asked about our father, who had developed a heart condition after diving into the lake on a very hot day to save a drowning woman. In the fourth grade, our young teacher made us put our arms behind our backs while we were seated, saying it was good for us; but it was very uncomfortable. In the fifth grade, we had a substitute whom we all disliked. One day, we brought vegetables of all kinds and some eggs, and while she was out of the room, we had a terrific time throwing the vegetables at the front of the room. The tomatoes especially made a splash; the other vegetables, a wonderful thumping sound; and the raw eggs crashed against the blackboard. The whole class was made to stay after school because no one would say how it all started.

There were a number of sixth grade classes, and I was so happy to be put in one housed on the school's top floor, accessible by a special staircase. My hope, as I had grown and gone from grade to grade, had been that I, too, would one day go up and down those special stairs. Our room was large and windowed on one side, and I sat next to the window. In back of me sat a boy who had no mother. To me this seemed so strange and awful. How could he live alone with his father? Who cleaned house? Who cooked? Who washed their clothes? He and I talked when possible. Our teacher, Miss Jergens, was pleasant and understanding. We began class each morning with songs and a story. I remember especially Kipling's "How the Elephant Got its Trunk" and "How the Chipmunk Got its Stripes." She had us put on plays. School became a refuge in that room and with that teacher. If only everyone could have such an outstanding teacher.

During the winter of that year, I was asked to substitute-teach in the first grade. Teachers were absent, and no substitutes could be found. I enjoyed it very much and was supported when necessary by the first-grade teacher in the next room. The children behaved well, and it was because of this experience that I decided to become a teacher. I can still see myself standing in front of the room, reading to the class.

There were no graduation ceremonies. We were given our report cards and told which junior high school we had been assigned to for the coming fall.

* * *

I had lived at home through the sixth grade, and then I left. I felt it was too much for my father and mother to take care of all of us children. And so, from the age of 11, I was on my own.

I immediately went to work for board and room and pocket money and continued to do so through the twelfth grade. Often the homes where I worked and resided were far from school, I often lacked carfare which made for hours of walking, and often my lunch was a thrown-together sandwich while the others around me had full cafeteria trays.

I entered the seventh grade at Collinwood junior high, determined to complete my education. The two years spent in that school were not the happiest. It was overcrowded, and we picked up hair lice.

On the other hand, it was at Collinwood that we were introduced to music, such as *The Mikado,* and taught the basics of cooking, as well as sewing and some embroidery. We also took gym, dancing, and art. For these I have always been grateful, for they turned out to be very useful. The whole area of American literature opened up to me, and I read avidly wherever and whenever I could, even in the school bathrooms. Once after school closed, I was found by the cleaning lady in the toilet, having forgotten time and place. A public library was close to the school. To me literature was precious. *The Scarlet Letter,* "The Song of Hiawatha," "Evangeline," and "The Gift of the Magi" stand out in the school course. Liking to read and being able to borrow books made life seem less barren.

In my situation, I didn't feel I could make friends. Several times I changed jobs and therefore residences when I thought to find a better position or I did not meet the needs of the household. In one home, my sphere was the kitchen and the back staircase. In another, I cleaned and helped cook. In an Orthodox Jewish home, I was asked not to stay during the week of Passover. Most were families with young children. Sometimes, I had a room next to the children or with them. At other times, I slept in an attic room, and once on a hideaway bed in the dining room. Through it all, I was approached only once, by a drunken guest, to whom I said, "Aren't you ashamed of yourself for drinking so much?" He snuck off. However, from working in these families, I learned a great deal about social manners, child care, and cooking.

Each family had its own ways; each couple was different and special. In two of them, the husband was a much older man, a widower, and probably married to his secretary or coworker. It was amusing to note how the younger wife tried to live up to her husband's demands. In one home, it was kippers and boiled potatoes for Sunday breakfast. In another, the couple was young, not well off, and with a young child. Since the wife sought to combine home and career, the husband had some chores, among them feeding the baby on the evening I came in late from school. Once, I found him holding a small burned pot out of the window, with the wind blowing the fumes back into the kitchen and the baby in its high chair gazing transfixed at the antics of her father. In another family, the young child refused to eat unless it was told stories so dramatic that in listening to them it opened its mouth automatically and downed whatever was on the spoon. In a fourth home, the two children, four and six years old, had whooping cough, and I had to hold their tummies while they whooped and brought up phlegm. Fortunately, I did not catch the disease. It was with this family that I learned to use an electric stove, the time it took to heat for cooking, and also the advantage of using the heat that remained in the oven to cook, say, prunes after the heat was turned off.

The Snow family stands out in my memory. Mrs. Snow wore her thick, long, light-chestnut hair in a braided crown. The couple had a beautiful home, built just opposite the new golf course. I helped cook and served at dinners. (I also gave French lessons to their two little daughters since I was taking it in high school. Not that they learned any, but the parents were proud to be able to say that their daughters were learning French.) I ate in the breakfast room with the children.

It was here that I had my first contact with a black girl just a little older than myself. She came to clean and iron. Through her I learned about the discrimination and exploitation of blacks. She was bitter and even complained about the difference in the treatment I was given. I tried to explain that I received almost no salary and was doing this to be able to get through school. She answered that even school was denied her because her family was in desperate need. Social services at the time were minimal or non-existent.

I also house-sat for the Snows, for which I was paid. They owned a superb police dog named Hector. As long as he spent the nights at home, I slept in one of the bedrooms, knowing Hector would take care of any intruders. But once, Hector stayed out for three nights! Alone in the residence, I decided that the safest place for me was in the nearest bathroom, since it could only be opened from the inside. There was no key or key hole. I piled blankets into the tub and slept in there, not caring whether any or every piece of furniture was taken away. Of course I never told the Snows, and luckily, the house was not broken into.

In my last year of school, not only did I live far from it and not only did I have to dust and prepare breakfast, but on my return I had to prepare dinner and clean the kitchen, often not getting to my room to study before 10 pm and staying up until 4 am doing my homework. On Saturdays, I worked in the electrical furnishing stand at Kresge's five-and-ten-cent store near the public square. We sold bulbs, plugs, wire by the yard, and the like. During the summers, I worked extra jobs to make more money. It was quite a feat staying in the upper third of my class while managing all that work.

* * *

Glenville High School, which I began to attend in 1923, was well structured. It had a truant officer, Joseph Bendler, and a social worker, Margaret Hastings. These two kept me from giving up. (I also received support from a Miss Maize, whom I met through Mr. Bendler.) Mr. Bendler took notice of me because of my absences. He came to understand my working/living situation and brought me to Miss Hastings' attention. She showed me great kindness. She had a cottage in the country and invited me to stay with her on several weekends. In the bedroom I occupied, I could hear an old windmill groaning away in the night. I never became accustomed to this sound, yet I preferred to awaken often in the night rather than not have the delight of being there. We had breakfast on a small terrace with the morning sun on us and goldfinches flying about. We worked in the garden, had a small lunch in the kitchen, then dined on the west terrace with the evening sun and, again, the goldfinches. There were other birds, but the finches were more in evidence. The wildflowers in the fields where we often walked in the evening also enchanted me. I kept in touch with Miss Hastings long after I had gone to Haiti.

News of my efforts to go on to college must have gotten around, for one day, my Latin teacher, Miss Campbell, left an envelope on my desk as she went about looking at our notebooks. I did not open it until after class. In it I found a $5 bill and a note saying, "Don't give it back and don't thank me. Some day do likewise." I had never had a conversation with her. Another time, I missed a math exam. When I returned to class, the teacher, whose name I've forgotten, said after I had explained my absence, "You don't have to take the exam. I'm sure you would have gotten a good grade as you usually do." I am not so sure, but I was very grateful. The one teacher who was not encouraging was a Bostonian who taught English in the eleventh grade. One day, she came out with, "I don't see why you are trying to go to college or how you will manage to do it." I looked at her and without saying a word walked out. Fortunately, in my last year, my English teacher was Miss Limback, a recent graduate of Wooster College. She, in contrast to the Bostonian, urged me to persevere. She drove me down to Wooster one weekend to see the campus and to speak with various people. Through her efforts and those of Miss Hastings, I did receive a tuition scholarship and did receive my bachelor of arts degree from Wooster.

I found my early adolescence painful. I had an awkward body; I seemed all arms and legs, and my hair was straight.

My hand-me-downs were not always the best fitting. Then at the age of 15, I began to be pretty despite my braids and the secondhand clothes, which I learned how to arrange to better effect. Our father refused to let us cut our hair. I wanted to cut mine, since bobbed hair had come into vogue, and I wanted to be like others. I took a pair of sewing shears and lopped off my braids. After our father gave me a good talking-to, he was obliged to finish the job properly. Then he gave in to my sisters. Clara Bow, at the time a wildly popular movie star with short hair and bangs, knee-high dresses, and rolled stockings, became our model.

I liked to dance. There were public dances, and for a modest sum one could spend the evening dancing with whoever asked. Several men came, as I did, just to dance. I went alone and came back alone. I was a bit ashamed of this activity, so I told no one about it. Only once did I see a schoolmate. Since he was as embarrassed as I was, he turned away. We never mentioned it in school.

Katherine had found that being a governess in a wealthy home was quite rewarding—no expenses for living, plus windfalls of dresses, from which I also profited. We saw each other on Sundays at home, where we were expected on our days off. We often dated together, not always in harmony and often as rivals. But these frictions were of short duration. We also went to the Hungarian get-togethers, where we danced the *czardas*, the national dance of Hungary. The family felt more at home in that atmosphere and was, of course, able to communicate in Hungarian. Our parents never really learned English but managed, with our help, to deal with official demands.

At the time, people seldom received at home or visited each other. The young met at the corner or at the movies. Most families we knew were first-generation immigrants. Most of the men were laborers or held very modest jobs. As a barber, our father had a certain standing. The slogan for the IWW *(the international labor union Industrial Workers of the World)*, "Workers of the World Unite," was everywhere. Eugene Debs at the time was the hope and our hero. Many discussions against "The Capitalists" took place. I was made to stay after school in junior high one day because I disliked the way our history teacher talked about the good that capitalism was doing, and I had shouted out, "You're speaking like that because you are being paid by the capitalists!" When we were children and throughout high school, the conversation at home turned constantly to the denied rights of the working class, the exploitation of the workers by the rich.

Since Glenville High School was in a district mostly inhabited by Jewish families, Passover was more important than Easter, and Hanukkah was as important as Christmas, although it was the Christian manifestations for which we were given vacations. It was at Glenville that I tasted matzo balls and gefilte fish for the first time; the cafeteria served them during Passover. Time off was given to Jewish students if the observance did not coincide with the Christian holiday.

What had me dumbfounded at school was the way some of the girls overdressed, as if they were going to a cocktail party or a reception: bejeweled, high-heeled, and made-up. I could not understand it.

My scoliosis, or curvature of the spine, was discovered in gym class. I was sent to Mount Sinai Hospital for physical therapy, performed by a young doctor. I was so shy that I put my middy blouse on backward so he wouldn't see my breasts. He was so angry that he shouted, "I only see your back. How can I help correct it if you hide it?" Did I ever blush and feel foolish. When I was in college, no one referred to the scoliosis. Perhaps the required swimming twice a week, the gym exercises, and the sports I played, including tennis and hiking, kept it under control. What might have later endangered it was horseback riding, which I did in the mountains of Haiti, but only for a few years. I could see that one hip had become slightly higher than the other and that one shoulder blade jutted out more. But since no one seemed to notice these anomalies, I forgot about them most of the time. The scoliosis did not interfere with my life, except recently in aging.

At Glenville, apart from a girl who took the same streetcar I did, I had only one friend. He sat either in front of me or behind me in several classes. He was interesting intellectually, and we had many conversations. His name was Lester. We were put together by everyone as "Esther and Lester" although we were just friends. He finished a year ahead of me, but I would encounter him again at Wooster College.

The subjects I liked best were English, Latin, and French. Math was a requirement, and I also liked it, since tenth-grade algebra was fairly easy, as was geometry. But I met my Waterloo in senior year: that year's algebra was Greek to me. I struggled through with a C or a B. Another headache was physics. Our teacher told me in the middle of the semester that he would have to fail me if I didn't study harder. So I studied harder. At exam time, to prevent cheating, he gave a yellow sheet of paper to one person and then a white one to the next person. He put two exams on the blackboard, one for the yellows, the other for the whites. Had I been given the white paper, I would have failed. I just happened to have studied the right subjects for the yellow. I was saved.

Biology was fine. We made albums with dried plants we found in the countryside. The course heightened my love for flowers and trees. I liked history and geography, and English and American Literature was a joy. I was so enthusiastic that I wrote papers on Poe, Kipling, and others outside of the class assignments for such teachers as Miss Kimberly and Miss Limback, and despite the Bostonian. In French, Miss Emerson taught us not only the language but told us about French customs and history so that the subject had meaning. Thanks to the two years with her, I could speak French when I went to Haiti, where it was and is the official language used by the educated. (The popular language Creole was and is spoken by everyone and is now written, too.) However, it was in Haiti that I was introduced to French literature, for my high school courses were mostly grammar and vocabulary-building with short stories.

For graduation, we had to wear a white dress. I searched around for this because I had wide shoulders, flat breasts (flapper style), and narrow hips. After many tries, I found one. On the appointed day, we went up on stage one by one to receive our diplomas.

I spent the summer working at the five-and-ten-cent store. In September, I left Cleveland for a few days for a much-needed rest with Katherine, who was a governess with a wealthy family near Chagrin Falls, where she took care of two young children. The home was in a lovely, quiet, wooded area and big enough so that my presence in no way interfered with the comings and goings of the household. However, I had been there only two or three days when I was informed by telephone that college had opened. So with just what I had with me, I returned to Cleveland and from there took the train for late registration at Wooster College in Wooster, Ohio.

Chapter Three

Wooster (1926-1930)

The tuition scholarship I'd received from Wooster was renewable each year, provided my grade average stayed at B or above. My first two objectives after registering were to obtain a room (since there were no vacancies in the on-campus dormitory) and then a job to pay for it and my meals.

I found a place to live in the home of a young couple. They were renting out two rooms, each for two girls, and I became the fourth. Each room had a double bed in it. We thought nothing of sleeping in the same bed. For years I had shared a bed with my sister Rose, each to her side. The house was at the bottom of a hill, with the college situated at the top on a plateau leading to Cleveland. The town of Wooster was in a valley, as were the college woods where we walked and picnicked. Walking up and down that steep hill was quite an exercise in the sun, rain, and snow.

I was fortunate to find employment with an older couple, the Fosses, Wooster College graduates, who had adopted a baby, now sixteen months old and recovering from a mastoid infection. I had had experience, so I took on the job with no qualms. I could also help in the kitchen. The house was too small for more than the family, which included Mrs. Foss' mother, so they paid for my room outside their home and later in a dormitory.

John Foss was a happy, outgoing child. It was my responsibility to take care of him from 2 pm to 6 pm. I managed to have my classes in the mornings throughout the four years (except for one semester of student teaching). When weather permitted, I took John for walks in his stroller. I often had dates on these walks. John became known on campus. In my third year, a professor of education asked to borrow him more than once. The Fosses were willing, and John came with me to class, where the professor gave him tests of one kind or another as demonstrations to the class. John was bright, and for him it was fun, as it was for us to watch him perform.

Besides caring for John, I waited at table for private dinners. Mrs. Foss had asked if I could serve, and then her guests began asking me to work at their parties. Soon I was quite busy. In fact, when I told classmates of the meals I'd had, several wanted to wait at table, too. I often gave one of my three housemates the jobs I couldn't take on. Few of the students knew how to serve as waiters, so before giving them any jobs, I showed them how it was done. We dressed in black, with a small white apron. Few Americans at the time had hired help. The mother was the homemaker and cook. Most of the food was put on the table, and each one helped himself, except when the father carved the chicken and the mother added the vegetables to the plate.

At the end of the first semester, of the four original girls in the young couple's house, only Mildred Meeker and I remained. But we requested other quarters because the young couple was in no way friendly: we could not have guests in to visit, and they showed no interest in us. Fortunately, in February 1927, we were able to move closer to the college, into the home of the assistant to the gym professor, where we had a large bedroom and shared the family bathroom. One of our windows overlooked a public garden, which in the spring was radiant with flowers, as were the woods, and birds were abundant, the air filled with their songs.

Two male classmates lived in the house next door, so many conversations took place between us at the window. It was at this time that I learned of my sister Katherine's marriage to a golf pro. No one had let me know that she had fallen in love. I later learned that she had met him in Venice, Florida, where the family for whom she was governess had been wintering. I never understood why she kept me in the dark.

Since neither Mildred nor I could afford to go home for the Easter holidays, we stayed in Wooster, although the college and dining room were closed. Luckily, I had some jobs waiting at table and could occasionally bring back leftover food. Otherwise, our diet was coffee and bread for breakfast, bread and raw cabbage with vinegar for lunch, and milk and bread for supper. We ate wild dandelion greens with vinegar once the cabbage was finished. We were very glad when the dining room reopened. During the two weeks, we did a lot of walking and reading, as well as studying, to pass the time.

Founded in 1866, Wooster was a Presbyterian liberal arts coeducational college that included courses in religion, two of which were obligatory. Through the church, missionaries were sent to Lahore and other parts of India. A good number of students were children or nephews and nieces of missionaries. The environment certainly must have contributed to my wanting to become a teaching missionary, or it might have been that this was one way I could see the world.

Chapel was held every day, with attendance taken. We freshmen were seated upstairs in the rear of the church, where most of the time we studied or wrote letters if the goings-on were not of interest to us. On Sundays, we were permitted to sit anywhere. In our sophomore year, we were moved downstairs to the rear pews. In our third year, we were seated in the center, and as seniors we were just behind the faculty, who took the front rows. One of my favorite dishes was fried liver with onions. But it was as a senior seated in chapel that I learned I could not digest onions cooked in this manner. Mildred was sitting next to me; we had been talking. Suddenly she said, "Esther, did you have onions for breakfast?" "No," I said, "I had them two days ago." What a blow—to have bad breath! So no more fried onions!

* * *

My sophomore year was far more enjoyable than my freshman year. Since I had been able to work in the summer for the Census Bureau of the Cleveland Board of Education, through the kindness and efforts of Mr. Bendler, the truant officer at Glenville High, I had some funds and felt I did not have to worry about where I would get the money to buy books and materials and a dress or two.

Again I lived off-campus. Mildred and I were housed even nearer school than before, in the home of a retired teacher, Miss Pendleton, and her widowed sister. Mildred and I were in one bedroom, while two other sophomore girls were next door. We all shared the one bathroom. We had our own staircase and our living room, which we only used as a passageway to our front door unless we invited a friend in. I did have friends in on occasion, but since we had no money, we did not entertain.

Harriet Walker, one of the girls in the other room, became a close friend. We took walks, discussed poetry, and so attached were we that we decided to room together in our third year when accommodations opened up in the dormitory on campus. (Mildred now had to work for board and room and had found attic quarters in a professor's home, while Ruby, the fourth girl, did not return to school.)

Mildred and I shared a large bed. In winter, when even our coats placed on top of the blankets could not keep us warm, we huddled together front to back. I still recall asking Mildred to turn over because I was tired of sleeping on that side. Once she had turned, we would snuggle together again like puppies for warmth.

Miss Pendleton's sister had just returned from thirty years as a missionary in Australia with her late husband, a Scotsman. What was interesting was that although born and bred in Wooster, she had to reapply for citizenship—as I later had to—after her long stay out of the country married to a foreigner. I became a citizen of the U.S. just after graduating from Wooster in August 1930. My father said he was a citizen of the world and would not take measures to become naturalized. But each of us four children born in Hungary took the test and was sworn in. (After I was married to Maurice and had lived in Haiti a while, my citizenship was revoked and was not returned to me until 1992 after I hired a lawyer to take my case to court in Cleveland.)

Miss Pendleton and her sister were very discreet and stayed out of our way, probably keeping to their rooms on their side of the house until we'd gone to class. Knowing our concentration on our studies, Miss Pendleton invited the four of us late afternoon each Thursday to have a cup of cocoa. She then brought us up to date on U.S. news. (At the time, newspapers rarely carried accounts of events happening outside the country, while radio was local, if anything, and of course there was no broadcast television as yet.)

Miss Pendleton lived next door to the Comptons, with whom I became acquainted. Their daughter had married a Mr. Rice and had gone out to India. During that year, the couple returned to Wooster for several weeks, and I spent some afternoons with Mrs. Rice and her parents. Before she left again for India, she gave me a pendant and bracelet made of clay and trimmed in blue and gold, which I kept for many years. One of the three sons was Arthur Compton, who in 1927 received the Nobel Prize in physics *for discovering the "Compton effect" (having to do with scattered X-ray particles, a step toward the atom bomb)*. The college commemorated this momentous occasion. We all gathered in the chapel, where Arthur explained the atom, of which I understood little. He was tall, very well built, and very handsome. We were so thrilled to share in this exciting event. *(Compton would go on to appear on the cover of* Time *magazine in 1936 and to head the forerunner of the Manhattan Project [whose bombs over Hiroshima and Nagasaki terminated the war in the Pacific]. In 1946, he was appointed Chancellor of Washington University in St. Louis but ran afoul of critics who said he moved too slowly in desegregating, since the school was the last major institution of higher learning in the city to do so [in 1952].)*

We were obliged to go swimming twice a week. From the Pendleton house, it was easy to get to the pool which was open several nights a week. We would put on our pajamas over our swimsuits and a coat on top, race to the gym, throw off the coat and pjs, and dive in and swim for what I think was an hour. Afterward, we dried ourselves, threw on the pjs and coat, and raced home, trying to keep the pajama legs from falling down. We were greatly embarrassed when we met anyone along the road. One of my classmates sometimes wore pjs to school because she was often late and had no time to dress. She had been threatened with a failing grade for disturbing the class so often with her late entrances. One time in winter, she was late. After jumping from her bed, she had thrown on a fur coat and run to class. The room was heated, and there she was wrapped in a fur coat. The whole class, knowing the reason for her keeping it on, snickered and grinned throughout the whole hour. The professor said nothing but must have suspected the reason.

I had never entered a swimming pool before I arrived at Wooster. As a child, I had lived close to the Euclid Beach Amusement Park on Lake Erie, which had sandy beaches. It cost nothing to enter the park. If one did not have money to spend on the attractions, one could sit on the benches or the grass, walk around to view the attractions, or go around the picnic tables for handouts. So, too, for swimming. It was our father who took us to the beach on summer Sundays. We wore homemade swimsuits and undressed and dressed in public. We learned to swim by splashing about, then managing to float or flailing about to keep our heads above water. At Wooster, I had almost four years of swimming. I tried several strokes, but the one I liked best was the side stroke. I practiced that, trying to whittle down the number of strokes it took to cross the length of the pool. At the exams, I was complimented on the style, rhythm, and length of my strokes. Later in Haiti, knowing how to swim proved an asset.

In high school, I had majored in English and Latin, with a minor in French. It might have been better if I had taken subjects other than Latin because on arriving at college, I learned that the three-and-a-half-years of Latin I'd done could have been accomplished in just one year at Wooster, with Virgil and Cicero in the next two years. If I had instead taken typing in high school, for example, it would have later saved me a lot of money on my college papers and my master's thesis at Teachers College in New York.

At Wooster, I decided to continue with English, finish the Latin requirement, and take up German. I also enrolled in classes in education so I could teach English in high school.

For one of my English courses, we had a teacher who kept picking up particles of lint with her fingers. This distracted me a bit, but the subject, Greek and Roman Influences in Modern Literature, was so fascinating that I accepted the annoyance. I was just a sophomore while the class was filled with juniors and seniors. But at the end of the term, I received the highest grade, ninety-eight, on the exam paper.

For the three years of German, the teacher was Miss Gingrich, an elderly woman of German origin. We called her Ginger (though not to her face). She wore either a wide black ribbon with a brooch around her neck or a boned gauze affair dating from the era before World War I. She fiddled with the brooch while we worked and worked. She was a hard taskmaster and often berated us for our laziness and lack of enthusiasm. I grew to like her and was invited several times to take tea with her at her home, where I tasted candied ginger for the first time. We missed her for the several days she was out with a broken arm. On that occasion, her sister was coming to stay with her, and in preparation for her arrival, Miss Gingrich cleaned her house, broken arm or not. She afterward confided that she could not let her sister come to a dirty house. Imagine! She opened for me the doors to the great literature of Germany—Goethe, Schiller, Heine, and others.

European history was fascinating because the young teacher, though often smirking and giggling, taught us well. She was enthusiastic and passed on the enthusiasm to us.

However, education classes, in my junior and senior years, were dull. We plodded through them with the two male teachers who seemed as bored as we were. But there was a benefit to me because both asked me to grade homework papers for 25 cents an hour. When I had too many, I passed them on to a friend to grade, telling her what to look for.

The junior-year class in religion was not terribly exciting. It was taught by an old returned missionary. We were able to do other homework and catch up on correspondence in that large class because we were shielded by the front rows of eager beavers. The teacher asked questions in alphabetical order so each student, as his or her name came closer to being called, would look up and pay attention. Because he marked our answers, we had to know what he was talking about. His questions most often could be answered by yes or no or right or wrong. He had the habit of putting his glasses above their usual place on his nose if the correct answer was positive, and below his nose if it was negative. Perhaps he knew what we were doing and did this to help us so that he would not have to scold. In preparation for the final exam, he gave us ahead of time one hundred fifty questions and their answers which we learned by heart, because from these he would pick ten questions for the actual exam.

The course in philosophy was a different matter. There was passionate debate, and both the teacher, a young preacher, and the class enjoyed the discussions. I also enjoyed my courses in American Political Theories and in Christian and Race Problems. All these were in my senior year.

For geology we had Mr. Versteeg, who was constantly at odds with the administration and roared out his grievances. But his very personality made us want to learn about the various geological eras, and I still remember quite a bit.

I cannot say the same for the man we had for biology in our third year—monotonous voice, a colorless individual who was absorbed by the diseases of fish. The course was so flat; he made it so uninteresting. Fortunately, his assistant in the lab, where we dissected frogs and so on, was animated, and I liked carrying out experiments and drawing the parts of plants and animals. But I was surprised and angry when the teacher approached me just before the final exam to say that since I had cheated, he might have to fail me. "Cheated?" I said. "How could I have cheated? Here is my notebook, and I swear I have done all this myself." "It may be," he said, "but you let a friend copy it, so you are as much to blame as she." I answered, "I have no friend in this class and whoever copied my work did it without my knowledge, perhaps while I was dissecting and taking notes, since I usually leave my notebook at my desk. I wonder if she even knew whose work she was copying." Well, evidently I was able to convince him of my honesty to some degree, but not entirely, for I was given a C, which I suppose he thought an acceptable compromise between the F he had threatened and the A I felt I deserved. I myself thought it was an injustice. (The following year the identity of the culprit was revealed.)

The only other class I did not enjoy was a psychology course having to do with tests and measurements. The young teacher was dry, and so were the various ways to test and measure. I experimented in how to answer exams and wrote how and why I did that so that the teacher would be aware it was deliberate. Some questions and their answers seemed so silly and superfluous. Moreover, it was the only class I ever had on a Saturday, so I often skipped it; I was indignant that the one-hour class should break up and interfere with the precious and otherwise free morning. At the end of the semester, the teacher asked me to stay after class. When we were alone, he said, "You have been impertinent. You have been deliberately absent too often. I should flunk you, but since I am sure you don't want to take the class over again and since I don't want to see you again in my class, I shall give you a D." It was the lowest grade I ever had in school. It depressed my average, but fortunately I was not obliged to give up my jobs or my scholarship. It made me pay, though, for my revolt and independence of thought. But was it also because Roland had graduated the previous June?

I had met Roland White my sophomore year and dated him the whole year. How we met I do not remember. He was a senior, only slightly taller than I. He may have been from a farm for he had large, rough hands. To earn board and room, he peeled potatoes for the men's dining room. But since he had free time in the afternoon, we went on walks with John Foss in the stroller. We also dated evenings for square dances. Modern dancing was not allowed on campus, a great disappointment to me because dancing had been my passion in high school. But square dances were permitted at Wooster and often held in the gymnasium. Roland and I were enthusiastic, if not accurate, dancers.

I still remember a walk we took on the first of June. It was sunny and warm. I had no hat. All at once Roland turned to me and said, "Esther, I didn't know you had freckles!" On reaching for a pocket mirror and taking a quick glance at my face, I saw that I was in full bloom and would have to be careful to keep out of the sun in the future. I had become pretty, but the freckles did detract from my newfound good looks.

The main reason I thought I was now better looking was because my straight hair, which I did not like, had been curled. Permanent waves had just come in. Although I had little money, I was determined to have a permanent, even though it cost $28, a huge sum at the time, and took four hours. Today, with clever haircuts and brushing, straight hair can be made into beautiful styles. In 1927-28, my hair was straight-straight and had no style. For me, the permanent was the most marvelous invention. Moreover, Mrs. Foss, in her great kindness, not only gave me some of the after-noon dresses she no longer wanted but also had them made over for me so that I was able to date dressed attractively. My social life brightened. I dated other men, but Roland, or Whitey as everyone called him, was my "steady." And he was a senior, and I just a sophomore!

Roland was to go on to Princeton Seminary, which at that time was fundamentalist. We never discussed religion, for I already had doubts about the divinity of Christ, his walking on water, and his five loaves and two fish, but these ideas I kept to myself, since I knew Roland believed in them. Even with Mildred, or "Mil" as we called her, I did not discuss them because her father was a minister. However, I had the feeling that she, too, was turning away from the organized church and some of the beliefs.

I learned to play bridge that year. Some of the girls already knew how and by watching them, I picked up the game. But it was not until my third year that I could take part during the very few hours I had free. I also picked up some information when I served at dinners, after which there usually was a bridge game. On a few afternoons, Mrs. Foss' mother showed me ways to play while I kept my eye on John, who, as he grew older, could play by himself on days he could not be taken out. Bridge was an important asset in the social life of Wooster, and it also proved to be so in Haiti. I was happy when our son John learned the game in college.

Besides taking care of John Foss, serving at dinners, and later correcting papers, I also had a job in the college library basement once or twice a week from 7 pm to 9 pm. Here were books for which professors had given assignments and which were held for their courses. They were lent to be read in the library only. I earned 25 cents an hour. In addition, I cleaned the apartment of the Dean of Women on Saturday mornings. After the first time, she was rarely there, so I could work expeditiously. For a while, she was handicapped by a broken arm. She asked if I could come help her dress in the morning and undress at night, which I willingly did.

From this experience, I got a few jobs helping to take care of people who had had an accident. One was the mother of the gym teacher, who had to go away for a conference for five days. It was exam time. I studied at her home and spent the night there. The night before one exam, Mildred replaced me. I just could not manage. Mildred came into the breach several times, for which I have always been grateful. Once or twice it took great persuasion, but she was the only person I could really count on.

* * *

At Wooster, the first-year girls who could find rooms on campus were generally housed in a very large mansion called Hoover Cottage. Those of us who lived off-campus ate in the basement of Hoover. In our second year, we had our meals in the main dining room. The waiters were men students, one or two of whom I occasionally dated.

Now in my third year, I was housed on campus in a two-story annex in the rear of the garden. To reach the main facilities, I had to go through a long, closed passageway that was called the esophagus. It was dark and dreary. I ate in the basement of Holden Hall, which was the senior women's residence.

In November, I was invited to Thanksgiving dinner at the McSweeneys', where I had often served before. Normally I ate in the kitchen with the old cook, a gruff, handicapped (one leg was shorter than the other) woman. John McSweeney had served in the U.S. House of Representatives, and we were all saddened when he lost his seat in 1928, at the same time that Alf Landon, the first Catholic candidate and a Democrat, lost to Republican Herbert Hoover in the presidential race.

Dinners at the McSweeneys' were elegant and lavish. Evening attire was *de rigueur*: ladies in evening finery and men in tuxedos. There were never fewer than two roasts at Mr. McSweeney's end of the table. He carved with relish while the guests carried on a light, scintillating conversation. After he put a good portion of meat on a plate, I carried it to the other end of the table, where Mrs. McSweeney served the vegetables. It was a very enjoyable ceremony.

At this Thanksgiving, I sat at the table with everyone else. I wore one of the two formal dresses that I had from Mrs. Foss' wardrobe. Since I had been asked to bring a guest, I chose a young man I'd been dating who attended a military academy not far from Wooster. He came back to town every weekend, and I liked him partly because of his military outfit, which he wore on dress-up occasions. At the McSweeneys', the young man was seated beside me, and at this dinner there was only one meat, a huge stuffed turkey. The McSweeneys performed their usual rituals, while the gravy and cranberry sauce were handed around. We ate. I was being very careful of my weight at the time. The young man seemingly was not, for first he opened his jacket at the collar, then one button, then another and another. It was when he had to loosen his belt that I decided he was a pig to be stuffing himself like that. I dropped him like a hotcake and refused to date him again.

(One holiday, I had nowhere to go. I must have told the McSweeneys' cook, who in turn must have said something to Mrs. McSweeney. The latter let me know that there was an extra room in the attic I could use. They, like the Fosses and others, were very generous to students, and I was very grateful.)

There were also occasions at Wooster when we were asked to dress up for dinner. I shall never forget my shock and surprise when once, in our junior year, I saw a classmate walk into the dining room wearing my best dress. I had two and had decided to wear the older, less elegant one so as to save the other—a black velvet, sleeveless fold-over with an artificial red flower where the fold was attached—for a greater occasion. We were all seated when the classmate rushed in. I doubt if she knew from whose closet she had taken the dress without permission. I was so amazed that all I did was open my mouth and gasp. I did not say a word, though inside I was boiling. Just as the dinner ended, she dashed out. I was detained since I had invited a guest, so I could not run after her. When I returned to my room, I immediately looked for the dress, and there it was. Since it was undamaged, I never mentioned the incident to the classmate, nor did I ever have anything to do with her again.

It would never have occurred to me to do such a thing. I would have either not gone to dinner or worn the best I had.

Mostly sophomores were housed on my floor, so as a junior, I had prestige and authority. Then I was named supervisor of the floor, which meant seeing that lights were off and that the large bathroom of five baths, five sinks, and five toilets was kept in order. (Our rooms only had washbasins.)

I was, also for the first time, part of a large, intimately intertwined group. Previously, contact with most of my classmates had been limited to the dining room, classes, dances, and picnics. Now in the dormitory, we shared the bathroom and ran into each other's rooms at all hours where the occupants were in all sorts of dress (or undress) and the rooms often in disarray. To me it was a whole new experience, and some of the freedom and dress were disconcerting. I remember inviting the German teacher Miss Gingrich for Sunday noon dinner in my senior year when I was lodged in the main building on the third floor. There were no elevators. As we arrived at the second floor, we ran into the girl who had worn her fur coat to class. She was hurrying down the hall to the common bathroom, quite naked except for a tiny fake tiger skin that she held up to her front. Miss Gingrich was shocked. She turned to me and gasped, "Is this allowed?" "Oh, she is quite dressed," I answered, "given the way some girls roam around here." How times and attitudes have changed!

Then I became part of a smaller group within that large group. I remember Peewee Piwanka, a small, slender girl from Shaker Heights, just outside Cleveland, whose parents invited me to have Sunday noon dinner several times. I never revealed where my parents resided, since Buckeye Road was not far from Shaker Heights in terms of distance, but in living standards it could have been miles and miles away. I think the Piwankas sensed this and were very kind to me because of it.

There was also Peg, whose maiden name I have forgotten, but I remember her married name because she wed Frank Celeste, whom she dated from her sophomore year on. She fainted on several occasions or was taken ill. We had to find Frank to take her to the dorm. Later, their son would become governor of Ohio.

Then there was Sarah, a big, heavy girl with a very Southern drawl. I recall she dated a very short, thin student.

We four were the nucleus; others joined us at various times. Harriet Walker, who had previously been a close friend, did not join. The minute we started to live together, we did not get along. The distance between us grew and grew, and by the end of the semester, she withdrew. Another student, Ruth Kinney (whom I did not know at all), was assigned to be my roommate. Ruth and I got along very well, each being careful not to disturb the other, nor to infringe on the allotted space. Fortunately, because I worked, I was out of the room most of the day. When we were together, we had all sorts of discussions.

At the end of the hall of the dormitory annex was a group of juniors who took me in, and when I had a bit of cash, I joined them for luncheon off-campus and several weekends away from the college. Was it vanity, curiosity, the need to feel accepted that made me happy to go about with these girls? This group was friendly with another group on the first floor with whom I later had an unpleasant experience.

I managed to keep my job with the Fosses. But I had a far more intense extracurricular life with my new responsibilities and with sports such as basketball, field hockey, and hiking.

I also joined the literary club, which took up much of what little free time I had. That year, they decided to put on a play, Oliver Goldsmith's *She Stoops To Conquer*. Those who wished to act in it had to try out. I read the play, and I very much wanted the part of Mrs. Hardcastle. Fortunately for me, one of our club members, a sophomore, sported quite masculine clothes and a boy's haircut and was pudgy and red-faced. She would be just right as the son if she could act, I thought. So I went to her, explained that we could make a team, and suggested we work out a scene where the two of us would be on stage alone. This we did. We were both cast, and the memorization began, as well as the acting gestures. The play was put on in the town auditorium for two evenings. We were a hit. Various people told me afterward that my acting was good and that I had an exceptional stage voice. This so encouraged me that I joined the Dramatics Club and appeared in two plays in my senior year, as well as doing publicity. However, I never matched my portrayal of Mrs. Hardcastle. When I arrived in New York City in the fall of 1930 after graduating from Wooster, I realized how many aspiring actors there were and how few really were success-ful. That is why I preferred to become a teacher.

I had also thought to become a writer. In high school, I had done several extracurricular papers. Edgar Allan Poe attracted me with his original, pessimistic, weird, and some-times macabre works. I continued writing, hoping to receive some encouragement, but nothing was up to recognition, even though I must have written well enough and originally enough that I received A's in Senior Composition and Theory in Criticism. Courses in English literature, especially Drama and Dramatics, were all absorbing.

Although I had gone with a group of students to see the original play *Porgy* in Cleveland, it was the Fosses who really introduced me to the theater—that is the professional one— and with whom I saw a number of plays. They drove from Wooster to Cleveland, where we had dinner at a restaurant, then went to the theater—mostly plays put on by a traveling company from New York. The Fosses loved the theater and each year went to New York for a week to take in several plays. I would stay overnight with John and his grandmother so that they would not be alone.

The Fosses also took me to a few football games out of town. They were careful to have cushions and blankets for themselves and for me, and after the games they took me to dinner before we returned to Wooster. They were as enthusiastic about football as I was, so we had lively conversations about the games and the players. I shall forever be grateful for their generosity and kindness.

In none of the many homes in which I worked throughout high school for board and room did I find the welcome and the kindness of the Fosses. Perhaps it was my fierce independence, my "I'll show you" attitude that kept those in the earlier households from becoming more friendly. Or was it the feeling I had of being exploited, of doing far more than I should have been asked to do? Of course, some were young couples without much money, needing help but unable to have a full-time maid.

An incident remains in my memory concerning Mildred. It was either in our junior or senior year that she offered her services to a group of students who, in their spare hours, worked on Saturdays with youngsters from one of the public schools. Mildred and a male student would be taking a group of ten or twelve boys into the college woods for a bonfire, with hot dogs and marshmallows. Mildred had asked me to help her out. Being free and willing on that Saturday, I accepted. It had snowed all day and night Friday, but the boys were undaunted. We started down the hill, dressed in slacks and sweaters, at least two of each. We came to the woods. The brook was frozen. There was a log connecting the two sides. Mildred had the food baskets, one in each hand. The young man and three boys crossed over. It was

Mildred's turn. She started across as if she were on a regular sidewalk. She slipped and fell in. She held the baskets high. Only her arms, chest, and head were visible. We thought she was standing deep in the water. No, she was sitting. The young man managed to retrieve the baskets, and Mildred managed to get out. What to do? She was heavy from the soaked clothes. We decided that I would take Mildred back up the hill. The young man would carry on. As we left, two of the boys fell in. We learned later that a big bonfire was built, the boys dried out, and the hot dogs and marshmallows were roasted and eaten.

Mildred and I started up the hill. Soon her wet clothes were frozen stiff. She could hardly move. I put my head (luckily, I was wearing a woolen cap) to the middle of her back and with great effort pushed her up the hill. She stopped and said, "Esther, I can't go further. Leave me. Go find help." I said, "No, you and I are going up this hill together." We did, to the first farmhouse. I knocked. A kind woman opened the door, saw Mildred's condition, and pulled us in to an open fireplace. We undressed Mildred because she could not bend her arms or legs. We rubbed her with alcohol, then I gave her half of my outer clothing. Using the crank telephone, I located a student who had a car and was willing to come pick us up. Once back at the dorm, we were lent enough clothing to dress Mildred so she could go to her residence. Interestingly enough, neither Mildred nor the drenched boys caught cold.

Wooster (1926-1930)

It was curious what would happen in the spring. Some frenzy would take hold of the male students, and the women followed. Since I had lived off-campus my first two years, I knew little about the spring panty raid. It was as a junior that I experienced this rite. It was a beautiful warm evening. The windows of the annex were open. Lights had been lowered when all of a sudden screams came up from the ground floor. I looked out and saw men trying to get in. The women downstairs ran through the hall, the esophagus, Holden Hall, and out the main front entrance. We on the second floor followed. Holden Hall, awakened, trailed after us. Where we raced to I don't remember. We finally landed in front of the small central square on one side of which was the chapel; on the opposite side, the library; and in the back, the main administration and class buildings. There we watched a student climb up the very tall flagpole. When he made it to the top, we all shouted, clapped, ran around in circles so to speak, and finally went back to the dormitory. In the meantime, some men had raided the dorm, picking panties off clothes lines, from drawers, and so on, to take back to their quarters as trophies. The prize went to the one who returned with the most. What was also odd was that there were no reprisals from the administration, no punishment, and all went back to normal by morning.

At the end of my third year, I packed my trunk during exam time so I could be off as soon as possible for my summer job with the Census Bureau, which was to start immediately. One evening, without notice or warning, while Ruth Kinney and I were studying, there was a knock at our door. On opening it, I saw the Dean of Women and a number of the downstairs group of girls behind her. Quite surprised and turning questioningly to Ruth, who was sometimes with this group, I admitted them. The dean took a chair; the others spread themselves about on our beds. My packed trunk was out in the hall, and I was asked to bring it in and unpack it. I suppose I could have refused or asked for the reason. But as I had nothing to hide, I obeyed and took out my belongings one by one and shook everything. Mrs. Foss had given me a $5 bill, and in order not to spend it, I had put it in the pocket of my dressing gown. Out it fell. For a minute I couldn't remember how it had gotten there. But then I thought the dean and the group would think I had stolen and hidden it, so I calmly said, "Mrs. Foss gave it to me and you may telephone her to verify this."

During the whole time of these proceedings, not one of the girls spoke. All was silence. When everything was unpacked, and even pockets turned out and shoes shaken, they all filed out. I folded and put back all my things, which included not only clothes and shoes, but books and knickknacks of one kind or another. Subsequently I learned from Ruth that the downstairs group had been missing various articles of clothing, hats, shoes, and so on, and since I had packed early, it was thought that I had taken them. I don't remember even having been in their quarters. When I returned to school in the fall, one of that group did not come back; it was under her bed, in her closet, and in her bureau drawers that many of the missing items were found. I also learned that it was she who had copied my biology lab notebook. The girls were ashamed of themselves for their suspicions of me.

This occurrence made me very wary of accusing any-one of anything just because of poverty or certain unusual actions. I do not remember the dean apologizing. What angered me was that I had cleaned her apartment for a year, often putting her affairs away without anything ever missing. A few girls thought I would not be back. One wrote to apologize. The good that came out of it was that in my senior year I was given a room to myself that I could deco-rate as I pleased and keep my own hours. I never told Mrs. Foss.

That summer in the Census Bureau, I was assigned to walk certain streets, going from house to house to register the names and ages of the possible school-age children. It was the area of Euclid Avenue near the town center, which had become a very poor section, inhabited mostly by black families. I certainly saw poverty, vulgarity, and homes in need of cleaning, but I also saw poor, genteel, well-groomed families. I later learned that a car from the Bureau cruised by every so often to watch me going in or coming out. I thought it was to see if I was on the job, but I was subse-quently told it was to see if I was safe. Several years later, Mr. Bendler was, unfortunately, bashed on the head by an irate father who happened to be home. When I took the census, I met no men.

In that area everyone spoke English. In another part of Cleveland where I was asked to work, the language was Slovak, with the families from various parts of Eastern Europe. I began to knock on doors. Here most lived in single, small houses with gardens of vegetables and flowers in front surrounded by a fence and a closed gate. Doors remained shut. Even a young woman raised suspicion. I was bewildered. How to have doors open? I had my job to do. There was a church nearby, and children were playing about. I sat down on the church steps, calling to several to come sit with me. They were in school and had learned some English. I told them about my job and asked them to teach me a few words of their language, which they did. One even accompanied me to her home. From then on I would knock and call out in Slovak, "Hello. How many children do you have?" Doors opened, usually with, "Come in, come in." I would apologize for not knowing more, but it didn't seem to matter. The children helped as interpreters, or we managed through our hands to indicate how many and how old the children were. Many, many years later in Paris, in the UN Nursery School I ran, I used the same method of learning a few words of the language of a child who knew neither French nor English and who felt lost in the foreign environment.

The students at Wooster were, for the most part, provincial—even I. One year, there was a male student from Iraq.

To us Iraq seemed at the end of the world. He stood out like a sore thumb. He was homely, with big feet that turned out as he walked. He spoke very poor English. Had he been handsome, perhaps we would have been kinder. We thought that Mildred went out with him as an act of charity. I was struck then by our provincialism.

Election time for the various posts in the different clubs came around. I never aspired to be president of the Literary Club but thought I would make a good secretary. So, as a candidate, I buttonholed classmates and club members to vote for me. One group of girls came to me to ask why I was running, since I was a foreigner. Well, that made me think. It was my foreign-sounding last name that seemed to put them off. It is true that very seldom was it pronounced properly. Rickenhauser or Rictover or other names were used. I always corrected the speaker, because I was proud of the name Reithoffer (which I found out later in Austria was considered a very good name). But that these girls in their third year of college should be upset by a last name that was different from most of those they had come to know was disconcerting.

I did not become secretary, but I did perform the job of manager of the Dramatics Club. This job actually interested me far more. It was I who did the advertising and promotion of the play we were to put on our senior year, Pirandello's *Right You Are, If You Think You Are*. I also had the very small part of the wife who appears dressed in black with a veil over her face at the very end of the play. I was too busy with my advertising chores to do more than that. But I still remember the sensation I made as I came on stage, simply because the character had been talked about during the entire length of the play without once appearing on stage and then all of a sudden, without warning, she was there. My only line was, "Right you are, if you think you are."

* * *

Then we were seniors. As I mentioned earlier, I was given a private room. During the summer, I had met a journalist from a Cleveland newspaper. He had been in Egypt and had brought back a life-size head in profile of a dark-skinned, large-eyed Nubian. I asked if I could borrow it for my room, now on the third floor in the main building of Holden Hall. Since the room gave on to the inner three-sided court, it was very quiet and had the morning sun. The head—which I promised to return at the end of the school year, and did— was the center of attraction. It was the only object on the wall seen immediately. I had found an old covering that went well with the head. A narrow cot was on the opposite side. The washbasin was in an alcove, hidden from view by a cur- tain of the same color as the beige walls. A dresser stood on the side of the entrance to the room, opposite the large window so that the eyes of someone coming into the room were caught by the head. The room was like a sanctuary—austere, without other objects to attract one's attention. To me it was a refuge.

As seniors, we were admired and sought after, not only by the younger women but by younger men, who could then boast that they had been out with a senior.

I taught an English literature class of third-year high school students every afternoon for the term and had to race down the hill to be on time at 2 pm. (Oddly, we were given only three hours' credit for the five hours a week of teaching.) The only special incident occurred when I had asked the students to write an essay or a short story. The papers were so well written that I wondered if there had been cheating. I asked their teacher about this. She suggested that I give them a theme right there in class without preparation. To my amazement and to her satisfaction, they did very well. The only student's name I recall is that of Maurice. It was so unusual at that time and place, that I can still see him standing up when I called his name to compliment him on his writing.

This was the year of "The Crash," for it was in early November when we heard about the Wall Street disaster. I knew of no one in our school who suffered from it. So many came from homes with modest incomes, largely through farming and its derivatives, and a few like me were from homes where all but the essential necessities were excluded. When we read that businessmen were jumping out of their office windows after learning of their stock-market losses, we hardly knew what the stock market was. We knew no one who held stocks. They were so far removed from our lives. We had no money and no stocks, so we lost none. No one withdrew from college and no one changed his or her way of doing things. That's how "The Crash" affected, or didn't affect, us at Wooster.

Spring semester 1930, our last! Of course all of us were excited and concerned about our credits and obligations.

In this last year at Wooster, I became better acquainted with Frances and Margaret Guille, fraternal twins who were very different from each other. If I remember correctly, they had transferred from another college and lived off-campus. Now they must have had a room in Holden Hall because I ran into them more often. I would not meet up with them again for years—until after my husband, our son, and I moved to Paris (in 1956) and I took a cruise to Greece during the 1962 spring vacation. As we were leaving Venice, I asked the purser to please seat me with a group in the dining room because I was alone. As I entered to look for my table, the first person my eyes fell upon was Margaret. I called out her name, and at the same time, she shouted mine. Although we had not seen each other in over thirty years, we had not changed so much that we could not recognize each other at first glance. I looked around the table, and there was Frances. Their tablemates were the two English women I had just met in the purser's office, and a French woman,

Jacqueline Bouvet, a friend of Frances' who also became a good friend of mine. From then on, our lives have often touched.

Mildred also became a lifelong friend and was the only one of my classmates that I dared invite to Cleveland to see my parents and the poverty in which we lived. My parents were living at the time in four rooms on 119th Street and Buckeye Road. There was a large kitchen, a living room off of which were their bedroom and a bath, and another bedroom off the kitchen. For a time, the living room functioned as the barber shop because business had fallen off and our father couldn't afford the rent on a separate shop. I don't think that I ever slept in that house. My sister Betty told me that she and our sister Sue slept in the kitchen, and our three brothers slept in one bedroom. I did have lunch there at times, but I managed to sleep in the attic bedroom of the homes where Rose had gone into service.

Mildred and I went to Cleveland to see a matinee of *Abie's Irish Rose.* I shall never forget the play, not only for its subject—a Jewish boy bringing home his Irish sweetheart and the consequences—but also for the mother's blue dress. It was long and had attached to it material of the same sort and color. I did not notice the extra material at first because she initially wore it in the back with the strings tied at her front. In the next act, she wore it in front as an apron. In the third act, it was used as a cape, and at the wedding as a turban. Moreover, instead of the usual orange blossoms at the wedding, Abie's mother decided it was silly to waste money on blossoms, so why not have oranges. This play and *Porgy* are the two I remember best of the Cleveland theater. About twenty years ago, Annette Metis, one of my former students at Mills College who is Jewish and became a dear friend, married an Irishman, and this event brought back the circumstances of the family from the play.

My mother was a good cook. Mildred and I had supper in the kitchen, my mother quite embarrassed but managing. (When my sister Katherine and I had some extra money, we were able to buy an inexpensive rug for the living room and later a set of dishes. It was the first time we had the same set of plates, cups, and serving dishes throughout the meal.) Then Mildred and I took the streetcar back to the public square, where we caught the last train to Wooster, and then walked up the college hill to our rooms. Wooster was such a quiet and peaceful place that we had no fear of walking about late at night. What we did fear was being caught for being out after hours, which at Wooster was 10 pm. I do not remember if we braved it or had received permission to come in late (since as seniors we did have some privileges).

As the end of the term approached, my student teaching was over. It was good to be free of that requirement and not have to go down the hill every weekday afternoon. The Fosses had moved from the small house near the college to a lovely new home farther away. My teaching had been from 2 pm to 3 pm, and from there I walked up to take

John out or play with him indoors and do odd chores. During the last term, the Fosses adopted another young boy and thus needed more help than I could give. But we must have worked out a schedule of some kind, for they went on paying for my board and room at college. Fortunately, the tuition scholarship had also continued.

My principal aim now was to find a teaching position. It was 1930, and the Depression had set in. How to track one down? The education professors put themselves at our disposal, giving us advice on how to go about it and suggesting possibilities and leads as to advertisements. There was no placement bureau at school. After some correspondence to various high schools in different Ohio towns, I was offered the position of English teacher in Bowling Green and the extracurricular job of coaching in basketball and track. I had been on the basketball team as rear guard and had earned a black-and-gold T in track, which I had sewn on my sweater pocket, as well as an H in hiking. So I thought I was quite ready, though nervous, to tackle both. There was no state exam. My diploma from Wooster was my license to teach. Therefore, I was all set, and I planned on going to Bowling Green during the summer to search for accommodations.

Graduation arrived. Many families came to see their off-spring graduate. Mine did not because I did not invite anyone. However, this did not prevent me from enjoying the pomp and ceremony in the cap and gown I had rented, as well as marching up onto the platform to receive the precious parchment and shake President Wishart's hand. I met some parents after the ceremony (*including Mildred's mother and her brother Ben, according to Barbara Wilkins, Mildred's niece, whom I located, remarkably, through the internet*), then hurried away to return the cap and gown and take the train for Cleveland. I could have a bed where my sister Rose was working, or I could serve as house-sitter for former employers on holiday.

Thus finished the four years at Wooster College, for which I have always been grateful. The experience was a life-saving one, crucial for my future. What would I have become without it?

With the knowledge of a sure position in Bowling Green—a feat in itself for a newly graduated teacher, since the Depression was becoming more and more severe—I left Wooster and went to work again for the Census Bureau. I needed a trousseau for my teaching job and money enough for expenses before the arrival of the first paycheck. I saved on food, often had but tea and toast for lunch, and even resorted to canned dog food—the only thing I found to eat in the house I was guarding. (It was not at all bad, and there were no ill effects. It happened because I had forgotten to buy something to eat while downtown, and there were no shops within walking distance in this exclusive residential area.) I went nowhere, saw no one. I read and discussed what I'd read with the young college student at the next desk in the Census office. I remember especially André Maurois'

Ariel and Nietzsche's *Thus Spake Zarathustra*, both of which he was also reading.

My friendship with the Comptons had given me the desire to become a teaching missionary in India. Thus some time ago, I had submitted an application to Hartford Seminary in Connecticut for my training and had been examined by a woman doctor to verify that I was a virgin, since one of the school's requirements for unmarried women at that time was virginity. The doctor had sent in the certificate, but there had been no further communication from Hartford. Then suddenly in mid-July, I received word that I had been granted a scholarship. I was very happy. I immediately notified the school authorities in Bowling Green of my change of plans, then worked through August. Armed with Hartford's confirmation, I packed my few belongings in a bag, bade farewell to my family, and was off on a Greyhound bus to Connecticut via New York City.

My parents were not very happy. They had had to accept my not helping to support the family on graduation from high school, and now here I was trotting off to the East Coast, when they had hoped that on leaving Wooster, I would finally be able to help them. (In 1928, I had taken out an insurance policy for $3,000 in their favor in case of my death.) Fortunately, Katherine gave them small sums, and Rose helped from her earnings. As I look back, I realize how selfish I must have seemed to them. On the other hand, since the age of 11, I had been on my own, not asking anything of them and giving small amounts when I felt I could from my meager earnings at school. (After going to Haiti, I sent a monthly sum for ten years. This I insisted on as only right since my husband Maurice gave the same figure to his widowed mother each month.)

Chapter Four

New York (1930-1931)

(At the end of this chapter and in subsequent chapters, a few Creole expressions are used. The equivalent in modern Kreyòl, which came into being in 1989 I'm told, is given in parentheses, along with the English translation.)

The bus ride east took twelve hours, since the highways were not what they are today, but then neither was the traffic. Arriving in Manhattan around 10 am, I had a four-hour wait until the bus for Hartford departed. What to do with the time? Five or six years earlier, I had been in New York for two nights. I had shared in the cost of an automobile trip there one summer, which someone from school had proposed. We were five—the high school student and her young man, her mother and her boyfriend, and me.

I think I was asked to go along to help pay car costs and hotel bills because most of the time we three women slept in one room and the two men in another. We were all on tight budgets. The two women paid for the two men, while each paid for his or her own food. We went to Canada by way of Niagara Falls. The others went on a trip to have a better view of the falls, while I stayed behind to look at them from the town. Then we went to Montreal, where I tasted the strong English tea, which, when milk was added, looked like coffee with cream. We stopped in Quebec to see the Plains of Abraham (*where the British capture of Quebec brought to an end the French and Indian War and France's ambitions in North America*). Passing through Sherbrooke, we eventually reached New York City, where by chance our modest hotel was near Columbia University. I toured the campus, never thinking I would see it again.

But evidently I must have thought about it in college. Now with the four-hour layover in Manhattan, I decided to go up to Columbia to see if I could get into a master's program in English literature. I hopped on the subway, and in no time I was in the English Department talking with a faculty member. She informed me that to get a master's would take at least two years and would require a great deal of reading and theater-going. I realized I would not have enough money and said so. After she saw my disappointment, she suggested I try Teachers College (TC), another division of Columbia, where a master's might be done in a year.

I hurried to the TC Registry, where two young ladies were handling the office. I recited my tale. They received me well and assured me it would not be a problem. On seeing my credentials, they proposed a loan scholarship. They even had a job for me. A newly arrived assistant professor, a woman with a four-year-old daughter, needed someone to help out. She had just moved into an apartment close by and was unpacking. Off I went, and I got the job. No more Hartford Seminary for me. I wired them, raced back to the bus terminal, retrieved my belongings from the locker, jumped into a taxi, and arrived at the professor's apartment in the early afternoon. I may have taken a taxi once or twice before in my life, but never did I have a faster and so daredevil a driver. We sped along, dodging other cars left and right. At the end of the ride, I could hardly get out of the taxi I shook so. As I look back, I think the driver did it on purpose to introduce a greenhorn to New York.

The job did not work out. The apartment had one bedroom. I slept on a divan in the living area, where we also ate. The place was in an unpacked state. My employer had no time to put it in order or to make proper meals. I had no set time or place to study. After two weeks, I decided that if I stayed there, I would not obtain my degree, so I looked for another job.

In the various homes in which I had worked throughout high school and college, I had picked up a great deal about good cooking and waiting at table. This now served me well, for a professor at Union Seminary, Dr. Fleming, or rather his wife, was on the lookout for a student who would cook and serve in exchange for room and board. I was interviewed and accepted.

The Flemings, who were Presbyterian, had been missionaries in India. He taught Comparative Religion, among other courses, at Union Seminary and was housed by the university. They did a lot of entertaining: personages from the school, missionaries, students, and friends. The apartment was spacious and quiet. It had at least four bedrooms and baths, even a small chapel at the far end of the center hall, plus two living rooms, one lined with books and giving on to the interior court of the seminary. The dining room, pantry, and kitchen overlooked West 122nd Street, as did a bath and the two maids' rooms, one of which was mine. It was just at 122nd Street that the IRT subway emerged to overhead tracks, and the sudden noise of the train rushing out often disturbed my sleep, even months after I had gone to Haiti. The other maid's room was occupied by a voice student attending the Juilliard School of Music close by. She dusted and cleaned, except for the kitchen area, which was my domain. When the Flemings were absent, I would visit the rest of the apartment.

This job worked out very well. Not only did I cook, set the table, and do the dishes, but I also sat at the table with whoever was invited. This was the marked difference from all the other homes where I'd worked, except for the Thanksgiving dinner at the McSweeneys' and the restaurant outings with the Fosses.

I seldom spoke, not because I was intimidated, but because the conversation was so interesting and on such a high intellectual level that I listened—as did the Flemings' daughter, who was 28 and worked somewhere in the city. From among the many guests, there were two who stood out. One was Charles Andrews, a friend and advisor to Mahatma Gandhi in the fight for freedom. Since he stayed for several nights, I had the pleasure of seeing him at breakfast and at dinner. His conversation was fascinating, mostly about India. The other was Reinhold Niebuhr, who had recently come to Union Seminary from Germany. He subsequently became an outstanding theologian. An English student who was also there later became his wife.

Mrs. Fleming was very economical. She did the shopping on Saturdays. We often had roast leg of lamb that winter. The hot roast was served on Sunday. It was served cold on Monday. It was made into a lamb stew with vegetables on Tuesday. On Wednesday, we added more vegetables and dumplings. We finished it on Thursday. On Sunday, there were important and/or distinguished guests, and then increasingly less important ones as the days went by. On Wednesdays and Thursdays, the guests were students only too glad to sit at a professor's table and be in a different atmosphere than the seminary or college dining room. Never had I seen a leg of lamb stretched to feed so many people.

No lunch was served in the family. Anyone at home at lunchtime took a piece of fruit and a glass of milk or something similar. I ate a sandwich in the TC cafeteria or went to a Chinese restaurant or had tea and toast. I was usually too busy to take time to come back to the apartment before 5:30 pm when I would prepare dinner.

* * *

Here I was in New York City. I was 21 years and nine months old. I must have been one of the youngest students at Teachers College. Most were, like my future husband Maurice, who was 27, coming to TC after several years out in the professional field. Because of my youth, I was quite popular. Compared to most of the women attending the school, I was attractive. At first, I was awed to be in such surroundings: the hallowed halls of Teachers College, Columbia University, one of the great schools of the world. Wooster had been among the top one hundred fifty best colleges in the U.S. Here was I now in one of the top ten, if not the top five!

We were fortunate to have some excellent and inspiring professors. I remember best Dr. Kilpatrick, who taught Educational Psychology. It was more philosophical than other courses like it. It was he who said, "One learns one's prejudices as well as one's prayers at the mother's knee," meaning when one is very young. (American friends have told me that the reason I could marry Maurice was because I was born in Hungary and did not come to the U.S. until I was five years old.) Another brilliant professor was Dr. Wilson, whose theory was that the only sure way of decreasing population growth was through education so that the desire for a better life for themselves and their children would make couples want to limit the number of offspring.

The reason I decided to major in Rural Education must have been because of the possibility of my going out to India. My interest in the subcontinent was further reinforced and expanded by my conversations with two early friends, both Indian, Prem Chan Lal and Rose Devasahyam.

I met Prem Chan Lal in one of my classes. I learned that he was the secretary to the leading Indian poet Rabindranath Tagore. To come into the latter's presence was an unusual honor, and I think one of the reasons I dated the tall, thin, wavy-haired, large-eyed, quiet man was because he was connected with the great man.

Thanks to International House and its Board members, we had access to opera and theater tickets we could never have afforded on our own. Very few nonwhites were seen in orchestra seats. Prem Chan Lal and I created a sensation at the Metropolitan Opera walking down the orchestra aisle to the fourth or fifth row center for Wagner's *Lohengrin*. The gasps and stares tickled us, and we could hardly keep straight faces. The singing was excellent, but the leads were physically so ill-matched that I watched them more than I listened. She was a huge Germanic woman; he, a small, thin Italian. When they entered the wedding chamber, it was ludicrous. When she lay on her side on the floor, her hips were so high that one could not see the bed. When the couple sat on the bed, the mattress dipped to the floor, and he slid toward her. Finally, on the balcony, when she swayed, the pillars holding the balcony swayed, too, and I feared its collapse. However, this circumstance did not abate my love for opera and my becoming familiar with many of the scores.

I had been to the theater in Cleveland, but once I saw plays in New York, I realized that it was here that theater in America was at its best and that the greatest actors and actresses performed on Broadway. Eva Le Gallienne's repertory company put on several plays that year, and although Le Gallienne was always Le Gallienne, we saw many of her shows, including *The Barretts of Wimpole Street.* I had read and admired Elizabeth Barrett Browning's *Sonnets to the Portuguese,* and I was enthralled. I also saw Alfred Lunt and Lynn Fontanne in *Elizabeth The Queen*. (Years later, I would experience the epitome of great theater when I had opportunities to go to London.)

Prem Chan Lal and I sat next to each other in the main Rural Education class, taught mostly by Mabel Carney. *(Professor Carney was head of TC's Department of Rural Education and an authority on the subject, a rara avis as a white female reformer and champion in the field of black education both at home and abroad.)*

Maurice Dartigue, who was Haitian, did not come into my consciousness at first. He was also in that class, as he was in several others. We began to exchange conversation, then he asked me to a Saturday night dance. He lived at International House, as did Prem Chan Lal. But Prem Chan Lal did not dance, and I loved to. Maurice danced very well. (I had several other partners. Among them were Gerard from Chile and George Clark, an American, who was studying law and permitted himself this one free evening to dance. He and I also went to the theater once or twice.)

Since none of us had much money, the restaurant we usually frequented was a Chinese one on Broadway at 124th Street. There we could have a bowl of soup—consisting of noodles, slices of roast pork, and bok choy—for 35 cents, or egg foo yong and tea for the same price. We were often joined by two young women, the Misses Kim, both of whom were working toward a doctorate. One of them, always in her Korean national dress, was a personage in the Korean College of Women. The other Miss Kim was the general secretary of the Chinese YWCA. I had three other women friends: Anne Cook, tall and elegant, up from Atlanta's Spellman College, who was already teaching; another African-American whose name I have forgotten, who said, "Esther, I have to work twice as hard to get half your grades"; and Rose Devasahyam, who became a missionary. (It was Rose who introduced me to

Indian food. Already I had to be careful about limiting spicy dishes, but this food I could not resist. It was to an Indian restaurant that Maurice and I went with the few friends who joined us after our wedding. It was cheap, abundant, and different.)

Compared to the rest of us, Anne Cook, who was living at International House, was rich. She offered me one of her gowns, which I gladly accepted since I had so few dress-up clothes. In general, I barely managed. I had no stockings. I sent an SOS to my sister Rose for a winter coat. She sent me two old ones, one of which I cut down for a long jacket and the other, a false caracal fur, I wore with reluctance because I did not like it at all. Mrs. Fleming procured a coat for me from somebody; so I did not freeze that very cold winter in New York, but I certainly shivered. The wind was often so strong that I had to wrap myself around a telephone pole not to be blown away.

Roland White (my steady from Wooster) and I had been corresponding. He was still at Princeton, and he came into New York to see me. He had changed, and so had I, and this was to be our last meeting. As if by common consent, without words, we realized that our relationship was finished. That was that.

I dated a number of men connected with either International House or my classes. One was Kalibala, a huge man, supposedly the son of a Ugandan chief, who complained bitterly that he did not have enough money to live at

International House (most who did had grants of one kind or another, as Maurice did) but could not find lodgings near the college because of his color. Indians and Chinese appeared to be more readily accepted, but blacks had great difficulty. Maurice was never confronted in my presence. His carriage, his elegance, his manners troubled some and restrained strangers from approaching, although we did receive looks and did hear remarks that we intentionally ignored. One evening, he and I dared go to the Cotton Club in Harlem and even danced. We were the only such couple, but no one moved away or refused to dance. Most seemed to be only surprised—even the waiters and the band.

There were private parties, but after being taken to one by Gerard the Chilean and to another by an American, I went no more. I was so naïve: I could not figure out why couples were disappearing, then reappearing, but I did not like it. Besides, there was too much smoke, too much drink, and too much futile conversation. I liked political or philosophical discussion or talk about the theater. At International House, there were all sorts of discussions by various groups on various topics, often based on the talk given by the Sunday evening supper speaker. These were stimulating and often heated.

For Thanksgiving, Mrs. Fleming said I could invite a guest, and I chose Maurice. He came, bringing as a gift a pound of ground Haitian coffee. I cooked the turkey with all the trimmings and even the pumpkin pie. The other student had a friend over, too, as did the daughter of the house. We received our guests in the living room (a novelty). I left to put the turkey and other food on the table. Dr. Fleming served the turkey and stuffing, while the rest was passed around. We three young women cleared the table, and Mrs. Fleming served the pie. She then asked Maurice to make the coffee. I went with him to the kitchen to give him the pot. When I saw him use a teaspoon to measure the coffee, I realized he had probably never made coffee in his life, so I took over the job.

By late November, I knew I was more interested in Maurice than in any of the other young men I'd gone out with. He was tall, well built, well dressed, polite, well mannered, and well spoken, although he had an accent. In class, he was serious and did not cheat. It was an eye-opener to see how some of our classmates—some in quite responsible positions—behaved. Our motto became, "We may fail, but this is better than passing by cheating."

As the days went by, he and I became more involved with each other and went about together. We often talked standing or sitting on the back stairs of the Flemings' apartment because I did not want him to see the tiny room that was mine. During the winter, I became quite ill, with a high fever. So that Maurice could come to see me, I asked the Flemings' daughter if I could use one of the guest bedrooms since her parents were away. Had Mrs. Fleming been there, she probably would have called a doctor and nursed me. Since she was not and her daughter worked, it was Maurice who went to the pharmacy and brought me what the pharmacist prescribed, Vicks VapoRub.

At International House, I encountered a former classmate who had lived near me in Holden Hall our last year at Wooster. We had not been friends then, but here in New York, we threw in together. She had found two male students older than we were. We formed a group and for a time often saw each other. But when I became part of Maurice's group, I slowly drew away from the three Americans.

Maurice's group was far more interesting. A few members stand out in my memory. Two were French: a Gaston Buron and Gigi (whose last name I've forgotten). It is she who gave Maurice and me the only present we received at our wedding, a homemade cushion cover. Then there was an Armenian studying to be an architect and a Romanian girl named Swarti. They carried on mostly in French. As the days went by, my two years of high school French returned. Since I understood most of the discussions but could not express myself, I sat back and listened. In fact, I was so quiet that when Maurice announced our marriage, his group appeared thunderstruck. Several said, "How do you know what she sounds like, what she thinks? We don't know if she can even say a whole sentence." This Maurice told me much later after he, from experience, had learned I could give as well as take in the way of speech and opinion.

Maurice introduced me to a few Haitians in New York. The vice-consul and his wife invited us to a Cuban restaurant, where I had my first taste of rice and beans and, for dessert, guava paste. I also came to know Adeline (nicknamed Didine) Maximilien, who would become a lifelong friend. In years to come, we would encounter her in New York, Port-au-Prince, Paris, and Rome. She once told me that Maurice could not have found a wife in Haitian society because he was too poor and too dark. I thought his color beautiful.

I'll never know how I managed, with classes, a job, studies, dates to the theater and to parties, plus Saturday evening dances and Sunday evening suppers at International House! It must have been that all the professors I had were generous and kind. I studied in the school library during the week and on Sunday afternoons. I must have just squeezed through (TC used a pass/fail system; no letter grades were given), and later that year I did obtain my degree.

* * *

First semester came to an end in February. Maurice, who had done a previous term at TC in 1926–1927, had completed his requirements and received his master's in Rural Education. He was to go back to Haiti at the end of March. That month was important to him. He was born in March; his father had died in March; and therefore he wanted us to be married in March. The very short civil ceremony took place on March 3, with Didine and John Carey (whom I don't remember at all) as witnesses. We then went to the Indian restaurant, but I suddenly walked out, throwing down the wedding ring, and headed back to 122nd Street because I thought Maurice was flirting with Didine—on our wedding day!

I do not recall how or when we made up, but we did because we consummated our marriage in a room Maurice had rented in Harlem. It was a front bedroom, quite spacious and adequately furnished. We met there a few afternoons and spent perhaps two nights together before he left for Haiti. The landlady looked at me with suspicion. Since the apartment door opened into a long hallway with both the bathroom and bedroom at the front, while the rest of the flat was at the back, I had no occasion to speak with her. Maurice had made all the arrangements. A few days before he returned to Haiti, Maurice and I were married religiously in the French Catholic Chapel near Columbia University on Morningside Heights. Since I was not Catholic, a side chapel was opened for us, and a young priest officiated. I promised to bring up the children we would have in the Catholic faith. This I eventually did, and our son John is (*nominally*) Catholic.

(*I would like to pause for a moment to consider how extraordinary it was that these two individuals ever met. To reach Teachers College, my mother had had to leave Hungary, struggle mightily to get a high school and college education, receive an eleventh-hour offer to attend Hartford Seminary and therefore turn her back on a teaching position that would have kept her in Ohio, change her mind (also at the last minute) about going to Connecticut and enroll at TC after realizing she hadn't enough money to pursue her first choice, literature studies elsewhere at Columbia. Had she deviated from this path at any point, it is highly unlikely that she would have encountered my father. If his own father hadn't died when he did, causing my father to abandon his plans for the law, had he not shifted into education and agriculture, had he completed his master's at TC all in one year, and had he not returned to TC for his final semester when he did, he would have never met my mother. It was, as they say in Yiddish,* beshert: *it was meant to be, despite all the odds.)*

In May, I finally told Mrs. Fleming of my marriage. I was setting the table. She entered the room saying she had not heard me talk of Maurice for some time. (She and I were in the habit of chatting together when she came to the kitchen to discuss menus and shopping.) I told her that he had gone back to Haiti and that I expected to follow him once I obtained my degree. Her reaction: that it was my heart that had spoken and not my head. My response: that might be so, but I was married and would join him when I had enough money to pay my passage. (So sure was I that it was with Maurice I wanted to be that it never occurred to me not to join him in Haiti.)

We had told no authorities of our marriage, and very few people knew about it. I wanted to keep my maiden name to finish the degree. Somehow a Harlem newspaper found out. Was it the landlady, the city clerk, one of the few friends who attended? I never knew, but the paper announced that a white woman student at Teachers College had married a Haitian. I doubt if many people knew where Haiti was. I didn't until I looked it up. (When I wired my parents telling them of the marriage and my going to Haiti, I added, "I don't know where it is, but I'm going.") On reaching the Rural Education class on the Monday following our wedding, some-one accosted me saying, "So you married Maurice Dartigue. You could have had any white man." I answered, "I was not looking for *any white man.* This is the man I wanted to marry." My voice gave her to understand that I wanted noth-ing more from her on the matter.

Mabel Carney wasn't convinced we'd wed and wanted to see the marriage certificate. She thought Maurice had left me. It was because of my marriage to Maurice that she became interested in Haiti. When she later learned that he had been named Director of Rural Education, she was pleased. After graduation, she begged me to write to her to let her know what Maurice was able to do, and we corresponded for years. When subsequently Maurice sent students from Haiti to Teachers College to be under her care, she helped in every way to make the students' stays profitable. I think she became quite proud of him and his achievements.

I decided that for my master's thesis I would do a paper on India since my original plan had been to go there. Moreover, from the stories I'd heard from Prem Chan Lal and Rose Devasahyam, I felt something should be written about the conditions and problems there. I did research, but I recall that although I accumulated a lot of material, I did not know how to condense, to synthesize. It rambled on, quite a hodgepodge. It is a wonder I received a passing grade. (At that time, I was convinced that only communism could save India, that only it could solve the problems of inequality and the disparities in income. How wrong I was in both cases. India is now free, but how far along has it actually come in terms of democracy and equality?) I'm sure it was Mabel Carney's generosity and interest that pulled me through. She was very kind, understanding, and patient. Being granted a master's was a gift for which I have ever been grateful.

I've forgotten how I obtained the summer/fall job as cook in the Robbins' household. He was Dean of the Cathedral of St. John the Divine in Manhattan, a tall, heavy-set, quiet man. She was thin, upright, and very English. I did not begin to cook until we reached their summer home in Heath, Massachusetts, but I did start to work for the couple at their Gramercy Park apartment. At the time, Gramercy Park was a quiet, elegant, and restricted residential area. I was there a week before we headed north. I had decided that the quickest and easiest way to have enough money to buy a few clothes and pay my way to Haiti was to cook. With all the experience I had gained at the Flemings', I knew I could manage—and do so more easily since now I had no studies to prepare. Lodged and fed, I could put most of my salary in the bank.

Heath was a small, nine o'clock town. It had dirt roads, crank telephones, bottled gas, and kerosene and coal stoves. Milk was brought straight from the dairy. There was a small grocery store, but meat was ordered from Pittsfield or purchased from a traveling butcher who showed up once a week. People like the Robbins came to get away from the heat and noise of New York City. Everyone knew everyone. When the telephone was cranked, anyone who wanted to could silently pick up their receiver and listen in and learn how much milk Mrs. X was ordering or if one of the children or a friend was coming up for the weekend and who would be sent to fetch them. (There was no public transportation.)

The Robbins had rebuilt an old, two-story, winged house and furnished it with New England antiques. For the help, they had added an annex off the kitchen. I rarely went into the main part of the house. The kitchen, pantry, and cooling shed were my spheres, apart from my room and bath in the annex. I enjoyed it all very much. I learned to use the kerosene stove, as well as the huge coal-burning one. The cooling shed was used for refrigeration, especially for the milk, which was set just above the ice on a shelf in a huge bowl so the cream could come to the surface and be skimmed off. I even learned how to make cottage cheese and butter. A gardener tilled a plot from which I gathered herbs or vegetables. I could ask him to get vegetables we did not have from a neighbor or farther afield. I made muffins of all kinds, especially from blueberries freshly picked, and Indian pudding in the oven of the big stove. Of course, shopping had to be done. I was driven to Pittsfield, where Mrs. Robbins and I did the necessary.

As the Flemings had, the Robbins entertained quite a bit. While I did the cooking, a student from Tallahassee, Florida, waited at table and did the house cleaning. We were company for each other. I heard about the amateur theater in the village and looked into it. A play dating from before the First World War was to be put on; it was titled *After Dark or Neither Maid, Wife, nor Widow*. I applied for the heroine's part and was accepted. It was great fun. Fortunately, rehearsals were held not far from the Robbins' house, so I could quickly run up after 9 pm, when dinner was done. I made my own mutton-sleeved red dress, which I wore throughout the play. For part of the décor, someone made a railroad train of cloth and wood with no depth that was carried across the stage on the run by two men at the appropriate time. My character's father who comes back at long last was portrayed by a summer resident, a clergyman from Washington, D.C. I've forgotten most of the play, except for when I recognized my father and cried out, "Father," and he cried out, "Daughter," and we fell into each other's arms. The theater was crowded.

People had come from all over to see it. It was pronounced a big success, and again I was told that I had acting ability and a good stage voice.

We formed a small group of young people who, like me, had jobs of one kind or another to make money. We borrowed books from the library, went on walks, swam in the Robbins' pool, and picked blueberries. Once, I was taken to a small cottage the Robbins had built in the woods of Vermont.

At summer's end, we closed the house and moved to the Robbins' New Jersey residence. It was built on the hills above the Hudson River and had well-tended gardens. It was a long, low house. I only saw the kitchen and our rooms. Here we spent part of the fall, with Dr. Robbins in New York one night a week for his work at the Cathedral. In this residence, we were quite isolated and had only the radio for entertainment and information. Even trips to New York were limited.

Finally, November arrived. Maurice wrote that it was no longer too hot and that he had found a home for us. I left the Robbins to stay in New York with a friend to shop and to buy my passage on a Dutch ship that plied the waters of the Caribbean, connecting Holland's holdings in the area. (It must be remembered that in 1931 only Haiti, the Dominican Republic, and Cuba were independent states in this region.)

It was my first experience on an ocean liner since my family's arrival from Hungary in 1914. To me it was very exciting. The more the ship heaved, the happier I was. It was very rough, especially as we passed Cape Hatteras.

I made my way to the top of the ship to watch it pitch and roll, holding on tightly to some object nailed to the boat. Few people were in the dining room, where the tablecloths had been wetted down to try to keep the glasses and plates in place and where the table tops had short fencing around them to at least keep everything on the table, even if things slipped around.

On the ship was a matronly American woman who introduced herself as the wife of the director (or maybe it was president) of a commercial enterprise in Haiti. She told me that the only words I needed to know in Creole were "Bum bagay la" *(or in modern Kreyòl, "Ban m bagay la"),* meaning "Give me that thing." I thought how sad that that was all this woman cared to learn about the basic language of the country in which she lived. (I myself became quite fluent in Creole.)

As we neared Haiti, the weather changed. It became warmer and warmer, quite balmy. When we landed in Port-au-Prince, it was hot for me, even in November.

Chapter Five

Haiti, Part I (1931-1934)

On this hot, muggy morning, my thoughts were only on how Maurice's family and friends would receive me. When the ship docked, there was Maurice anxiously looking up, and on seeing me, he rushed up the gangplank to take me in his arms. He was normally a very reserved person, but in this instance, he let himself go. Then we went to the cabin and sought porters to carry my suitcases. After the formalities of Customs and Immigration, he led me to a car belonging to a friend, who drove us to our quarters: two rooms giving onto the ground-floor front porch of a rooming house (or *pension de famille,* as the French call such accommodations).

The *pension* was on one side of the Champs de Mars, a large open square like a commons, with the *gendarmerie* opposite, grandstands to the left, and a row of houses and one of the city's two movie theaters to the right. On our side were several other *pensions,* a café, a bakery, and the other movie house. The front porch, shaded by vines and separated from the street by a garden and trees, served as the *pension's* dining area. I had only a quick look at all this after dropping off my luggage because Maurice's family had prepared the noon dinner and was waiting for us to arrive.

The other members of the Dartigue clan consisted of his gray-haired mother Régina; his two older sisters Thérèse and Renée; his younger brother Jehan; and his two much older aunts, his mother's sisters Maria and Amarante Duperval, who'd had a dry goods store in the town of Les Cayes *(pronounced Lay Keye, as in 'eye')* and had retired to be with Régina.

Jean Baptiste, the family's late patriarch, had been an orator and a jurist with a national reputation, known for his honesty and integrity. He had been a pre-eminent lawyer in Les Cayes (and some of the surrounding towns), and he was elected a *député* (the equivalent of congressman) for a short time but refused to run again. In 1912, Tancrède Auguste, the President of Haiti (and Liliane Nadal's maternal grandfather) appointed him Governor of the South. Two years later, he was asked to march on Port-au-Prince at the head of his regional army and assume the presidency of Haiti; but he said no, he didn't want to become president by means that were not constitutional. In 1915, he was again offered the presidency, but he flatly refused because he said that in this case, he did not want to be anyone's puppet *(under the American Occupation, which had just begun).* Shortly thereafter, he did accept the position of Minister of Agriculture and Public Works, which is what brought the family to Port-au-Prince. But after eight months, he resigned and returned to his law practice, commuting between Les Cayes and the capital.

He could have been rich, but he cared nothing for money, working pro bono for those who couldn't afford to pay and charging moderate fees to those who could. The central government owed him an enormous sum because, during the country's unstable years (1911-1915), as Governor of the South he'd kept his military units calm by paying the soldiers their salaries and pharmacy bills out of his own pocket, which the government could not afford to do and for which he was to be reimbursed. Just before his death, in 1924 (six months after a stroke), the International Claims Commission paid him an adjusted figure of what the Haitian state owed him. He gave a large part of it to the man who had pushed through the claim for him. The relatively little remaining was a combination of some cash but mostly bonds that the public had no confidence in. The family was urged to sell the bonds before they became totally worthless. That and the monies clients owed him but conveniently ignored at his passing explain why Jean Baptiste unwittingly left his family badly off financially.

Maurice had had to quit law school and enroll in the Central *(later, National)* School of Agriculture set up by the American

Occupation at Damien, where tuition was minimal and where he was able to secure a part-time job to help support the family. Thérèse and Renée, who, like most women of their class, had not held jobs, also went to work, the former as a clerk at the Bank of Canada, while the latter gave lessons to children at home. Jehan remained in school to complete his baccalaureate before enrolling in law-school evening classes while working during the day. This experience made Maurice extremely careful thereafter about money.

All this I learned a bit later. Maurice had not said much about his circumstances, nor did I expect much. But as we entered the family courtyard, it was obvious the Dartigues had a very modest income. It was a rented house, just below Sacré-Coeur church. There were no rugs on the floors; the living room was quite bare, except for an upright piano; and the dining room was also Spartan, other than the worn-out table and chairs. Maria and Amarante occupied the back bedroom; Thérèse and Renée, the middle one; and Maurice, Jehan, and their mother, the large front one.

A neighbor who spoke English had been invited to dinner to help me in my first contacts, although Maurice and Jehan were fluent in English. Perhaps the family thought my little French was not adequate enough to break the ice. But I plunged right in and, I'm sure, amused them with my translated English. However, I did not want to put a barrier of language between us and so struggled on. Moreover, the neighbor irritated me by all the advice she kept giving. I thought to myself that I would find out on my own or ask Maurice. As we ate, I smiled to myself for, to honor me, imported canned goods had been prepared—sliced ham, peas, and, for dessert, peaches—all quite expensive, whereas I had been looking forward to Haitian stewed chicken, rice and beans, and locally grown fruit. When dinner was over, Maurice said we had to hurry back to our quarters to pack a few things because we were going for a few days to a hotel in Kenscoff, a village high in the hills. It seemed this was to be our honeymoon.

Well, it was a fiasco. The road to Kenscoff was of dirt and very narrow. It curved in and around the mountains. I had often been carsick before, and now going quickly from the ship into the heat of Port-au-Prince, then up the mountains was too much. I barely made it. At the hotel, we were given a cold, damp room with the toilets downstairs. With all the changes in temperature, I became ill and used the staircase many times as I went back and forth. Evidently, the custom in Haiti for newlyweds was to shack up. After two days, I begged Maurice to take me back to Port-au-Prince. I preferred to be sick in private, with bathroom close at hand.

The food at the *pension* was not the best. There were several bachelors in residence, one or two of them in bad financial straits whom the owner did not want to throw out. Since not enough money was coming in, we sometimes were served a peasant dish, *maïs moulu ac pois (mayi moulen ak pwa,* i.e., cornmeal mush with kidney-bean sauce). Since my condition did not improve, off to the hospital I went, where

I stayed for a week. The medical facility had been built by the Americans during the Occupation. It had a large, two-story, central building and several small one-story buildings, in one of which were the private patients. The rooms all faced the wide, plant-shaded veranda. Friends visited in the afternoon, gathering on the veranda. I was honored by the visit of the Anglican prelate Bishop Carson, who became a friend despite the fact that he realized I would never become a believer or a churchgoer. To pay the bill, Maurice had to borrow money from a well-known moneylender who charged 20% interest a week! Back at the *pension* I had to be very careful of what I ate, but even with these precautions, I had bouts of dysentery. These would plague me during my entire fifteen-year stay in Haiti.

Maurice returned to work, and I kept our rooms in order. Our bedroom had formerly been the central hall of the *pension.* The main staircase leading to the second floor had been blocked off with a sort of partition to create the room, and a tent-like ceiling let in the light from the staircase window above. We had access to a toilet and a hastily put-together shower. It was when I was resting one afternoon, that on looking upward I saw one of the guests who had forgotten not to use these stairs (there was another flight at the back of the *pension*) and was staring at me lying on the bed as he descended. From that time on, I was wary of using that room during the day and implored Maurice to get us out of there as soon as possible.

Maurice later told me that the owner of the *pension* owed him money and offered to repay him in this way. He had accepted the offer knowing that otherwise he would never see any of the money. He realized how uncomfortable it was for me—the lack of real privacy and the food unfit for my needs—and so we began to look about for a house to rent.

* * *

At the first ball I attended in Port-au-Prince, I created a sort of sensation. It was my initial appearance in "society." I had been talked about, had been seen in town here and there, and had been introduced to a few people. But here was almost everyone, including the dowagers and chaperones, as well as dignitaries. The dowagers were sitting in a long row on the right side of the entrance, the length of the large dance floor of the Bellevue Club, located behind Sacré-Coeur, on the hills leading to Pacot. As we entered, my arm on Maurice's, we could hear the sudden stirring and see the heads turn from us to the neighbors. I do not remember whether I did it on purpose or not, but I had chosen a bright red material out of which I fashioned a gown of various triangles, a sleeveless bodice, and a huge bow on my *derrière*. I painted my fingernails and toenails red and wore open-toed, gold, high-heeled slippers. Well! I had a lovely time, and for days my dress and my dancing were the talk of the town.

* * *

Everyone grew roses in their gardens to sell to the florist since, prior to airplanes and greater private wealth, no flowers were imported, and roses were the main flower to be sent for weddings, funerals, and so on.

If there were no weddings, funerals, receptions, or baptisms to attend, the main afternoon activity was to either go visiting or be ready to receive people after 5 pm without notice or with a note brought by messenger—usually one's yard boy—to announce the visit. Few people had telephones, whereas everybody had a yard boy who took care of the grounds, polished the wooden floors with a coconut brush, scrubbed the tile floors, churned the ice cream, and ran errands. (*Because wages for household help were impossibly low, most of the bourgeoisie, regardless of income, could afford one or more domestic employees.*) Many homes in that area were within walking distance of one another, and the yard boy would be posted as a lookout so that one could hurry to be ready and be sitting on the front porch to properly greet the visitors on their arrival. (And if one received a visit, one always returned it in the very near future.)

Gossip was the principal ingredient of the conversations. One afternoon, I was at the home of my mother-in-law. The yard boy announced someone heading toward the house. I did not want to take part, so I withdrew and peered through the curtain. As the person ascended the stairs to the front porch, I could see that she was bursting to impart some news. I later heard the goodbyes and looked out at her departing figure. By the way she held herself and walked, I had the feeling she was very pleased with herself and with the gossip she'd passed on. It was extraordinary how news, often distorted and untrue, got around. I was often amused and sometimes indignant about the gossip circulated concerning me, the family, and Maurice. One bit of gossip was that I would not stay the year. Another was that Maurice and I were to divorce. After we moved into a rented house up on a hill, visits to us were far less frequent. People learned that if a visit was not announced long beforehand, I might not be home, for I could be out walking, playing tennis or bridge, or helping Résia Vincent (the president's sister) in her charity work.

* * *

Maurice decided we should go to Les Cayes, the town in which he was born and had lived until the age of 12 when the family moved to Port-au-Prince. The car ride was interesting:

we first went along the shoreline, then cut across the mountainous interior along the valley, crossing the same river at least twenty times, back and forth, as it pursued its difficult way to the sea. The road was wide enough for just one car at a time. Some crossings had primitive toll gates because this part of the road was on private property and the landowner wanted his due. It took us a full day. (Now with the new, improved, paved road bypassing much of the river, it takes just three hours.)

Les Cayes was small and sleepy. At one time, it was quite busy as a port, but most of the shipping had been diverted to Port-au-Prince, Gonaïves, and Cap Haïtien (Cape Haitian). We stayed with Amalia Bermingham, Maurice's aunt (his father's half sister), her son Lionel (who was in the import-export business), and Lionel's wife. *(Lionel was twice-married, but I don't know which spouse this was: Gilberte Villedrouin or Paulette Rouzier, a distant cousin of our good friends the Rouziers.)* They had a spacious home upstairs, with a large grocery store and depot downstairs. We were installed in the guest room where, we were told, President Vincent had slept when he visited the town. Here, for the first time, I had a proper Haitian breakfast. In Haiti, it is the custom to serve a small cup—a demitasse—of strong, hot coffee, well sugared, at 6:30 am, the aroma from which filled the house, followed at 7:30 by a copious meal of eggs, sliced avocado, toasted cassava, and any other dish one asked for. The table bore seasonal fruit, condiments, and imported fish—dried and salted, such as cod; or in oils; or smoked, such as herring.

Then we went about the town visiting various relatives. I became quite confused as to the connections and never did get them straight. I only had an inkling of how many families the Dartigues were affiliated with when years later the death notice of a cousin named Louis Durand appeared in the papers. *(We were related to the Durands in two ways: my father's aunt Carmen Duperval [his mother's half sister] was the wife of Louis Durand, while his aunt Amalia's son-in-law's sister Halida Hall wed Georges J.-B. Durand.)*

In addition to the Berminghams and Durands, there were the Rousseaus (through Maurice's paternal grandmother Rose), the Durochers (Maurice's maternal grandmother Doris), the Dupervals (Maurice's mother), the Voigts (through Maurice's other aunt Carmen, his father's sister), the Marescots (Louise Bergeaud, one of Maurice's first cousins, married Marcel Marescot), and the Durets *(Carmen Duperval Durand's daughter Amélie wed Jules Duret)*.

Kinships among other families with ties to us were interconnected, even complicated. There were the Léons *(to whom we were related in a number of ways:* through Maurice's aunt Amalia, who was a Léon; *through his aunt Carmen Duperval Durand's son Abel, who wed Etie Léon, a sister of* Rulx [*the 'lx' is pronounced like 'lix' as in, say, Felix*] Léon, an eminent physician and former Director of Public Health and Hygiene, *whose grand-uncle was Amalia's father; and through my father's grand-aunt Louise [Rose Rousseau*

Dartigue's sister], whose daughter Angèle Delerme married Rodolphe Léon, a first cousin of Rulx Léon).

There were also the Halls (Amalia's daughter Gabrielle wed François Edouard Hall, *while Rulx Léon's aunt Missis Léon married Edouard Joseph Hall, who was François Edouard's first cousin)*; the Duviviers *(Edouard Joseph Hall's mother Ermina was a Duvivier, who wed Théodore Joseph Hall, whose sister Rose Cecile Hall Léon was Missis Léon Hall's mother, Rulx Léon's grandmother, and Amalia Léon Bermingham's aunt)*; and the Bonnefils (Amalia's grandson Edouard II François Hall married Gisèle Bonnefil, *whose first cousin Maria Bonnefil had wed Duvivier Hall, Edouard Joseph Hall's brother).*

These were the closest, most all from Les Cayes, and largely from the second half of the 19th century. However, when I met and understood other family groups, I could not think why the Dartigue family never had reunions and family parties or kept up with one another. Maurice and I might have gathered the family at our son John's baptism, say, but Maurice never suggested it.

The name Dartigue began as Artigas in Portugal long, long ago, according to a specialized Larousse publication on the origins of French names, and DNA testing traces one of the male markers to Caceres, in western Spain, not far from the Portuguese border. Over time, the name's bearers proceeded across Spain and over the Pyrenees into southwestern France, where the second 'a' usually became 'ue'; the name, in some cases, acquired an 'l' or a 'd', while the 's' was kept or dropped; and in other instances, a suffix was added. Today in France, one can find such variations as Dartigue, Lartigue, Dartigues, and Dartiguenave and, in the south-western region, more than a dozen little towns called, among others, Artigues and L'Artigue, Artigat and Artiguedieu, and Bious-Artigues, some of which my parents came upon when they drove through the Basses-Pyrénées in 1958.

The male founder of the Dartigue line in Haiti was French, but his identity remains unknown. Fact and fancy have floated about for years, and it has sometimes been diffi-cult to separate the two. One relative told my mother that the first Dartigue in Haiti was named Saint-Cyr and had a son with a métisse *(the term to describe, in the tortuous racial classifications of the day, a girl born of a Caucasian father and a native Indian mother). Another relative told my mother that our ancestor was a naval lieutenant who came to Cap Français (the previous name for Cape Haitian) in 1798 and had a son with a* métisse. *However, a recent search of the French Maritime Archives in Vincennes, just at Paris' door, indicated that the naval lieutenant's last name was actually Lartigue. In his book,* Les Marrons de la liberté, *Jean Fouchard wrote that in Haiti the L of Lartigue at some point morphed into a D; but who can say whether it applied to our family. A tale twice told—by my Oncle (i.e., Uncle) Jehan to his son/my cousin Jehan Henri and by my mother to me—suggested that the family name had once been De*

L'Artigue, abruptly trimmed to Dartigue after the French Revolution (1789) to mitigate the chance of its bearer losing his head to the guillotine, but that, too, is unverified. In 1785, the Affiches Américaines *(the leading newspaper of the day) carried an item concerning "Marie-Catherine Mercy, dite Dartigue Longue," who was identified as a freed slave and a* métisse *and who resided in Les Cayes, where at least five generations of Dartigues were born. A 1775 edition of the* Affiches Américaines *mentioned an Ibo slave for sale, one of whose prior owners was named Dartigue.*

My first cousin Marie-José NZengou-Tayo, Oncle Jehan's eldest, has long had a strong interest in uncovering our common past. In May 2012, during the course of a scholarly conference in Guadeloupe, she made time to consult the island's principal library for M.L.E. Moreau de Saint-Méry's sprawling, three-volume, hard-to-find study of Haiti, published in the 1790s. (It, however, proved worthless to our purpose because Saint-Méry paid little attention to the country's South and Southwest, which is where Les Cayes is located). In August, during a ten-day visit to Haiti (from her home in Kingston, Jamaica, where she is an Associate Professor of French Literature at the University of the West Indies), she had intended to make a day trip to Les Cayes; but an unexpected hitch arose, and the visit will be scheduled for another time in the future. She later found on the internet a possible branch of our family residing in Venezuela. We'd been vaguely aware of the name but certainly not the location, and we essentially know nothing about them, including if and how we are related.

Most importantly, just a short time ago, Marie-José made a stunning discovery on the internet: an acte de naissance *(more formal than an American birth certificate) dated 1799, executed in Les Cayes and witnessed by a saddler known as Jean Baptiste Dartigue, exactly the same name given to our grandfather, who would not be born for another sixty-three years! Although this did not solve the riddle of the first French Dartigue to set foot in Haiti, it eliminated the naval lieutenant as a possibility once and for all; gave us a new ancestor we had never known about; seemed to indicate that one or more generations of Dartigues might have preceded him in Haiti and specifically in Les Cayes, possibly shifting the arrival of the Frenchman to around 1750 (if not before), as opposed to the late 18th century we'd been assuming all along; and made us wonder further if Marie-Catherine Mercy had been the* métisse *several had made reference to.*

Although Saint-Cyr Dartigue was no longer in contention as the originator of the family line, he was certainly not a fantasy. In fact, there may have been two Saint-Cyrs, for in the 1970s my mother found an 1823 confirmation of trans-ported merchandise and an 1884 property sale, both involv-ing a Saint-Cyr Dartigue and both notarized in Les Cayes. This could mean either one very long-lived individual or a father and son. My mother wrote in her account for me that, according to our cousin Rulx Léon, a genealogist by hobby, the Saint-Cyr of 1884 had been a Justice of the Peace in the district of Les Cayes, who, according to my Tante (i.e., Aunt) Renée, had a son Calaf with a mulâtre *(defined as part black and part white. Her name is unfortunately lost, as are most of Les Cayes' municipal records, consumed in a fire in the early 1900s.) My mother learned that* Calaf married Rose Rousseau, known as Belle Brune (both for her color and her beauty), whose father had been a *commandant* (the U.S. equivalent of major) in the Haitian army during the Haitian Revolution (1791–1804) and who, post-independence, was the first military commander of the *Commune* (municipal district) of Port-Salut, not far from Les Cayes. *Calaf and Rose had five children together—three girls and two boys, one of whom, Jean Baptiste, born in 1862, was my grandfather. In time, he became engaged to Gabrielle Duperval. However, she fell fatally ill (tuberculosis) and on her deathbed extracted a promise that he would wed her older sister Régina, which he dutifully did.*

* * *

The trip to Les Cayes was for family. Other visits took us inland, for sightseeing or for Maurice's job-related inspections. He wanted me to see the farm-schools and rural schools that had been put in his charge. He was understandably quite proud of what he was trying to do. The farm-schools had been created by the American Occupation in 1924 to improve the country's agriculture by educating the rural young. The teachers and the schools were to be the guiding lights and town centers. Already he believed in school and community cooperation. He also believed in pragmatic education, not just theoretical literary schooling.

Off we started from Port-au-Prince early one morning with provisions in the form of food, drinking water, and five-gallon tin containers of gasoline, for nothing was available, except in a few towns through which we'd pass. The roads were, for the most part, unpaved and rutted. Anything could happen, so we also had tools with which to dig out the car, if necessary. We had a good chauffeur who managed very well. I sat in front, where the bumping was less severe. Maurice had a wonderful quality: he could nap on the open road between stops. I, on the other hand, felt every jolt. In the small town of Saint-Louis, we paused for a cup of hot coffee. Maurice said it was a must because it was the best brew in Haiti, which had excellent coffee everywhere and prided itself on this specialty. We stopped near Saint-Marc at a farm-school where the classroom and workshop were well-organized and clean, and the gardens, thriving under the recent rains. On we drove to Gonaïves to lunch quickly with friends.

Haiti is a very small country, only some 10,000 square miles, yet its climate and geography have as many variations as a much larger one. There are rivers, plains, valleys, high mountains, lush green areas, and an arid one called La Savane Désolée (a really desolate savannah), which we passed through with the early afternoon sun beating down on us and the stench rising from several sulfur sources. This was after the comparatively cool green fields of the Artibonite Valley. When we finally started up Puilboro Mountain, it was such a relief, both physical and mental. Going higher and higher, back and forth, around curves, deeper and deeper into the hills, I was impressed by the beautiful scenery. Later, after seeing the Swiss mountains, I thought of Puilboro as the Alps in miniature, but as stunning and refreshing. We arrived in the evening at Chatard, the only post-primary farm-school, with about thirty boys as interns. Maurice had been the first head of this school for nine months before receiving the grant in 1930 to finish his master's at Teachers College. It was now only eighteen months later, so several of the teachers and students he had known were still there. Of course, we had a warm welcome, an excellent Haitian supper, and conversation about what had happened since he'd left. We were given a room and in the morning shown the classrooms, workshop, dormitory, gardens, and animals. We would return several times, but this first visit stands out.

We drove to Plaisance on our way down toward the Cape. In Plaisance, we stopped in the presbytery of the parish church to meet Père Codada, one of the first Haitians to become a priest. Up to that time, most all the priests had come from France, with a few from French Canada. Père

Codada was fascinating, aware of his status and differences, and regaled us with anecdotes.

Having still to visit several more schools, we left Père Codada to wind our way down to the Limbé River, over which we crossed on a bridge so rickety that the car had to go very slowly so as not to weaken it further. Fortunately, it was still there on our return; later in a storm, it broke up and had to have major repairs.

We visited a school near Limonade and went on to the church where the Emperor Henri Christophe was supposed to have had his first stroke. We also passed Marmalade before proceeding to Cape Haitian, where some vestiges of the colonial city remain, making it completely different from Port-au-Prince, which burned down twice and never had been as glorious in colonial times as the Cape. In the morning, we motored to the town of Milot, to which President Vincent later gave money to have a round chapel built, duplicating the one that had existed before the Revolution. Along the road to Milot were ruins of large gateways, the only remains of the colonial homes and properties destroyed during the Haitian Revolution.

I had already read about Henri Christophe and the great fortress La Citadelle Laferrière (the Citadel) he had built on a mountain as a lookout for a possible return of and invasion by Napoleon's troops or any other foreign army. Just before arriving at the foot of the hill we would ascend to the Citadel, we visited the ruins of Christophe's palace, Sans-Souci.

It must have been a vast and magnificent structure. Now, other than the intact, wide staircase leading into the palace, there remains only a roofless, hollow, broken-wall shell. But the huge tree under which Christophe sat to hear complaints, give advice, or serve punishment still stands.

We began the climb on horseback, up the winding, very narrow mountain path to reach the base of the Citadel, whose huge high walls jut out as if the edifice were an extension of the angular mountain, like the prow of a ship. It was in poor shape, not having been repaired since Christophe's time, but still awe-inspiring. Fortunately, it had been built very well, and despite the years of neglect and adverse weather, it still stood strong. It was several stories high, and we went from the prison cells at the lowest level, up through halls with old cannons pointing toward the Cape and the surrounding sea and piles of rusted cannonballs beside each emplacement. At the top of the Citadel was the parade ground, and in between were rooms without doors that must have been barracks. All this was constructed for the most part by hand labor. The cost in human life was enormous.

It was on later inspection trips that we reached Ounaminthe in the northeast, almost on the border with the Dominican Republic, as well as Hinche and Lascahobas, also near the Dominican border but farther south. From one area to another were largely hamlets and a few villages without electricity or water, except for water sources or streams. When I later learned that the annual national budget for the entire Haitian government with its functionaries (including teachers) was only $8,000,000 for a country of at least 3,000,000 people, I could understand the lack of facilities and the reason Haiti was referred to as the poorest country in the Western Hemisphere. Its only two natural resources were the pine forest, yet unexploited, and bauxite, soon to be exploited and soon exhausted. Agriculture alone was the mainstay of over 90% of the population, much of it done with primitive tools. There was some cattle raising and fishing, generally for local consumption; sugar, cotton, and their derivatives were the main exports.

* * *

The American Occupation of Haiti, lasting nearly twenty years (1915–1934), was another of those shameful overseas military adventures cloaked in flag-waving dissembling to hide the self-interest at its core. From 1911 to 1915, Haiti experienced considerable instability, with a revolving door of presidents (six in all—four sent into exile and two dying in office [one possibly murdered]). Rival political factions jockeyed with each other. Restoring law and order in Haiti was essential, said the U.S. propaganda machine, while the military was tacitly instructed to protect American and certain foreign businesses.

With World War I raging in Europe (but America not yet involved), one of the U.S. government aims was to exert a counterweight to the small German community that had inhabited Haiti for years (during the course of the 19th century) and, it was said, controlled some 80% of the country's commerce at the time. The Germans had skirted the constitutional ban on foreign ownership by marrying into the families of the Haitian upper class, something any red-blooded white American could have done, except for the teensy matter of racial prejudice. (In fact, once the Occupation was underway, the tension on that score became palpable, as did American arrogance.) Thus an additional U.S. goal was to rewrite the Haitian constitution to eliminate the foreign ownership clause, permitting Americans to launch an economic invasion.

Once the richest of France's colonies, Haiti had gained its independence through a slave revolt that dragged on for thirteen years (an unlucky omen of what was to come). The French exacted a price for this freedom by imposing ruinous reparations. By 1915, the country was borrowing heavily from U.S. and French banks to service its huge national debt, and the fear of a default, as well as a deep concern that the next Haitian president might be violently anti-American, allowed the U.S. government to give itself even more reasons for intervention. With State Department support, a group of American investors had already acquired control of Haiti's one commercial bank and with it the government treasury, and now with the Occupation, no Haitian government decision could be made without the express consent of American civilian overseers. (Iraq, anyone?)

There was some good to emerge from the Occupation in addition to the farm-schools, including the construction of bridges, hospitals, schools, public buildings, and miles and miles of roads.

The Occupation began to clear out as early as 1932; soldiers and other personnel and their families were leaving for good. This opened up a whole area of recently built cottages, tailored to American standards. It was the Occupation that brought the American bathroom to Haiti. Until its arrival, even in the most luxurious homes, people had washbasins in their bedrooms or there was a small room near the bedrooms with washbasin, water pitcher, and chamber pot (or else a *chaise percée* [pierced chair] with the pot underneath.) The maid or the yard boy brought down the slop jar. Drinking water was kept cool in large earthenware jars, and water was brought upstairs in pitchers to fill the washbasins. To freshen up before meal times, there was a small tank with a spigot attached to the wall and a basin with a flat back to catch the water. A little towel hung close by. For bathing, the small swimming pool in the garden was used, although some had makeshift showers in the backyard. Toilets were outdoor privies.

Consequently, when the Americans arrived, they demanded bathrooms. These were put into the new houses in the recently opened hill area of Pacot, where streets had been marked out and water brought down from a source higher up in the hills. Electric poles were erected, and a private electric company was installed to generate and distribute power. Maurice and I were lucky to find and be able to rent one of these relatively new houses, which was a two-bedroom bungalow. The view from the front porch, which was shaded in part by a vine called "rice and beans" (because it had small red and white flowers mixed up in the same cluster), was stunning. No house on the opposite side impeded this vista, which spread to the mountains across from the valley and allowed us to see a part of Lake Azuéï (also known as Etang Saumâtre), which extended to the Dominican border. We faced north, and the reflection of the morning and evening sun was often breathtaking. This view gave me great pleasure.

Maurice and I had very few belongings: a large bed whose springs and mattress he had ordered all the way from Chicago (probably from Montgomery Ward), a folding bed that became our living-room couch, a set of drawers, and a mirror. Our dining table was a board on trestles; our chairs, the kind with straw seats sold in the marketplace. Someone had given us a large mahogany, cloth-covered beach chair in which one could sit or lie back. On the porch were more straw chairs and a large kitchen table left by the former occupants. We usually ate and worked out there. The previous owners had also abandoned a small three-shelf collapsible bookcase, held together by wooden pegs, which I still have with me in Paris *(and which I now have in Los Angeles)*.

A pantry stood behind the living room, while the kitchen was in the backyard, attached to the maid's room. I insisted on investing in a refrigerator and a small electric stove with oven. I wanted to do the cooking. The maid could help me prepare vegetables and clean up afterward. She did her own cooking outdoors, and she washed the clothes outside, too.

I still remember my first helper, Ophise. She was young, pretty, and well groomed. She addressed me as "Madame" and always used the third person singular when speaking to me. We got along very well. Only once did she really upset me. My sister Rose had sent me three beautiful evening gowns, and I had worn them several times. (In Haiti at the time, one dressed for dinner parties.) I had decided they needed cleaning and had put them out on a chair in the spare bedroom. While awaiting Maurice with the car (he had bought one secondhand), I went to chat with a neighbor. Upon my return, on entering the front yard, I saw the three dresses hanging up in the backyard, dripping wet, with their colors running. It was a terrible blow. I could not scold Ophise, because she had thought to be of service. The only thing I could say to her was that she was not to take anything from that room without my telling her to do so.

After several months, Ophise asked if she could visit her family in the country for a few days. I granted her the holiday, and she was to return after ten days. Fifteen went by. Then came the news through a maid farther down the road who was from the same village as Ophise, Petit Trou de Nippe: Ophise had died after eating too many green mangoes. I was very much saddened by the news, and I must say I never had another helper like her.

On the road in back of us, in a similar house, lived Tamara Baussan and her husband Robert. She had been born in Baku, Azerbaijan, of Jewish parents who had fled with her to Constantinople in 1917 at the start of the Bolshevik Revolution. Two years later, they managed to get to Nice, in southern France, and then to Paris, where Tamara studied to become a secretary and where she met Robert, whose father had sent him from Haiti to study architecture. They married just before he returned to Haiti, arriving six months before I did. He was teaching at the School of Applied Sciences and was already building small homes. They had very little money, as did we. My friendship with Tamara grew partly because of our common circumstances—tight budgets and ingenuity in concocting dishes at little cost for entertaining. We exchanged recipes and went for walks. Through the Baussans, we met the group of Haitians who had been in France. Tamara and I even decided to have our children at the same time, but when she announced her first pregnancy, I told her we were not ready because we could not yet afford to have a child.

By the time she was pregnant with her second child, I was expecting our son John. But Tamara and I had not seen each other for at least two years. Robert could not bear Americans, and since I was American, he did everything to break up the friendship. What was interesting was that late in our pregnancies, Tamara telephoned to ask if she could come to see me in the house we had built, which was close to the one they had constructed. Even with our protruding fronts, we fell into each other's arms. John was born on September 12, 1940; Tamara's son Jacques, on October 15.

* * *

Maurice and I had to watch carefully what little money we had. We were never in debt, but we were often strapped financially. In addition to paying our monthly bills, a set sum was given to Maurice's family, and an equal amount was sent to mine in Ohio.

Twice during our first year, Maurice had become quite angry with me. The first time was because I wanted very much to have the two ends of the couch concealed by small bookshelves that could also act as end tables. I had saved a little bit of kitchen money and knew I could have them made and painted for $3 each. When they arrived, I placed them, then put books inside and on top a vase of wildflowers I had picked in the fields above our house. I thought Maurice would be very happy. On the contrary, he became irate when he saw them and asked how I could waste the little we had on such superfluous items. I was so upset that I walked out of the house into the dark night and stayed out for a good hour. When I returned, nothing more was said by either of us.

The second time he was in the right. I had joined a bridge group. I liked playing bridge and liked the group. Whereas at Wooster we had played for a prize, here the group played for money. One week I lost $10, a huge sum for our budget. Of course, I honored the debt, but I had to ask Maurice for the money. He was indeed furious and said, "You choose: either bridge or me." From then on, I played with others for fun but never again with the first group, and as I made other friends who did not play bridge, I slowly dropped it.

* * *

In the course of my first six months in Haiti, I became involved in a lot of different activities. For some of them, I would go down from Pacot into town and return on foot. I had also nursed Maurice through a dreadful case of bronchitis. He caught it while lying on the bedroom floor beside the slotted door to the porch after we'd had a quarrel. The doctor had come and put iodine all over his back. This made Maurice perspire a great deal, and both he and the bed sheets had to be changed several times a night. I did not sleep, watching his breathing, ready to give him a drink, wipe his wet brow, and administer medicine. One night his mother came to relieve me; another night, his brother. Sheets and pajamas were washed and ironed daily. My temperature went from the normal 37 degrees Centigrade to 35 (*i.e., 98.6*

Fahrenheit to 93.3). I had become anemic, and our house on the hill was very hot. The doctor ordered a change of climate for me. Kenscoff was suggested. I insisted on the U.S.A.

I wrote to the Robbins, and they agreed to have me work for them again in Heath, Massachusetts, for three months. Maurice accepted my going because my job, this time as housecleaner and waitress, would pay for my boat fare. My sister Rose came as cook, so we were together. Again I joined the theater group, although I do not remember the play we did, in which I had a much smaller role. It was fun to be out of the heat and away from problems and responsibilities.

* * *

I fell in love with Furcy *(pronounced Fur-see)*, a hamlet more than 4000 feet above sea level, the first time I saw it, in 1933. I was staying without Maurice in a little house in Kenscoff that Tamara and her husband shared with Liliane and Joseph Nadal. A dear friend had come up from town, Jacques Roumain, Liliane's brother, a poet and author. (His *Gouverneurs de la rosée* [Masters of the Dew], published shortly after his death in 1944, would go on to be translated into at least forty languages. *[The English version is by Langston Hughes and Mercer Cook.]*) He proposed a picnic to Furcy, which delighted me since I had heard of it but had never been. With a yard boy carrying the food basket, we started up the mountain. I was impressed with La Découverte, but when I saw Furcy in the distance below, surrounded by still other mountains, I was enthralled. After walking down a stony path to level ground, Jacques suggested we make our way at an angle to another mountain and a small area of pine trees where we could have our lunch in the cool shade. I thought, "This is for me"—primitive, uncluttered, quiet except for animal noises, no cars, and only peasants here and there. On another visit, in the company of other friends, we walked beyond the pines and down a steep hill to a pool that had been carved out by nature as the waters from above dashed down toward the sea. It was called Bassin Bleu, so blue were its waters. We took off our outer clothing and plunged in. It was wonderful.

I went up to Furcy a few more times with Tamara and others, and then when Marie-Thérèse Grant, a Haitian married to an American who had been a marine in the Occupation, asked if I would take her two young daughters, Ghislaine and Nicole, to stay in their house, I was more than willing. Although she loved Furcy and had spent many summers there, Marie-Thérèse could no longer do so because of a heart condition. Through our conversations (I'd been giving her daughters gym classes for a while), she realized how fond of Furcy I was. (Ghislaine, who came to be nicknamed Fatboy *[though the source has been forgotten]*, and I grew very close, and of all my Haitian friends, I've known her the longest, more than sixty years.)

The girls and I spent two months in Furcy. The house had a living/dining room and two or three bedrooms, one behind the other, furnished only with the strict necessities. A covered porch ran the length of the house and along the front. The residence was opposite the church, with a small, shaded open space between them. On Sundays, we sat on the front porch to watch the comings and goings. After church, the young gallants rode around the open space to show off their horsemanship. A very limited market was held. The city people exchanged greetings, and on occasion some dropped in on us. However, most of the time we sat on the side porch, which gave onto a narrow garden. The kitchen was at the end of this side porch, and if we saw people coming from the road to Kenscoff whom we did not want to see, we would race through the kitchen, out behind the privy, and hide ourselves in the growing fields in the back of the property. The girls and I slept in the biggest bedroom, in front. When Maurice came up on weekends, sleeping arrangements were changed, with the girls going into a back bedroom and the doors closed. Marie-Thérèse sent up food every week and gave me money to buy fresh fruits and vegetables from the passing market women. The cook was local, so the food was not too good. Occasionally, I did some of the cooking.

In a short time, Maurice and I decided to buy property in Furcy—although we had no intention of purchasing the bit of land we did acquire. We had wanted something nearer the main road. But most of the land had already been bought up or was in litigation. When I first saw the property we'd been told about, I was unhappy. It was halfway down the hill from a secondary road and the torrential rains had made deep gullies in the footpath that crisscrossed it. It had also been eroded from wrong planting and was barren. Only the morning sun and the mountain opposite it convinced me to buy it. The slope of the hill was at first steep, then leveled off halfway down before sloping steeply again down to the ravine below. We chose the area of level ground for the site of our shack so as to have the view and not have any house built in front of us. We hoped one day to buy the rest of the upper hill.

The property was shaped like a giant baseball diamond, each side roughly 100 meters (328 feet) long, and had over a dozen owners. We said we would deal with only one. A man named Vilmin brought me a tin box filled with papers. We sat under a tall pine tree. He asked me to look through the papers and choose the one I thought applied to this parcel of land, which had been given to his great-grandfather by the State as payment for his service as a soldier. I opened a paper and read parts of it, putting it into Creole. He would say, "It's not that one." I went on to the next paper and so on until I finally found the right one. He gave it to me to take to the lawyer and surveyor to do the necessary. What was remarkable was that Vilmin had such confidence that I would do the right thing and not try to cheat him in some way. Later, we bought from him the remaining upper part of the hill, altogether some seven acres (2.8 hectares).

We filled the huge gullies, first with trash, weeds, any-thing, then added landfill, which eventually became grass. We put the path the peasants used over on the side of the hill and planted cacti at the head of the property, cutting off the road in this way. We also had other gullies dug across the upper part of the hill from one side to the other as runoffs so that the water from the heavy rains did not deluge our property.

We found a honeysuckle vine on the land, one of the few good things able to grow, and we let it continue. It often perfumed the area. Once the shack was installed, we planted nasturtiums around it, and they prospered too. Later, we added sisal to hold the earth in place during rains, and we planted trees, many, many trees. We kept planting them because, although the saplings survived, they did not seem to grow, the soil was so poor. When we went back in 1950, they hadn't seemed to budge. In 1957, they had increased in size but only a bit. Finally in 1961, they started to reach upward, and then in 1973, I was astonished to find a thick tall pinewood above and below our shack. The only way we could see the stunning view of Morne La Selle (Saddle Mountain) was through small open spaces between branches.

The distinctive odors of pine, eucalyptus, and red gera-nium were easily detected in the clean, clean air. And there were birds: turtle doves, mourning doves, tiny humming-birds, love birds, canaries. Their songs could be heard all around. There were also crows and quail.

141

In the last twilight of the Occupation, we learned that the Americans were selling the simple homes they had put up in Kenscoff to rest and get away from the heat and noise of Port-au-Prince. The houses had wooden floors, tin roofs, and tin sides halfway up, with mosquito wire netting around the upper half. We bought one. Whether it was the Americans or the local peasants who took it apart, I don't remember. But it was brought over the hills in sections by the peasants to our property in Furcy, where wooden piles had been put in on the side facing the mountains, while the rest of the shack would sit on firm ground. It was reconstructed as two rooms (living/dining room and bedroom); a lean-to leading off from the living room was added as a tiny dressing area where guests could wash their hands or change clothes; and beyond that was the kitchen. More tin roofing was installed to make the walls solid bottom to top, and little windows were inserted in front (they did not open) to let in light, as well as wooden shutters on one side that opened during the day toward the mountains in the distance. We put up a three-foot wall to keep the land from sliding down. (Later, we added a free-standing room for John's nursemaid.)

* * *

My arrival in Haiti in 1931 came shortly after Résia Vincent's return. She had lived in New Jersey for several years, teaching French in private schools, and now put her energies into charitable works. Her bachelor brother Sténio had been elected President of Haiti the year before. She was generally referred to as Mademoiselle *(or Mlle, for short)* Vincent in deference to her age (60) and her position as first lady. She took over two vast rooms at the end of the left wing of the National Palace (which fronts a small square right next to the *gendarmerie,* which in turn leads to the Champs de Mars). The palace is oblong in shape, with two wings at either end and a dome in the middle, and is white-washed. A windowed-in corridor runs the entire length of the wing (although a middle section was taken over by the kitchen). In the front part were the president's quarters, with his offices. Mlle Vincent had made a pleasant, small, informal dining area hidden from the rest of the wide corridor by large, potted green plants. She initiated Thursday afternoons for receiving, and soon these gatherings became popular with the Haitian ladies, the American ladies of the Occupation, and the American business people. She and I became friends, as much as a 60-year-old, highly placed woman could with a 23-year-old whose husband was a functionary, and it was because of my friendship with her that Maurice and I were invited to dine at the palace from time to time.

On one occasion, in 1934, we were to meet the Duke and Duchess of Kent, newly married and on their honeymoon. It intrigued us that Haiti would have been included in their

Caribbean tour. The Bigios were English and had a beautiful home in the hills, situated on several acres, with a well-
cared-for garden near the house, quite removed from the
street so that the royal couple could be secluded and undis-
turbed. The Duke and Duchess had consented to one reception. They were charming. Princess Marina was beautiful and
gracious. She received us normally; we did not curtsy. She
appeared embarrassed when a woman, supposedly a Greek
(the princess was Greek by birth), did try. It seemed so silly
under the circumstances.

Earlier that year, in July, President Franklin Roosevelt
came by ship to Cape Haitian to formally announce the
end of the American Occupation as a gesture of the Good
Neighbor Policy. Maurice, as part of the government, was
there, having gone up by car. President Vincent hosted the
reception in Roosevelt's honor. Fortunately for me, I was also
present, due to the kindness of Mlle Vincent, for whom a
military plane had been offered so that she wouldn't be tired
out from a twelve-hour, hot and dusty road journey. She,
Mme Léon Laleau (wife of the Minister of Foreign Affairs),
and I had the plane to ourselves and were at the Cape within
an hour. Roosevelt came from the port by car. A ramp had
been placed over the entrance steps of the reception hall
to permit the president, who had had polio, to be wheeled
up. With difficulty he was helped out of the car. Flanked by
his two sons and wearing heavy leg braces, Roosevelt managed with great dignity to mount the ramp on foot. He filled

us with great admiration. I can still picture him refusing his handicap, determined to enter the hall with all the solemnity of his role as President of the United States. It was most moving and impressive.

The U.S. Marines as a group left in August 1934, but until 1947 there remained advisers of one kind or another—in the financial office, in Customs, in the army, and in health, as well as those in the American Consulate and Legation *(which would become a full-fledged Embassy in 1943).*

* * *

I held several jobs, though some were voluntary. The first, to augment our income, was teaching two girls, a ten-year-old and an eight-year-old, recently returned from the U.S., where they had been born. Their father, a well-known Haitian pianist who had been making his way in New York, had suddenly died of a heart attack, leaving his wife without any other possibility than returning to her family in Haiti. But after six weeks, I gave that work up since I did not have proper books and the girls were quickly integrating into their new milieu and fast forgetting their English. I told the mother that since they were going to be living in Haiti, they would be happier going to a French-language school and being with the other children. Besides, it would save her money.

Then I directed a group of girls in games and gymnastics. I'd gotten a call from Marie-Thérèse Grant, asking if I would give gym lessons for pay to her two girls. I said I would if at least eight girls in all could be found to make up the group. She managed to do this, and twice a week I went to Pétionville to lead the girls on the Grant tennis court. Then André Chevalier, an older Haitian friend of Maurice's to whom we paid Sunday visits, asked if I would be willing to put on a public exhibition of gymnastic exercises for a sports event to be held soon in the city stadium. I said I would do it on a voluntary basis. We gathered twenty girls of the bourgeoisie whose parents had granted permission on two conditions: first, that I would be on stage with the group, and second, that the girls would be properly attired. I promised both and decided on white bloomers (although shorts had just come into vogue) and short-sleeved middy blouses such as I had worn in high school. The girls practiced the different movements.

The Sunday afternoon came. President Vincent honored the event with his presence. The girls and I went on stage, went through our routines, and were loudly applauded. It was the first time young ladies of the bourgeoisie had performed in public. Two professional women singers also appeared. The president congratulated them and gave them each a bouquet of flowers. He did not congratulate me or give me flowers. I was miffed. A week or two later, there was a reception in the palace garden. Evidently, the president had been informed of my irritation. During the party, the Chief of Protocol approached me to say that the president would like to speak with me. Maurice and I went up to where he was standing. He then said how charmed he had been with the performance of the young ladies and handed me a bouquet. I thanked him, and after a few minutes, Maurice and I walked away. I thought it very silly to be strolling about with a large bouquet of flowers, so I set it down on a chair and later forgot to retrieve it to take home.

(*My mother introduced girls' volleyball and basketball to Haiti.*) I was then asked by André Chevalier if I wanted to help him create two volleyball teams, which I was willing to do since I had played both volleyball and basketball at Wooster. We gave exhibition games, and after a number of months, he broached the subject of putting on such games to make money. Here I begged off because I did not wish to become involved in any money-making schemes with him or anyone else.

My one visit to the Dominican Republic I owe to André. The subject arose when Maurice and I were paying a visit to him and his family. André said that President Rafael Trujillo had invited him to come to the Dominican Republic by a military plane he would send. In addition to the pilot, there would be room for five people, but as neither his wife Blanche nor his daughter Odette (who was part of the volleyball team) wished to go, he invited us to join him and two journalists, who would file reports. I was delighted, and Maurice was able to obtain a leave of absence from work. We spent three or four days in the capital of Santo Domingo. The men met with Trujillo. We were then shown various points of interest, especially the cathedral, which dates from colonial times and has on display a most unusual trunk that supposedly belonged to Columbus.

I shall never forget the return flight. Trujillo had given one of the journalists, Stéphen Alexis, a fighting rooster, which had been tied up inside a burlap bag. I asked the men to give their impressions of the visit, which precipitated an animated conversation. We had forgotten all about the rooster when suddenly there was a loud, vigorous crowing, and instinctively everyone looked out the plane's windows to see where the sound was coming from. Then we realized how foolish we were and turned our heads to the center of the small plane where the rooster was standing with his head outside the bag.

* * *

Maurice and I left Pacot because it was too hot and rented a furnished house that the owners used only during the three summer months. It was in Pétionville, at the time a summer village and today a town with permanent residents. There was no electricity. People used kerosene lamps and either charcoal or kerosene stoves. What I liked was that the heat was less wearing at that altitude. During the winter, we actually needed blankets. We had to sleep separately because the big bed in one of the rooms had a huge lump in the middle, preventing any communication between the two sides, while the bed in the other room was too narrow for two. We ate on the back porch, which also served as a pantry. When we had guests, we set the table in the small living room. I realized later how selfish I was to cause Maurice to drive so far each day downtown and then out to Damien, north of Port-au-Prince. But he was very patient with me, and he even let me have a dog, although he didn't much care for either dogs or cats.

There was a large backyard with several tall trees in which a flock of crows lived. Such goings-on! Such a racket! The yard was constantly alive with their chatter, their cries, their flying about. Thank goodness that with darkness they settled down. They were never drawn to the light of the kerosene lamp on the supper table, nor did they have any quarrels with our dog. Sadly, the dog was killed in an accident.

* * *

I continued the gym group on the Grant tennis court and had several students for English conversation lessons, including Mme *[Germaine]* Léger. One of the students taught me something very important: never to spend up to the last cent. She believed in putting some money aside for an emergency or a rainy day. She said that after she married, her husband gave her two *gourdes* a day for marketing. (That was the equivalent of about 40 cents of a U.S. dollar.) Of that she put away 50 centimes (or 10 American cents), one fourth of the allotted money, and she had managed. I decided to do the same. It was in this way that I was able to buy my first secondhand, table-top sewing machine, with hand-turned wheel, on which I made my dresses. Later, I traded it in for a used electric knee-shaft machine.

Maurice proposed that I go help teachers in a school near his office. I could accompany him in the morning, and he would take me back home at lunchtime, when school let out. There were two teachers with more than sixty girls in the room. On the first day, my presence provoked an attack of epilepsy in one girl and a feeling of unease in the teachers and the other pupils. After two days, it seemed best that I not return. Besides, for me, the heat in the crowded school room was more than I could bear. I shall always admire those two young women, making the effort to teach under such conditions.

* * *

In February 1934, I learned that my brother Otto had died after an auto accident. While I had been fortunate, for the most part, in the teachers I had had in high school, Otto had not had a single one who understood his needs. He hated school and often did not go or was put outside in the hall or sent to the principal for misbehaving and impertinence. Moreover, father and son did not get along. Otto ran away three times while I was still at home. Once, he went as far as Detroit. He had a friend down the street whose uncle was a streetcar conductor from whom the friend stole streetcar tickets to sell at lower prices. A policeman caught them trying to make a sale, and Otto was beaten by our father. Otto and I felt that leather strap quite often, he because he did not measure up to what our father expected of him and I because I did not always obey or was punished for things that were not my fault. The beatings drove me to find school a safe harbor and learning a joy. They drove my brother to despair. He revolted against father and school. After I left home, I saw him only once or twice and did not like what I saw. He abandoned school and held some kind of job. The accident happened in the early hours of the morning in the dead of winter *(following, said Uncle John Reithoffer, a party for my Uncle Art's 19th birthday)*. It was Otto's first outing after recovering from an illness. The car in which he was riding sought to pass another, got its wheels caught in streetcar tracks, skidded, and crashed into an iron pole just where Otto was seated. He died in the hospital an hour later. It was the money from his insurance that permitted the family to buy the house they moved to in rural Ohio. So in the end, he did leave a legacy.

It was also around this time that my brother-in-law Jehan received a grant to study at Cornell. He already had a law degree and was employed at Damien, but he wanted to know more about agriculture and production. His year in the U.S. put a strain on our finances for, although my sisters-in-law Thérèse and Renée both worked, the absence of income from Jehan made it hard for all of us. But we managed and Jehan came back with a degree that permitted him to have a promotion and better pay. It also benefited him later when he left Damien and the agriculture center and became a partner in Darbouco, a firm dealing with agricultural necessities— machines, seeds, soil-enrichment products, and so on—for he knew what it was all about and could give advice. The company, with a branch in Pétionville, is now run by his son/ my nephew Jehan Henri.

Chapter Six

Haiti, Part II (1934-1940)

Knowing we would have to leave the Pétionville house in June, we began to look for a large house in town. Maurice and André Liautaud had suggested I start a nursery and lower-elementary school based on American educational philosophy. After all, they said, I had the requirements and the license. Maurice had taken my diploma, a large 18-inch x 12-inch parchment to the inspector, who gave his authorization after Maurice showed him that he was holding the document upside down.

After some searching, we found a house *(belonging to Marie-Thérèse Grant's family)* that would serve both our personal and my professional needs. It had been empty for some time and was supposedly haunted. There were two very large rooms and a big back porch on the ground floor, and two large rooms with a bath and kitchen upstairs. It was near Sacré-Coeur, far from the street, and reached by a long driveway that ran between two houses fronting the street. It had a two-car garage and a big yard with two mango trees providing shade.

We made the garage into a classroom and did the same with the back porch, where I was to take over the youngest group of students. At the end of the porch was a partitioned area that became a dollhouse. A ledge near it was used as a table and lunch counter, holding the canteens of food sent by the families at noon for those staying in school for lunch. Different tables were set up. The largest, round with twelve low chairs, served for group activities and also for lunch. One big room was used for dancing, exercises, and, from 1 pm to 3 pm, the resting room for the youngest.

Maurice and I used the upstairs as our private quarters and lived there for three years. We were disturbed at first by various thumping night noises until we realized they came from a small turret where a family of rats had taken lodging. The thumps were caused by their jumping from step to step on the stairs leading from the turret to our quarters as they foraged for food. We took care of that. Also, the turret had to be nailed closed because during storms the wooden shutters flapped in the wind, and several times the birds from the yard trees (which were tall enough that their branches extended over the roof of the house) found their way into the turret but not their way out. They made all sorts of noises.

Too, the birds would drop what seemed like stones on the roof every so often, which made a sudden, loud, unexpected sound and thus would startle a sleeper. After Maurice and I moved out to Thorland, our quarters were turned over to the school's older children.

We called the school L'Ecole Moderne, and the language used, of course, was French. It never was a large school, having at most sixty to seventy children in four classrooms. The hardest task was to find teachers who did not use the memorization and recitation method (the typical French approach). I did find a good teacher for the older kids in Marie Labastille, who was enthusiastic and liked to teach. A Mlle Durocher did well with the younger children. The in-betweens, who were in the converted garage, never had a good instructor. The children learned, but not by way of dis-cussion, discovery, projects, or research at their level.

We organized plays and a parents' day and, with the older ones, went on field trips. I no longer had time to continue the gymnastics group Marie-Thérèse Grant had put together. But we instituted a gym class at school, which was held in the yard, and when the preschoolers were resting, I took it over. Among the children I remember at the school were the Grant girls, Fatboy and Nicole, and the Nadal twins, Jacqueline, who is no more but whom we saw a lot of in Paris, and Marie-José, who became a painter and coauthor (with Gérald Bloncourt) of *La Peinture haïtienne/Haitian Arts*. Marie-José told me a few years ago that she still remembered that it was I who taught her that mixing yellow and blue would produce green. The Nadals' cousins Daniel Roumain and Marcel, Marie-Thérèse, and Raymond Villard were also in the school, along with Daniel Hibbert, Colette De Lespinasse, Nicole Séjourné, Ivan Ethéart, and the Déjoie children—Jessie, Marise, and Louis, who a few years ago became a candidate for the presidency of Haiti.

I also remember the Bigio boys—David and Ben— and their sister Lily, who was the first to fly out from the garage classroom to pick up the mango just landing with a thump from the fully laden tree. There were, additionally, Ginette and Ghislaine Rouzier, Mi Ki *[Michaëlla]* Léger, the Lafontants, Gaston Baussan, and the Roy boys—Yvan and Reynold—whose mother Ghyslaine was told by the palm reader Mme *(short for Madame)* May that she would have three husbands, and she did. (After divorcing Fritz Roy, she wed André Liautaud, who was Maurice's good friend, became our son John's godfather, and was appointed ambassador to the U.S. She had three more sons with André: Frantz, Claude-Hervé, and Ghysandre *(who was also known as Zoupite)*. After André's untimely death in 1951, Ghyslaine married Pierre Liautaud, *André's first cousin once removed*.)

I gave Marie Labastille complete autonomy. I looked into the other classrooms occasionally, but I was too absorbed with my preschool group to give much attention elsewhere. With the several responsibilities (including the collection of fees) and with the heat to which I could not adjust during all the years we spent in Haiti, I slowly wore out. The trip I made to the U.S. (in 1935) or the stays in the mountains, in either Kenscoff or Furcy, helped me to continue working.

Fortunately for me, Marie Labastille became a good friend. She lived with her mother but could absent herself at any time. She often stayed with me while Maurice was in the States, and several times we went up to Furcy together to the Grant house during winter and spring holidays. She liked to hike and to read, so we hit it off very well. She did not mind the primitiveness of the cottage or the simple food, or the lack of heating when at night the temperature dropped to almost freezing. It was very cold in the early morning, and we would start the day with three sweaters and three slacks. By noon, with the sun fully up, we would be down to one sweater and one pair of slacks, and at about 3 pm, we would start putting clothes back on. In the evening, reading by kerosene lamps, we put our hands in a folded pillow and hated taking a hand out from the improvised muff to turn a page. We even tried turning the pages with our noses. Our main delight was walking—often to the end of the hills on which the house stood, to the west to see the sunset, to Bassin Bleu or to La Découverte, or down the valleys, carrying on all sorts of discussions. We were told to go accompanied into the valley since some of the peasants were hostile to city people and might chase us. We went alone and the only thing that happened was that we were both stung by wasps. Consequently, we never went back there.

Ti (*meaning 'little' in Creole, derived from the French 'petit'*) Joe, the *gérant* (or guardian) for the Grant property, must have been six-and-a-half-feet tall or more. He looked huge, whereas most peasants were short. When he rode a mountain horse, his feet almost touched the ground. He lived in a hut in one of the valleys, but was always at the house early. One day when I walked out to the front, I saw hanging from a small tree an object made of various bits of feather and fur. Ti Joe was there, and I asked him what it was. He answered that it was a *wanga* (*possibly the forerunner of the voodoo dolls of New Orleans*) and that the person for whom it was intended would understand if he passed the house. I said, "You take it off right away. If you want to put up a *wanga*, you do it at your house, not at ours." My voice must have sounded angry and carried weight, for he took it down immediately. Another time, we found on the footpath outside the house leading to the cemetery the trunk of a banana plant with a piece of wood stuck in its center. I asked Ti Joe what this meant. He answered that it was another *wanga*, adding that this did not concern city people. Those were the only two *wanga* I ever saw, but I heard of many placed about, either to ward off evil or to punish someone.

Marie Labastille's best friend at the time was Lucienne Mangonès, who was to be married the day after we were to come down from Furcy. Marie and I had walked hatless a great deal in the midday sun, which was hot, and it had also been windy. The night before our descent, we both burst out with full-blown cold/herpes sores on our lips, which had swollen to double their usual size. We had to go to the wedding, of course, but we couldn't let ourselves be seen like that. Once in town, we sent the yard boy first to one friend then to another, with a note asking for a hat with veil. Finally, the veiled hats arrived. We went off to the wedding but refused to eat or drink so we would not have to lift our veils. Too much sun without a hat always produced these sores, and I quickly learned never to go out unprotected.

* * *

Until the Sylvain sisters—Yvonne, Jeanne, Suzanne, and Madeleine—I think I was the only woman in Haiti to have a college degree. Yvonne became the first woman to practice medicine. Jeanne earned a degree in Social Work at Catholic University in Washington, D.C. Suzanne was the first woman with a PhD in ethnology and wrote several books on the Creole language and on women's advancement in both Haiti and Africa. Madeleine, who had gotten a law degree, was a feminist, too. (*Many years later, in 1985, my mother would write an article about the four sisters for the Paris-based Association France-Haïti's Bulletin.*)

Madeleine asked me to join her in forming the first women's movement, which I did with Maurice's consent. The organization was called La Ligue Feminine d'Action

Sociale *(The Women's League of Social Action),* and under its auspices I was asked to give a talk in April 1935 on the education of women in Haiti. Well, the conference, which took place at the Centre d'Etudes Universitaires, created a sensation because I came right out and said that the women were poorly educated. Even though the rural schools were open to girls (through Maurice's efforts), only 10% of the rural school population attended class and of that 10% only one-third or less were girls. Moreover, since there were many dropouts, the peasant girls typically had one or two years of school attendance, hardly enough to make a difference. The group between the peasant class and the upper class was not much better off. Some went for eight years, mostly to the private schools run by various religious orders. The children of the upper class also attended these schools which were based on the French program and where the emphasis was on proper behavior, manners, and savoir-faire at social occasions, with a little bit of art, literature, embroidery, and music thrown in. What was remarkable was how well Haitian women managed with the little education they received.

The audience, mostly of upper-class women, was indignant. Not only did they not understand that I was including in my remarks the peasants and the *petite bourgeoisie,* but they thought that I was dividing the upper class into lower, middle, and upper. It never occurred to them that the others—the peasants and the *petite bourgeoisie*—could be taken into consideration. How could I be interested in those groups?

The newspapers were full of my talk. A few thought it courageous and necessary. Some thought I was ill-bred to speak so directly, that it was an affront to the welcome I had been given by that very society I was criticizing. One woman wrote that she agreed with me but I should have put on evening gloves—meaning I should have been more discreet in my remarks. I later learned that my talk and the reactions to it had diverted the attention of the newspapers from a delicate and critical situation in the government. I imagine Maurice must have heard remarks but he never said a word to me.

However, I did not stay long with the women's movement. Several quite aggressive women took hold of it, and I was not ready to fight for the cause in that way. Besides, I was continuing to have health problems and was more interested in getting on with my school.

* * *

That summer, to escape the heat, Marie Labastille and I went for courses (practice teaching, music for children, and "The Activity Program in the Primary School") at Teachers College in New York. I do not remember how much I was able to offer her for the trip or whether she paid for herself.

We had reserved rooms at International House, and when we arrived, the registrar refused to believe that we were the Haitians expected. We said, "Oh, yes, we are." He responded, "You can't be. You're white." It took some time to prove who we were. We spent our mornings in class and our afternoons studying or sightseeing. Marie had school friends in Manhattan, girls who had been with her in boarding school in France. She invited me to meet them, and when our courses were over, we stayed with one whose parents were away visiting in Europe.

* * *

In 1935, Marie-Thérèse Grant sadly succumbed to the heart disease that had kept her bedridden for years. In fact, I had never seen her out of bed; she had managed her household from there. At the time, there were no funeral parlors in Haiti. The deceased was prepared and put in his or her coffin at home. The custom was that the minute one heard the church bell toll, one asked for whom it was, and without dressing up, one went to the home of the deceased to mourn or help. Since the Grants lived in Pétionville, a messenger came with the news. Leaving word for Maurice, I managed to get there in time to see the neighbors putting makeup on Marie-Thérèse, already dressed and in the coffin. She was buried that afternoon after the church service.

Subsequently, her husband Tommy asked me if I knew of anyone who would come as governess for the two girls, and I thought of my college roommate Mildred. When I had left Wooster for New York in 1930, Mildred had taken a job in a private school in San Juan, Puerto Rico. We had corresponded, and I had learned that she was quite unhappy. Behind the façade of a proper school, she had witnessed the teachers' backbiting, intrigue, and rivalry, for which she was not prepared. So I invited her to visit us in Haiti, and there she met Tommy, who hired her.

A year later, in 1937, Tommy and Mildred wed. But they had a rocky time of it, and in 1940 Mildred left the marriage and Haiti and went to live with her brother Ben in Chicago. She took a course in library science, landed a job with the National Safety Council of America, and stayed with that organization until retirement. Much later, during visits to the U.S. from Paris, I went to Chicago to see her and one year traveled as far as Yosemite National Park, where she was on holiday. She in turn came to see us twice in Paris. In 1980, Fatboy invited her to Haiti, knowing I would be there for a few weeks. Two years later, at her brother's home, Mildred married again, to Alex Coutts.

* * *

Mlle Vincent's greatest achievement was the creation of a boarding school in La Saline, a poverty-stricken area just outside Port-au-Prince. Its doors opened in 1935. Of course, as sister of the president, she was able to get things done and ask for favors not easily granted to others. In this case, she took over a building that she converted into a school, the ground floor of which was used for classrooms, a dining room, a chapel, and a small visitors' lounge. The upstairs was turned into a dormitory for one hundred girls. On the property was a large open hangar where she installed the kitchen with huge brick stoves holding giant cauldrons, a clothes-washing area, and showers and toilets. I helped by sewing dozens of sheets and nightgowns cut from bolts of muslin begged from dry goods stores and destined for the future students. (I worked so much in the heat that my blood pressure went way down.)

To have the means to make all these changes, buy cots, make clothes, and so on, Mlle Vincent put on all sorts of popular affairs. The most outstanding and unusual was when she took over the greater part of the Champs de Mars, putting up a dance floor, hiring a band, and installing a simple restaurant, gambling booths, and attractions with prizes. It was an enormous production for Haiti. I sold dances—that is, I danced with anyone who paid $5 a dance—and I made $50 on each of the two evenings of the affair.

At first, Mlle Vincent thought to have lay teachers for her school, and I believed that I might be of help in some capacity. But she decided it was best to have an order of nuns with no attachments, wholly devoted to service. Perhaps it was with the help of the Papal Nuncio that she learned about the Italian order of the Salesian Sisters. Soon five nuns appeared who remained in Haiti for the rest of their lives. The Mother Superior must have been 40 years old. The other four were young—two quite rosy-cheeked—and enthusiastic. They put in a garden and raised guinea pigs to ensure vegetables and added protein. One of them, the *économe (the person who handles a household's finances)*, went into town on foot sometimes to buy and sometimes to beg for quantities of food, such as macaroni, made by the Nadal brothers. Years later, I saw her still going about, much heavier, much slower, with feet hurting. These nuns were really devoted, and they finally received aid from the large charitable organizations Caritas and Oxfam. They added on to the building, putting up schoolrooms for the children of La Saline. One Sister also went out into the marketplace to teach the rudiments of the three Rs and simple sewing. When the Mother Superior retired, she went up into the hills and began a similar institution there. It became a boarding school for girls whose parents had gone to work in the States. Even later, a secondary school was started. In both, a tuition was required as well as a fee for the boarding facility. Mlle Vincent gave all her fortune to La Saline to build a church on the grounds, and so did a wealthy widow for the school in the hills.

Once all was ready, one hundred worthy girls were found to enter La Saline, the purpose of which was to train them to become skilled maids. They were to be taught the three Rs, cooking, cleaning, laundry, sewing, and other household tasks. They prepared a trousseau to take with them upon finishing. The school is still in operation. Today, it prepares girls to become secretaries, professional dressmakers, and so forth.

While Mlle Vincent was putting all this together, she was also creating a leisure club, which would become known as Thorland *(pronounced Tore-land)*, to fund the school. Again she was able to obtain property belonging to the government, which had lent it to an American group that had tried to grow rubber. Part of the property was occupied by the rubber trees, as well as some low buildings. On the largest of these buildings, she added a second floor as a dancing and dining area and had a bar, a tea room, a kitchen, and lavatories put in on the ground floor. She had four tennis courts built, as well as cabins, additional lavatories, and a swimming pool. She had an engineer go high up into the hills, where he capped a freshwater source and piped it down to Thorland, so there was plenty of water for the entire property. (When the Salesian Sisters took over the premises after the club was abandoned, they had little water available to them because people all along the pipeline had siphoned off water for their homes. Consequently, for drinking water the nuns put in a well [found for them by a water hunter] in an area where the salt water of the bay had not seeped in.)

When the club was ready, three hundred families became members. I was surprised when Mlle Vincent asked me to manage it. How did she come to the conclusion that I could or would run it? I still had my school, which I'd been operating for three years. But, with Maurice's consent, I took the challenge and became the facility's Director and a member of the Board of the Fondation Vincent pour l'œuvre des Enfants Assistés *(The Vincent Foundation for the Disadvantaged Children's Charity),* which oversaw the school and the club.

Maurice and I moved out to Thorland into a cement house that was spacious for a couple. It was a low, screened-in building with a large living room, bedroom, dining room, porch, kitchen, closets, shower, and toilet. Our house sat quite independently and had its own driveway. It was on the opposite side of the large property, separated by a wide field from another building, which had been converted into the clubhouse.

Despite the screens on our house, I had malaria three times while we lived in Thorland, once having a 110-degree fever that made me tremble with cold. We were at a party at Liliane and Joseph Nadal's. I was laughed at for complaining of being cold when everyone was saying how hot it was for the season. I finally begged Maurice to take me home. He put me to bed, piled blankets on me, heard my teeth chattering, saw me still trembling and shaking, and so called the doctor in town to please come, although it was past 10 pm. The doctor took my temperature and announced the disease. I lost eleven pounds in as many days, and Maurice and David Hammond, who had also been at the party, had to eat their words: "These women who are always complaining about their health." Another malaria attack later came on with a persistent ache in the small of my back. After two days, I could no longer stand it. Maurice drove me into town to see our doctor, who exclaimed, "It's good you came. Had you waited till tomorrow, it might have been too late." Some years later, when I was at New York Hospital in Manhattan, I warned the young doctors that I might have fever as the sun went down due to recurring malaria. "Thank goodness you told us," they cried. "We would never have thought of it." After Maurice and I moved out of Thorland, in 1940, I never had another attack.

I continued to direct my school while running Thorland. But it was too much, and I had to give up the former. With a few exceptions, it had been hard to find the kind of teachers we needed, and parents paid badly. L'Ecole Moderne had been a challenge and had exhausted me. As I look back, I wonder if it was out of kindness that friends sent their children, or if they really believed in our kind of school.

* * *

Maurice and I liked to entertain, even in our earliest days when we had almost no money. Because of my past cooking experience, I was able to put together dinners costing much less than those done by others. At Thorland, we continued entertaining at our own home with our own help. If we used the club, we paid like any club member. We were determined not to take advantage of my position.

We had quite a circle of friends, very few connected with Maurice and his work. They were mostly those to whom we had paid visits and met at parties, dances, or receptions who had invited us to their homes and whom we found interesting or fun to be with. They were largely Haitian or, like me, married to a Haitian, and generally our age. Of course, there were other friendships, some of short duration or circumstantial since we entertained foreigners passing through Port-au-Prince, or friends of friends.

Fortunately for me, I was able to have Marie Labastille stay with me at Thorland, too. As I have mentioned, rumors were always rampant, and although Maurice had confidence in my loyalty to him, had I not had Marie there, all sorts of gossip would have been flying about. Our son John's coming was announced to me four times before I was ever pregnant. Once an 18-year-old who had come to Thorland to play tennis walked around me, saying, "Are you really expecting?" My first thought was, "How can this young man possibly be interested in whether I am pregnant or not?" Were the young so short of conversation that such a subject could be a part of it?

Thorland was very busy. The staff consisted of four or five waiters, one or two cooks, and six gardeners. The waiters

were able to make sandwiches, but the cook(s) and I prepared the dinners, sometimes for fifty or eighty people at a
time. We put on tennis matches, swimming competitions,
table-tennis tournaments, charity balls, dinners, lunches. At
the time, the road from Port-au-Prince to Thorland was quite
unencumbered. (There were several large properties along
the road, which later, when broken up, produced an ever-
growing population, filled the road with people, cars, trucks,
and *tap-taps* (a form of transportation, a gaily painted pickup truck). A tanning factory was subsequently built, emit-
ting dreadful odors, so that the pleasure of going out to the
club lessened.) But while President Vincent was in office and
before the proliferation of restaurants and hotels catering to
large parties, Thorland was *the* place to go. It also had the
only protected, enclosed sea-swimming area. But apart from
that, we did not build any facilities, and the bathers came
to the clubhouse for refreshments. Few frequented the sea
beach, preferring to be in the shaded gardens near the pool
and tennis courts.

Thorland was the only leisure club open to all who paid the
monthly fee of three dollars. A collector was hired whose job
it was to go around town to pick up that amount. Although
the club had more than three hundred members, perhaps
one hundred or fewer used the facilities on a regular basis.
The young especially were grateful and often spent the day at
the pool. Tennis groups came for the afternoon. We catered
to tourists from passenger ships for luncheons and of course

had dinner dances to raise money for the Salesian Sisters. (We aimed for $350 a month, with more at Christmas.)

After Maurice and I moved out of Thorland and into our new house in Turgeau in 1940, I spent usually part of each day in Thorland and was always present for large dinners and parties. Antoine Dupoux was the club's overseer, daily manager, and cashier, and with the waiters, he handled small luncheons and the afternoon swimming and tennis groups. There had been a few managers before him; but it was he who proved he could do the job, and the club functioned quite well. (He later told me that I had taught him a great deal.)

* * *

It was only at official gatherings that Americans mixed with Haitians; in ordinary, everyday social life, there was very little contact. The Americans had their private clubs, and the Haitians, theirs. Very few of the Americans had learned French, and few Haitians knew English or else refused to speak it as a matter of national pride. So at these functions, there were the American women decked out in their finery, struggling to communicate with Haitians in the only way they could: in Creole, the language of the people, which amused me. The one Haitian the Americans always actively sought out, however, was Résia Vincent, the president's sister. They vied with each other to have her as honored guest at their luncheons and afternoon teas; after all, since the president was a bachelor, she was the First Lady of Haiti.

Many of the Americans were prejudiced, but certainly not all. One example were the Krolls, who became very, very close friends of ours. One day, Mildred said, "Esther, Margaretta Kroll is not like the rest of the Americans." Mildred had met her at the library of the American club called Pétionville Club, frequented exclusively by Americans. I had met Margaretta's husband Fred before they were married. Fred was the son of the Episcopal bishop for Haiti. He had been born in Hawaii, and his godmother, I remember his saying, was of Hawaiian royalty (*Queen Liliokalani, Fred Kroll Jr. told me in an e-mail*). He was three years younger than I, and when I first met him, he was still in college, at the University of Virginia.

Margaretta was a graduate of Bryn Mawr and had come to Haiti to visit an American classmate who worked at the American Legation. I did not see much of Fred until I met Margaretta at a reception, where we chatted with each other. Their son, nicknamed Ti Fred, was born four years before our son John. The Krolls joined the club at Thorland, so we saw more of them. We kept up with them long after we'd all left Haiti. In the late 1950s, Fred worked in Paris for two years; they then came back to Paris for almost yearly visits in the 1960s and returned from time to time in the 1970s and early 1980s. While we were in Burundi, they were in Kenya, after which I visited them in Morocco. We saw them while they were again living in Haiti in the 1970s, and in the 1980s I caught up with them in Sarasota, Florida, and at Grey Gables in Ojai, California, a retirement village where I briefly thought to live after Maurice's death. It was remarkable how our paths would cross time and again. The Krolls' great asset was bridge. They played it well, and it opened doors everywhere in the world they were stationed.

Another American couple we got to know well was Peggy and Bill Krauss, who came to Haiti around 1939. He was a journalist and wanted to write. They had little money until he passed the exam for vice-consul and became part of the American Consulate. Through them I met newspaper columnist Walter Lippmann and Harlem Renaissance novelist Zora Neale Hurston. The Krausses had become friends of the Krolls and had rented the made-over thatched peasant house with a lovely informal garden that Fred and Margaretta had relinquished for a fine new dwelling. When Maurice and I moved from Thorland to Turgeau, the Krausses took over the home we left. The first successful story Bill wrote and sold was to *The Saturday Evening Post* magazine about the hundreds of frogs croaking at night in the woods and gardens of Thorland. Many years later in Paris, Bill became the ghostwriter for ambassadors to OECD (Organisation for Economic Co-operation and Development) and had short articles printed in the *International Herald-Tribune*. They lived for many years in Paris while we were there, and, like the Krolls, went back to Haiti for a time in the 1970s and to

Grey Gables in the 1980s. We also saw them in Tangier and in the south of France.

How we came to know David Hammond I do not remember. He was an American vice-consul, and since he often came to Thorland, it is probably in chatting with him there that we became fast friends. (When I was free, I often went around the tea room and gardens [where there were tables and chairs] to converse with members and their guests.) He was living with a friend, Tom Henderson, who was also with the consulate, and they regaled us with tales of superstitions and horror stories they had picked up during their stay in Haiti. David's nickname was Coco Chéri, though how that came to pass I don't recall, either. (It was common for Haitians to be given nicknames, but not for Americans. There was an attempt to saddle Maurice and me with Momo and Tètè, respectively, but I quickly put a stop to that.) When Henderson was transferred, David took a smaller house. He then went on leave to his hometown of Price, Utah, and brought back a bride. There were festivities for them among the Americans. We were invited to none. It was two weeks after their arrival that David brought Marion to Thorland. We became good friends, but time and again Marion would telephone to say that the consul had advised them not to see Haitians. Naturally, this was political, but it seeped into the social life as well. Once in 1939, while we lived in Thorland, Maurice hoped to interest the Americans in what he was trying to do in the rural schools and invited a group to see a short movie and photographs. We arranged the screened-in porch, made food, and prepared drinks. The guests came, sat down, and watched the film. When it was over, I offered food and drinks. Only one, Mrs. Pixley, accepted. The others left immediately. It was not that perhaps they were not hungry or thirsty, but it was the way they acted—as if we were contaminated.

Marion left David after an unhappy three years. David was more content as a bachelor. He stayed on until after our son John was born, then was transferred to Spain, where he remained until after the war. We never saw him again but kept up with him by letter or telephone until his death in 1969, after a car accident in Malawi, where he'd been working with a charitable organization. Marion and I still correspond, and she came to France for two weeks some years ago. I in turn saw her and her husband Vernon Pearce twice at their home in Los Gatos, California, when visiting John in Los Angeles in the 1980s.

Another of the lasting friendships was with Eleanor and George Simpson. He was a sociologist and had come to Haiti to study peasant customs, especially their religion—voodoo. He decided to live near Plaisance, not far from Chatard, for six months, leaving his wife and two young children in Port-au-Prince. I visited Eleanor quite often, sensing how she must feel to be in a foreign country, not knowing the language. Her sister stayed with her for a time, as did her mother. George came once or twice a month to see the family, bringing written material for Eleanor to type and taking provisions back for his stay in the mountains. When he had completed his project but before he could have it published, the excellent book by Malcolm Herskovitz *Life in a Haitian Valley* came out (in 1937) and has since become a classic. George used the material he had collected for a series of articles and later went on to write an important textbook, *Racial and Cultural Minorities*, with his associate, Milton Yinger. (It was updated in successive editions as things changed in America.) George was also one of the first to look into the Rastafarian movement in Jamaica, whose members believe they descend from Ethiopian forebearers and not from enslaved people in other parts of Africa. George rose to be head of the Department of Sociology at Oberlin College in Ohio.

These were our principal connections with Americans until Maurice became minister in 1941. Subsequently, we had contacts with not only American officials, but those of several countries, especially from South and Central America. This was my reason for learning Spanish.

* * *

Maurice and I had driven into town from Thorland when news came of the massacre of Haitians in the Dominican Republic. This was in 1937, and we were in the area of Croix des Bossales. It was there that I witnessed my first *couri (or kouri)*—crowds panicking and running in several directions. It was quite frightening. The rumor was that Dominican President Rafael Trujillo was on the march with an army to attack Haiti. Maurice stopped the car, and we watched the vendors throwing their wares back into their baskets, lifting the baskets high, looking for the quickest way out of the square, and heading for it. When most of the crowd had left, Maurice managed to turn the car around, and we started for Thorland. We no sooner had arrived when Mildred telephoned to say that the lights were out in town, that we should seek safety because anything could happen. We decided to stay put. We had several oil lamps if the lights should go out. They did not. There was no panic in our area or in Carrefour, a small town farther on.

But for days, all was tense. There were more alarms and more *couri.* Rumors of all sorts were going about. The palace was on the alert for fear of an uprising. I realized that Mlle Vincent would feel deserted, so I decided to go into town to see her. Mine was the only car on the street. The palace gates were shut. I got out and said that I had come to pay my respects to Mlle Vincent. Since there were no telephones on the grounds, a soldier had to be sent up to give the message. He returned, the gates opened, and I can still see myself walking up the very wide stairs that led from the driveway to the palace entrance, with guards at either end of each step. I was not afraid. I wanted everyone to see that a friend in need is a friend indeed. I do not remember whether

I had considered that as a white and a foreigner, it was easier and safer for me than for a Haitian. In 1946, when it was
my turn to be in danger, Mlle Vincent stayed away. I never
really forgave her for this sign of cowardliness. Perhaps my
gesture was only bravado. Most people stayed at home to
see what the outcome would be. President Vincent kept his
job. If there was a plot to overthrow him, it did not materialize. Rumors of plots were common. The massacres and
their consequences might have put the presidency in jeop-
ardy. Questions arose. Why did Trujillo decide to have the
Haitian cane cutters killed? Why had he not rounded them up
and sent them back once the cane cutting was done? A few
months before this, Trujillo had been in Haiti. (He had visited
Thorland in the company of the president and Mlle Vincent,
and I had been introduced to him.) Had he come for negotia-
tions? Had they failed? It was estimated that at least fifteen
thousand Haitians were murdered.

The massacres did bring out the hostility of the Haitian
proletariat for the upper class. There was some pillaging
even in private homes. I knew of one intrepid house owner,
a tiny, frail woman who had gone out on an errand. At that
time, doors were not locked. Several women from the poor
section of town had worked their way up to Sacré-Coeur.
They spotted the open windows of this small house, and
not seeing anyone around, they boldly went up the front
steps and through the door. They were filling their baskets with odds and ends and enjoying themselves when in

walked the owner. Arms akimbo, she gave them a talking-to, insisted they empty their baskets, and then told them to be off. Without a word, one after the other they left, and once out of the house, they fled down the street. The owner called out for her maid, only to find she had hidden herself in a closet, trembling with fear. The maid also received a tongue-lashing, and all she said was, "Madame, you are you, but who am I?"

* * *

The French cruiser *Jeanne d'Arc* stopped in Port-au-Prince for four or five days, and there were all manner of festivities. We were invited to visit the ship. I became friendly with one of the young officers, who was a good dancer for a Frenchman. He took us to his cabin, and when I saw his personal refrigerator, I exclaimed, "Are you spoiled! Such luxury!" "Oh, no," said he, "we are not spoiled; we are cherished, for they know we will all be killed in the coming war." It saddened me to realize that this could be true. They were so young. On their last evening in port, they gave a ball aboard ship. Maurice refused to go, and I could not go without him. I was so angry. I broke a half-dozen glass-framed pictures, knowing I could put them together again, and they made a great clatter as they shattered on the floor. It did me good. (*The* Jeanne d'Arc, *launched in*

1930, fortunately survived the war and was not decommis-
sioned until 1964.)

* * *

In the summer of 1939, I made my second trip to Canada. I had hoped to go to France, where most of the group with whom we socialized had either studied or visited. (In fact, some of them were more interested in what went on in France than in Haiti!) I had picked up information about authors and other intellectuals and wanted so much to see this paradise for Haitians. But after talking it over with Maurice, I realized that the time was not right since the news from Europe was not reassuring. So I chose Quebec, where Maurice's friend, Auguste Viatte, was teaching at Laval University. (Maurice and he had first met in 1927 in New York, when Viatte was a professor at Hunter College.) I could improve my French and take in some sights at the same time. Arriving in July, I found my way to the university to register and asked where I could lodge. The suggestion was a *pension* called La Protection des Jeunes Filles Catholiques. Well, I was neither a young girl nor Catholic, but I was accepted. There were any number of young ladies, but some residents must have been more than 70 or 80 years old, in wheelchairs, who never appeared in the dining room but on some days were taken out on the porch while the bedding was changed, which was done every two weeks.

Quebec is a town of many churches. I counted thirty steeples from my window. Many tolled the hours, some even the quarter hours. We seemed to hear church bells all the time. In the dining room, I met several young women who had come from the interior of Canada and would return there once they made enough money to put together a trousseau. They spoke an odd French, which I tried to comprehend but not always with success. Others had different regional accents that made their French equally hard to understand.

In those days, Laval was a school for men. But in the summer, women were permitted, especially nuns who taught in the parochial schools, because a law had been passed obliging all teachers to have a degree. At the time, nuns wore the *coiffe* (starched bonnet). There were at least twenty different kinds, and in my spare moments I tried to count them. This was fun, since we had chapel every morning where we were all collected together.

Perhaps nuns did not need a lavatory, but I did. I went from floor to floor, only to find men's accommodations. I went to the registrar's desk. A cleric waited on me, and I explained the situation. He admitted that no one had thought about it. I told him that with urinals just inside the door, it was embarrassing for a woman to walk in and come upon a man using one. He did not know what could be done. I asked him to let me take care of it. I would put a notice on the door of the second-floor lavatory. The men could have the first floor. Armed with a piece of cardboard and black crayon,

I made a "Ladies Only" sign and tacked it up. I must have been the only person to use it because I never encountered another human being while in there.

The courses at the university lasted almost four weeks and were interesting. They consisted of French composition, grammar, conversation, and Canadian literature (which I had never heard of). I visited the Viattes, who were getting ready to leave for France for a holiday, and I went on a tour to Lac Saint-Jean. I thought it odd to have all signs in two languages, but then later a young Canadian on my bus going to the States found it odd to see signs in English only.

When the courses ended, I visited my family in Cleveland and traveled to New York, where I stayed with one of Marie Labastille's friends, Irene, who became a dear friend of mine and with whom I've kept up to this day. *(Irene would marry Walter Kent, but I don't recall that I ever knew her maiden name.)* Her family's apartment, on West 123rd or 124th Street, was small. Her parents had the bedroom, while Irene slept in the parlor, closed off at night to be her bedroom. Her sister slept in the dining room. It was because her sister was away that I could use the bed. None of us had very much money. Irene had been in Haiti as Marie's guest, and because we had seen each other very often there, I felt I could ask the family to take me in. This was the year of the World's Fair in New York, and for me its most interesting feature was the exposition of paintings. Irene's mother accompanied me. Her father no longer left the apartment; the radio was his connection to the outside world, and he listened most of the day, just as some people watch TV today.

Irene's best friends were Viola Kantrowitz and her husband Sidney, a dentist, and they became our friends. Later, when we moved to Great Neck, it was through Viola that we met her cousins Dorothy Lang and Lena Five and their mother, Mrs. Gurin. Lena was married to Helge, a Norwegian, and one of their daughters, Cora, was in the same class as our son John.

* * *

It was through Mlle Vincent's charity that I became friends with Marie Lavaud. She was Joseph Nadal's sister, and Maurice had known her since adolescence. She and her husband Franck had been living in the provinces, but Franck's army promotion had brought the family to Port-au-Prince. On one occasion, Marie and I prepared for a charity ball for which Franck lent us a military club. After we left Haiti, we did not see the Lavauds again for ten years, until we moved to Paris.

* * *

In early 1940, I helped Maurice with the chapter on education in Haiti for the yearbook issued in 1942 by the International

Institute of Teachers College, *Education in Latin American Countries,* published in French, English, and Spanish. It was edited by Isaac Leon Kandel, who was the most important figure in international education of his time, under whom Maurice had studied, and who had asked Maurice for the chapter.

I never held a position in Maurice's department or in any other government service. The Thorland Club, which I managed, was private.

* * *

After my three bouts of malaria in Thorland, I was determined to live in the hills, where the disease was much less prevalent. Maurice and I had been looking for a property to buy and finally found one that pleased us. It had an 80-foot frontage and narrowed to a point 500 feet back. It was like a slice of pie. The front yard was about 40 feet deep, part of it wooded, so the house would be protected from passersby. This was followed by a clear space, about 150 feet deep, for the projected house. There was another wooded area behind the house, and then a grassy, gentle slope in the back to the side, which on wash days we covered with wet sheets and towels to be bleached and dried in the sun and wetted every so often by our laundress, Clémencia, who stayed with us from the time we entered the house up to the time we left it, in 1946.

The property had originally been bought for $500 by Alfred Vieux for one of his six daughters. She, however, preferred Pétionville, and he sold it to us for $600. It was high on the hill called Turgeau (and because this section was even higher, it was called Haut Turgeau). At the end of the road was the Source, an outlet of the piping that gave part of the city its water from much farther up in the hills. At that time, those hills were deeply wooded, and there was as much water as anyone could want. Today, the area is covered with houses, and if people are lucky, they receive water for two or three hours a day, if that much. Some have put up large gasoline drums and/or filled cement reservoirs of various sizes, running from a yard square and a yard high to standard swimming pools, in order to have water for household purposes. Drinking water is bought in one-gallon and five-gallon glass containers. (In the past, Source water was boiled for drinking, but it is not clean enough for that today.)

We chose as architect a friend, the supposed Marquis de Veyrac, who had fled France (we never learned why), arrived in Haiti in the late Thirties, and, we thought, was almost penniless. He was charming, very polite. He did not show us his credentials. We may have been taking a great chance. There were a number of Haitian architects quite capable of building the house, but we chose him. The house is still standing, so he must have known something about architecture.

With the $4000 we had saved, De Veyrac was able to construct a two-story, retangular home. On the ground floor was an entry, an L-shaped living room that included a dining area, and a staircase to the upper floor. There was a pantry and *office* (as an indoor kitchen is called in Haiti) that led out to an open-air area with a charcoal brick stove and ledge. Off to the right, attached to the house, were two maid's rooms and the maids' bathroom with shower, flush toilet, and sink. I think these were the first such accommodations for help in Haiti. Most everywhere else, there were only latrines and kitchen sinks or pitchers of water for washing. One of the help was responsible for the bathroom's cleanliness, with each taking a week's turn. I told them that if it was not kept clean, I would lock it up. But I never had to do this.

We would live mostly in the very large room upstairs where we had a big window put in that had a magnificent view of the bay and the mountains (this is where we break-fasted every morning), a smaller window overlooking the terrace and garden in back, and a third window looking onto a neighbor's property. Off this family room was a large bed-room, bath, and dressing room. This last was converted into a very small bedroom when we realized that I was pregnant. In the Spring of 1940, we moved in, having furnished the house with odds and ends bought or given from here and there, as have all the homes in which I have lived.

The beautiful trees on the property, unfortunately, har-bored huge nests of termites, and we were constantly fight-ing their invasions, as well as those of giant cockroaches some two inches long and with a large wingspan. We put mosquito netting over our beds, not for mosquitoes but for the flying roaches and the occasional bat, since our windows stayed open night and day. The windows were wooden-slatted shutters, and we closed them only against the sun or rain or in our absence.

Maurice must have been in the U.S. when the strongest earthquake tremors hit Port-au-Prince. We were already in the new house, but John was not yet born. The quake was so unnerving that I jumped from the bed to open the bedroom's closed door but could not find the doorknob. It seemed as though the door was swinging from side to side. It was really I who swayed because I appeared not to be able to stand straight. Neighborhood dogs were making a dreadful noise with their barking. The moon was bright. The suddenness, the barking, the quake's strength, and the length of time it lasted were frightening. It finally subsided, as did the dogs. A smaller quake took place while we were still living in Thorland, and another happened when John was about four years old. He and I were breakfasting upstairs. The table shook, and I said, "John, stop shaking the table." He answered, "I'm not shaking it." And then I realized it was an earthquake.

CLEVELAND. At age 14, with older sister Katherine (top) (1923)

WOOSTER. Graduation (1930)

NEW YORK. In front of International House, with Maurice (left) and Rose Devasahyam (right) (1931)

HAITI. February 1937

HAITI. Her beloved Furcy
(summer 1938)

HAITI. On a tennis break at Thorland, the leisure club she ran
for charity (1939)

HAITI. Holding newborn son John, with
Maurice, Didine Maximilien (kneeling),
and Tamara Baussan (1940)

HAITI. With John in Kenscoff
(summer 1942)

HAITI. With Maurice and John (1942)

HAITI. At the Lycée Pétion, with (left to right), Charles de Catalogne, unknown man, Elizabeth Moffat White (wife of the American ambassador), Maurice, and Ulrick Duvivier (1944)

HAITI. With Maurice (left) and Jean Fouchard (ca.1945)

Chapter Seven

Haiti, Part III (1940-1946)

I had been told that I had a curved uterus and probably could not have children. Whether the curve had changed during the previous eight years of marriage, I don't know, but our son John was conceived on the initial try. In Haiti, most newly married couples had their first children within a year or two of their wedding, and in some cases after seven months. Up to then, Maurice and I had been very careful since we didn't think we should have children until we could afford to support them. But at the end of 1939, our general practitioner, Dr. Naumann, told us that we had better get on with it because I was not getting any younger and it would be harder and harder to give birth.

We did not announce the baby's arrival, but it was finally evident. It happened at Thorland. I was playing tennis with a friend, and we were picking up our tennis balls since we had not been able to find a ball boy. At one point, I could not reach over my front to pick up the balls. My friend said, "Esther, I do believe that you are really pregnant," and I answered, "Yes, I am, five months along." And of course, she spread the news. I was very big the final weeks. I felt like an elephant, especially in bed, where I could not find a comfortable position. One of our men friends remarked how misshapen my body had become, whereas another said, "Your face is alight with expectancy. It is a joy to behold." Maurice took it all very calmly, but I'm sure he was very happy to become a father. After it became known that I was expecting, several childless couples came to ask us what we had done to conceive. Since we had not had a child, they thought I had had an operation or had taken medicine of some kind. They could not believe we had done nothing.

I almost lost John twice—when I had my last bout of malaria at Thorland and, later at seven months, from overdoing. To keep him, I had to stay lying down for a week. I also suffered from amoebic dysentery and could hardly eat anything. For the three weeks before John arrived, I had little more than boiled *mirliton*, a light-green, squash-like vegetable with less taste than zucchini and even less vitamin and mineral content. It was remarkable that John was born as well as he was. I can only credit Nature. He was ten days overdue when he finally decided to come out. The temperature was as warm outside the womb as it had been inside, so we did not have to dress him too much in swaddling clothes. This was at about 11 or 11:30 am on Thursday, September 12, 1940.

The birth was not easy. Pains had started the night before which kept me up most of the night, walking back and forth in the upstairs of our new home. Dr. Naumann came at 7 am and told me to keep on walking. Since the bed seemed too soft, Maurice went downtown to find a board, which he brought back at 10:30 am, to slide under the mattress. He left the house, and the ordeal began. I started to scream with pain. The doctor said, "Stop! The workers who are building the house in back will hear you!" I answered, "To hell with them!" I continued to let out screams. He again urged me to stop. I yelled at him, "Who is having the baby, you or me?"

It was dreadful. John's head became stuck. I could see it—that is, the top of it—in the full-length mirror opposite me. The doctor kept saying, "Push, push, or the baby will be asphyxiated!" So I did, tearing the flesh. At the same time, he took hold of the head and finally wriggled him out. John was screaming and continued through the afternoon and night. I kept saying that he might be hungry, but the doctor explained that the baby was to have nothing but a bit of boiled water sweetened with a little sugar. I am sure John felt abandoned because of the doctor's Spartan attitude.

Mlle Vincent and her good friend Loulou *[Lucie]* Faubert came to see me. I was still upstairs after John's birth. I had not thought about godparents, but in the course of the visit, Loulou said, "Naturally it is

Résia who will be the godmother." I could not say no (but my choice would have been Marie Labastille). Maurice chose André Liautaud.

We had been invited to several christening parties, had not gone to them, but had sent presents. We thought they were stupid. So we did not have one for John following his baptism. For some silly reason, the mother of the child to be baptized did not go to the church ceremony, and it was my sister-in-law Renée who held John until the actual act, when Mlle Vincent took him in her arms. André Liautaud was in the U.S. at the time, so my brother-in-law Jehan took his place. Back at our house after the service, the godparents were served champagne. Mlle Vincent left, and only Maurice's family was present. Maurice had not suggested our having a party and of course in my family there never had been a party. Did we want to be different? Or did we not want to spend the money? We refused to go into debt. The new house had taken all our savings, and we would have to spend more if we felt we needed to enlarge it. Of course, there were no gifts, but we did not want any. I was surprised when a friend turned up with one, and she scolded me for not having announced the birth to her. (We had told only the family and the godparents.)

John's first few months were absorbing, so there was little social life for me. In fact, our whole way of life changed. For a time, we kept regular hours—no parties, no staying out late.

* * *

John had a digestive disorder of some kind. After I could no longer breast-feed him, we tried him out on cow's milk, then goat's and donkey's, then certain prepared milks, but nothing suited him. Finally, we managed to get formula from the U.S. and asked people who made official visits abroad to bring some back. But this did not work, either, and we donated the unused portions to the maternity and children's ward in the main hospital in town.

When John was about two-and-a-half, we were told he had childhood tuberculosis, allegedly contracted from a nursemaid. The doctor who made the diagnosis had just returned from France, having specialized in the field and wanting to open a sanatorium. Naturally, Maurice and I were frightened. On the advice of an American friend by the name of Pearson (first name forgotten), whose hometown was Asheville, North Carolina, which had a reputation for helping people with TB, John and I flew to the States. (We were able to do so because Maurice was minister.) During the train ride from Miami to Asheville, John became very sick. I had let him crawl on the floor, and perhaps he had picked something up, since he began to have diarrhea and fever. I called the conductor, who had the train stopped and found a doctor in whatever town we were in. The doctor looked him over but said he could do nothing and went off.

We were met in Asheville by Pearson's sister, who had contacted a nursing home and a specialist for us. I immediately called a doctor who gave John the right medicine. We really had to be careful about what he ate and drank. We installed ourselves in a bedroom with two single beds and a bath. I suppose I should have asked for a crib for John since he crawled about in the bed and never slept well. I put up a rope around it to hold him in, but several times I found him about to fall off at the foot of the bed. It seems I slept lightly because I awoke just in time each time. The food was good. I went downstairs for meals and brought up something for John, which most often he refused. We continued in Asheville for a while, but there was no amelioration in John's condition. I decided the alleged specialist did not know much about children's illnesses, and I was very pessimistic. I made up my mind to take John to Duke Hospital in Durham, North Carolina, which had a department for childhood diseases. I gave up the room at the nursing home but asked them to keep most of our clothes there. I said goodbye to the friends I had made.

It was a long train ride. Once in Durham, we went directly to the hospital, where John was admitted and placed in a special, isolated cubicle because of the possibility of TB, whereupon he burst into tears. The head of the department was of the opinion that John needed to learn English in order to communicate with the nurses and therefore should not be able to see me; consequently, all I could do was peek at John from behind some curtains. I felt awful seeing him cry.

I found a room for myself that turned out to be very uncomfortable, and there was no place nearby to eat. So I went back to Asheville. I telephoned Duke every other day from there. At the end of three weeks, I was told I could come pick John up. After collecting all our belongings, I headed back to Durham. What was my happiness when my first view of him was on a three-wheeled scooter, his foot pushing it as fast as it could in a race with another child up and down the corridor! I knew then that he was all right and that the doctor in Port-au-Prince had made a terrible mistake.

A young doctor at Duke gave me a report. He said John's upper respiratory ailments—such as sore throat, chest colds—could possibly be interpreted as tuberculosis; but John had been given a freshly made vaccine for testing TB and had shown no symptoms. However, he did have celiac disease (which explained his digestive problems), which could be fought, said the doctor, by liver injections or a syrup of liver. These would supply what John lacked. The hospital also recommended mashed ripe bananas, scraped apple, and scraped lean beef. (*In time I would outgrow the disorder, and years later, it was shown, with a specific test, that I'd never had celiac but something which at the time had been lumped under that heading.*)

We took the train for Miami, where we were able to get a plane for Haiti, again because of Maurice's position. I noticed that John never stood up when he was alone but squatted, and I decided that it was because in the hospital, a net had been placed over his bed and tied down so that he could not climb out or fall out. It took some days for him to get over this habit.

On reaching our house in Turgeau, John instantly recognized Henri (who worked for us in various capacities), shouted out his name, and ran directly to him. I then took John upstairs and put him to bed. Not having slept properly in over two months, he fell immediately asleep. It was so wonderful to know that he was free of TB. A few months later, I saw on the street the maid who had supposedly been ill and dying of TB when she had been with us. She seemed hale and hardy. Were the X-rays mixed up, or did the doctor in Haiti read factors into them from his great desire to put up a sanatorium?

In accordance with Duke's instructions, we kept starches and fats out of John's diet, but this was very hard. So he could have some companionship, I invited a few children on the Turgeau hill for a play group. (Because of his strict diet, it made more sense to have children come over to our house than for him to visit others.) Three American children from one family, the Curtises, who were attached to the American Embassy, walked up from Mont Joli three times a week and were joined by a little Canadian girl who lived just a few houses away, as did a little American boy. There is a photo in our album of John's third birthday, when I served Jell-O embedded with sliced bananas as a birthday cake since he could not have ice cream or cake because of the milk, butter, and flour.

* * *

It was around this time that John had the beginnings of diphtheria. I found two white stripes in his throat, and we were all given shots. I remember asking the doctor to give one to Monique, John's nursemaid. He looked at me in a funny way but finally gave her one, too.

We had had bad luck with nursemaids until Monique came along. Most had been inefficient and ignorant and hard to teach, and each had had different expressions and swear words, which John picked up quickly without knowing what they meant. Monique stayed with us until we left the country. She was young, pretty, well groomed, and careful. When we went out for the evening, we would put a mattress in John's room and have her sleep there (rather than in her own room).

We never had a night watchman since friends were so dissatisfied with theirs. Once, when I went downstairs in the morning, I realized there had been someone in the house during the night since several things were missing, even from the refrigerator. In fact, one of the desserts had a mark on it as if a finger had been poked into it. Another morning, when John and I were in Furcy, Maurice could not find his trousers. He looked everywhere, and finally it was Henri who discovered them in the back garden. During the night, someone had come up the stairs to the second floor, grabbed the pants, and gone out a window and down into the garden. After looking through the pockets, he had taken the money and left the pants. From then on, that window was kept closed.

* * *

The Haitian presidential elections came in the spring of 1941. At the time, Haitian women did not have the right to vote, so this only concerned the men. President Vincent had been encouraged to step down. I knew that Elie Lescot was the Haitian ambassador to Washington, but I had never met him. It was he who became president, and soon after his election, Maurice came home to say that he had been asked by Lescot to be his Minister of Education, Agriculture and Labor. *(While touring the country as a candidate, Lescot had marveled at the state of the rural schools and said that if elected, he would choose the one responsible to be his head of Education.)*

That same spring, Maurice was sent as a delegate to the Dominican Republic for a few days. Trujillo invited the group to visit his country home, where he showed off his two hundred suits and many horses. Was he trying to make amends for the massacres of 1937?

The years Maurice was minister roughly coincided with the war years. He was appointed in May 1941. The war was already on in Europe. The United States declared war against the Axis powers after the Japanese attack on Pearl Harbor on December 7, 1941. President Lescot did the same on the same day. Franklin Roosevelt was still U.S. President, and relations between Haiti and the U.S. were friendly. In fact, President Lescot depended on this friendship and used it to help Haiti.

The creation of SHADA (Société Haïtiano-Américaine pour le Développement Agricole, or Haitian-American Agricultural Development Corporation) in 1941 was a joint effort between Haiti and the U.S. to grow rubber in Haiti and also to find an acceptable substitute for rubber. This had been prompted by the grave concern that the Japanese would take control of the rubber-producing areas of Southeast Asia. The project was placed under the Ministry of Agriculture and thus absorbed a great deal of Maurice's time. (He was also made Vice President of the undertaking.) Because of this, there were many more contacts with Americans who were brought in as professors and for certain other positions, as well as with Americans already living in Haiti who managed to obtain posts of one kind or another at various levels of importance in the new company. As minister, Maurice was in touch with the American officialdom from the vice-consul on up, as well as with representatives of other countries, such as Peru, the Dominican Republic, Mexico, France, and Cuba (of those I remember best).

But in no way did we give up our personal friends; we added on our official entertaining and socializing. I spent my days at Thorland or with John—because of the long drive and the threat of malaria, I never took John to Thorland— or I helped Mlle Vincent with La Saline, while two mornings a week I was with the sewing group we had organized to make hospital gowns and layettes for the maternity ward in the main public hospital in Port-au-Prince. It was a hectic time.

The war did not affect us too much. Since gasoline was rationed, we had to have special tickets to buy it, but we did not feel deprived. I do remember hiding the tickets so they would not be stolen (since they could be sold for a good sum of money) and then not finding them when I was in desperate need of gas. I knew they were in the linen closet, but on which shelf and under what item? After taking everything out seven times, I was ready to undo every folded sheet, pillow case, and towel when I finally recalled that I had placed the money in a fold of the shelf paper on one of the shelves. What a relief!

Nor was Thorland greatly affected by World War II or by the lack of tourists since there were enough local members. Even with the presidential elections in May 1941 and the change from President Vincent to President Lescot, the club remained in full activity, since the new president and his wife were always cordial. However, after the fall of Lescot in 1946, Thorland declined.

* * *

Before Hitler invaded Poland, many Haitians had said that what Hitler did in Germany concerned only the German people. After the occupation of Poland, however, voices were raised against Hitler and his armies, for now it concerned everyone. There were many discussions. A group of Germans and their offspring born in Haiti formed a Heil Hitler group. We looked upon them with disdain. One of our younger Haitian friends had married a handsome German who, once war was declared, left Haiti by way of the Dominican Republic and later turned up in Germany as a *Gauleiter,* or so we were informed. *(A* Gauleiter *could be described as the Nazi Party's highest-ranking political leader at the regional level [though, I'm told, it was not a very important position].)* Another man who disappeared was probably picked up by a German U-boat since his empty car was found early one morning at the port of a town south of Port-au-Prince. He had married an American woman, and perhaps he had found a way to unburden himself. He was never heard from again.

Once we were at war, some of the German men who had been born in Haiti were sent to prison. Others who were German nationals living in Haiti were taken by the Americans and placed in internment camps in various states. This happened to Carl Heinrich Voigt, the husband of Maurice's paternal aunt Carmen. *He was a fourth-generation-in-Haiti German national. In 1904, he had dispatched his wife and children to Germany, where Voigts had lived for centuries in Uetersen, just outside Hamburg, because he thought the children could receive a better education there than in Haiti.* Before I came to Port-au-Prince, Carl Heinrich had had a big store in town, which had been consumed in a fire, and was left penniless. He subsequently lost his teeth and suffered from diabetes. In 1944, during his internment as an enemy alien in Fort Lincoln in Bismarck, North Dakota, he wrote to me, praising the Americans because he had been given treatment for his diabetes and a new set of teeth. At war's end, he was offered the choice of returning to Haiti or going to Germany. He chose the latter, of course, where he was reunited at long last with his family.

Dr. Naumann, our general practitioner, was German, and we continued our relationship with him until the atrocities against the Jews came to be known. I couldn't bring myself to use him after that. However, we had difficulty finding another doctor whom we liked and in whom we could have confidence, especially for our son.

* * *

During President Vincent's regime, on those occasions when Maurice and I were invited to receptions, we were placed, understandably, at the very end of the horseshoe-shaped table. Now, with Maurice's position as minister, we found ourselves seated at the top near the guest of honor. The visit of President Isaias Medina of Venezuela was a great event because of the special link between the two coun-tries. In 1815, Simon Bolivar had sought asylum in Haiti, and President Alexandre Pétion had given him arms and two ships with which to return to fight the Spanish in the north-ern area of South America that ultimately became Venezuela, Colombia, Panama, Ecuador, and Bolivia. Without Haiti's support, we wondered if Bolivar could have returned and gained freedom for that part of the southern hemisphere. For Medina's visit, the magazine *Cahiers d'Haïti* published a special issue dedicated to Bolivar and to the friendship of Haiti and Venezuela. At the presidential dinner, I was seated to the left of President Medina. We carried on a conversation in his poor English and my rudimentary Spanish. But carry it on we did. Fortunately, I have always been able to make conversation and had recently taken Spanish lessons. Here they came in handy.

At another dinner, it was my English that gave me a seat next to the honored guest, Dr. Max Bond, who headed a commission to strengthen Haitian-American relations. He spoke only English.

At various occasions, the Peruvian minister and I sym-pathized with each other because both he and I were try-ing to gain weight but could not. My usual weight was 120 pounds, but because of my recurring intestinal problems, I was down to 100. (What his reason was I don't know, but as a result, much of our conversation turned on that subject.) Naturally, for me this made for a mannequin size and an elegant look in clothes, but it prevented me from even tasting the dishes served at all these dinners. I took as little as possible, waltzed it around the plate, put the fork to my lips a few times, and pretended to eat. What I did do was talk, hoping my way of eating would go unnoticed.

The Mexican ambassador was a frequent visitor at Thorland, along with his two daughters with whom he often played tennis, and we became friends. We discussed food, and they were eager to have a real Haitian dinner. We invited them for chicken cooked the Haitian way and for rice and beans (Haiti's national dish), yams, *malanga* (a starchy vegetable), Caribbean sweet potatoes (very different from the American variety), both ripe and green boiled plantains, and coconut ice cream made with crushed ice in the old-fashioned ice cream churn, turned by the yard boy, who knew just how long it took and would have it ready at the moment it was to be served.

The ambassador in turn invited us for a Mexican meal. He ordered food from Mexico especially for the occasion. The other guest was a bank manager we knew who was part Haitian and part French. I ate what I could, which was not much, but enjoyed watching the three men. There was one dish consisting of fish in a sauce. The ambassador spoke highly of it before it was served. I took none. Each man took a portion. They ate, they swallowed, and soon their foreheads glistened with perspiration. Then it rolled down their faces in streams. The dish was so highly spiced that even they were surprised. The sherbet that followed was greatly appreciated.

I remember one of the buffet suppers at the American consul's home because of what I overheard. There must have been twenty or so guests. Most had finished the main course and were sitting in small groups chatting, waiting to be relieved of their plates. A few moved around as I did, going out onto the terrace to see the night sky and feel the soft breeze. On re-entering, I happened to pass a seated group of four ladies, one of whom was the American minister's wife. She was just saying, "Oh, Mr. Dartigue, we didn't think he had it in him, but just after a few weeks..." I could catch no more since I was moving on. I recall thinking, "So, just because he is modest, does not show off, nor cater to you, you thought he didn't have what it takes!"

On another occasion, the American ambassador and his wife came to our home for dinner. He was white-haired and elderly. The meal had gone well, and after it, we sat in the living room. I noticed that he was nodding off, and I was determined that he would not go to sleep at my dinner. So I sat down next to him and kept him in conversation until it was time for the party to break up. As I look back, it must have been torture for him, just as it had been a strain on me. It was later that I learned that he invariably went to sleep after dinner wherever he happened to be.

We held a cocktail party that Maurice wanted to have or thought he had to have. The situation between the Haitian members of the Board of SHADA and the American president/director was strained, to say the least. So here were Haitians and Americans drinking and chatting as if all was well. Knowing the circumstances and what everyone was really thinking, I admired them all for their and our hypocrisy. On the other hand, when everyone had finally gone, I hoped never to have to go through such an ordeal again.

* * *

President Lescot and his wife had a large family, if I remember rightly: five sons and two daughters. The palace was used for official entertaining. They acquired a manor house just off the main road to Pétionville that had belonged to the senior Elliotts. When Mr. Elliott retired as director (or president) of HASCO (the Haitian-American Sugar Company), he and his wife preferred to return to the U.S. and thus sold their home, known as the Manoir des Lauriers *[The Laurels]*. This is where the Lescots did their private entertaining. We were invited several times, and I remember especially one New Year's Eve. The party was held on the flat top of the house, which was a covered terrace. There was a dining area as well as an informal sitting area. The view of Port-au-Prince, the bay, and the mountains was stunning. That evening, I ate smoked turkey for the first time. I was sitting at President Lescot's right, and it made him happy when I told him I had never had it before and did not know it even existed. How he managed to have it and pink champagne, I did not ask. The war was on, but he was the President of Haiti, so for him it must not have been a great problem. I still prefer fresh turkey, but it was a novelty. Just recently in Paris, his youngest son, who has spent most of his life in France, gave me his arm to go into dinner. I told him that the gesture took me back fifty years when his father had done the same under very different circumstances.

President Lescot had arranged for the arrival of the French theater group headed by Louis Jouvet, the famous French actor. A buffet supper was held for them at the palace. We also invited the troupe to Thorland for a ball that was being given for a charity. I greeted them, then sat with Jouvet, who held forth with a number of young Haitians gathered around him. It was because of the war that we had this pleasure. Such an excellent theatrical company would have never touched Haiti, had Europe and Asia been open to receiving them. But only North and South America were available to them, and apart from certain areas in Canada and a certain group in Latin America, the company could not be appreciated as well as they could be in Haiti, where French was *the* language, as well as the culture and education. They spent several weeks there, during which they mounted such productions as *Dr. Knock* and Paul Claudel's *L'Annonce faite à Marie (The Tidings Brought to Mary)*.

A group of French intellectuals, also invited by President Lescot, visited Haiti in the winter of 1943–1944. It included André Maurois, the writer of biographies; Jacques Maritain, the Catholic philosopher; André Breton, the "pope" of Surrealism; Geneviève Tabouis, a well-known journalist who from New York edited a weekly newspaper, *Pour la Victoire (For Victory)*; and Henri Torrès, trial lawyer, prolific writer, leftist, and, while in New York, editor-in-chief of the newspaper *La Voix de France (The Voice of France)*. We had the friendliest relationship with Maurois. We had read his books, knew he'd had to flee the Germans, as had some of the others, and had found refuge in New York. Our conversations were a great pleasure at the various luncheons and dinners, one of which Maurice gave at Cabane Choucoune, the highly popular nightclub/restaurant, at which Maurois was the guest of honor. I recall our discussing the importance of selecting the right adjective, as well as Austrian writer Stefan Zweig's suicide in 1942. For his second marriage, Zweig had wed a woman much younger than himself. Maurois said that his own wife had been at his side since their youth, through thick and thin, and perhaps had Zweig still been with his first wife, who would have grown old along with him, he would not have felt the desperation that pushed him to take his life. *(Actually, Zweig suffered from depression throughout his adult life and created a number of literary characters who could be said to represent him and who committed suicide in the course of their stories. Zweig probably came to realize the futility of his running—from Vienna to London to New York to Rio. The final straw may have been the complete isolation in which he found himself in Rio [aside from his second wife Lotte, who, always of delicate health, joined her husband in death—by barbiturates.])*

* * *

Because of the summer courses Maurice held for the country's secondary school teachers, I had the pleasure of renewing my acquaintance with Auguste Viatte, whom I had visited in Quebec in 1939. How Maurice was able to have him and others come for a month on the tight government budget he had, I can't imagine, but he did. The American, Canadian, and French governments also sent scholars. These included W.E.B. DuBois, who gave a talk on "The Conception of Education," criticizing the Haitian upper class for not helping the wider population to have access to a full run of schooling, health care, and the country's culture, and writer-educator Alain Locke, champion of the Harlem Renaissance, who offered a series of conferences on the theme of civilization and democracy. Mercer Cook, former Howard University professor, headed for two years an American government mission of teachers to train Haitians to better teach English. We became lifelong friends with him and his wife Vashti. (He would later become the first black American to head in Paris the Voice of America, and one of the first to represent the U.S. as ambassador, first to Niger and then to Senegal and Gambia. We renewed contact with the Cooks in Paris, Dakar, and Washington, D.C.) Among those the French paid to have come was the poet, professor, and French National Assembly deputy Aimé Césaire, of Martinique.

My parents occasionally received gifts from visitors to Haiti, including The Negro in Art, *one of Alain Locke's books, inscribed with "a remembrance of Haiti," and* a basket of beautiful roses from Nelson Rockefeller, then U.S. Undersecretary of State for the Latin American republics.

It was by happenstance that I was in town when Viatte came to Haiti because, for the most part John and I were up in Furcy to get away from the heat, which very much affected me but did not seem to bother Maurice and his team or the foreigners.

Furcy was a saving grace for me. I even thought to be buried up there. Just above where our property met the road was a little cemetery with a few graves and small tombs covered with moss. From there the view of Morne La Selle was stunning. I loved Furcy because it was as yet little touched. For me it was a paradise and such a relief. I do not think Maurice liked it as much as I did, but he accepted it. The very simplicity of our lives in Furcy during those summer months was a joy and a distinct contrast to the protocol, intrigue, and pomposity of life in town, where the circle was very limited and everyone knew everyone. Once a friend asked how I could stay in Furcy for two to three months without coming down, and I answered, "The better to listen to all the old jokes and gossip." The round of receptions, dinners, and obligations was constant, especially after Maurice became minister. The casual wear of today was just not permitted then. In town, we dressed for any and all occasions, in silk, chiffon, organza, with hat, gloves, and high-heeled pumps. I recall once being hard put for a hat. I had seen in a magazine a Lilly Daché creation made of two flat lace rounds about six inches in diameter, held together by a wide black ribbon tied in the back. I took two sisal doilies normally used under finger bowls, threaded a black sash through them in the same manner as in the photograph, and wore it. Later, when we had a formal dinner at the house, I had to undo the hat to have enough doilies.

After many tries with various seamstresses, I decided to design and make my own dresses, since we needed so many changes of clothes—or so we thought. The wife of the American minister had no such problem. She wore the same chiffon afternoon dress at least a dozen times. It was not a question of money. We felt that she just didn't want to be bothered and that the social gatherings in Haiti were not worth the effort. On the other hand, the wife of the first secretary of the American ministry kept us gasping with her dazzling wardrobe. She was tall, willowy, beautiful, and charming. Even Maurice was eager to chat or dance with her. After wearing a dress two or three times, she would give it to Mlle Vincent to sell for the benefit of the Salesian Sisters. We thought this was a generous gesture and liked her the more for it.

* * *

The Haitian upper class had a poor opinion of the Dominicans, and I suppose the Dominicans had a poor opinion of the Haitians. Back in the early 1820s, General Jean Pierre Boyer, who became president of Haiti after the death of Pétion, managed to put the Dominican Republic under Haitian rule for nearly twenty-five years. Perhaps this fact made the Haitian élite feel superior. On the other hand, the Dominicans had dealt only with the poor Haitian cane cutters. However, I will say that the Haitian upper class had acquired a polish and a veneer that was not so evident in the homes and receptions of the representatives of the Dominican Republic.

One event amused us. It must have been the final reception given by the Dominican ambassador before his return home. (We were acquainted with the family because the father and daughter came often to Thorland.) There was a dressed table in one area of the receiving rooms. When I approached it, my eyes opened wide because in the center was a large enamel washbasin filled with a sort of potato salad, and the ambassador was urging his guests to partake of it. Later, the ambassador himself served individual hot savory meat pastries from a large emptied Chesterfield cigarette carton (one could not fail to see the lettering printed on the outside of the box). I didn't have anything but was bemused when the ambassador asked his American counterpart to have a meat pastry from this box. Was the reception an afterthought? Had the money for it not been sent until everything was packed? There certainly was a lot of gossip among the Haitians on the Dominican art of receiving. Perhaps cold finger foods and drinks would have been enough.

In contrast, at Thorland on one occasion, we were to receive several hundred guests, foreign doctors with or without their wives, as well as Haitian doctors and dignitaries of one sort or another. A committee of women had been formed and came to Thorland to discuss the luncheon with me. I begged to have paper plates. "Oh, no!" said the ladies. "The plates must be at least of earthenware, if they can't be of china." So we rented plates and wine glasses since Thorland could not provide more than two hundred, and cloth napkins as well, since paper ones would not do. Mlle Vincent arranged the tables, Loulou Faubert mixed the salads, and I handled the meats and the desserts. About ten charming young Haitian women were to act as hostesses, and they came to the affair beautifully attired. On the other hand, the foreign doctors and their wives arrived dressed in shorts and tennis shoes, as if going to a picnic.

I remember another dinner at Thorland, ordered for eighty people by a group of engineers, some of whom had studied in France. It was to be a five-course French dinner, one of which would be rabbit. Rabbits were scarce, but I managed to find twelve by asking around and going out to the villages since there were none in Port-au-Prince. The day of the dinner came, and the rabbits had to be killed. No one knew how to do this—not the cooks, the waiters, or the gardeners. Fortunately, I recalled how my father had done it, and although I found it distressful, I did what was necessary and showed the group, since all the help had gathered around to witness the procedure. After I had taken care of two, the cooks took over.

The animals were cut up, marinated, and roasted with a sauce. We were proud of ourselves. After the hors d'oeuvres and fish dishes were served, it came time for the rabbit course, which was carried upstairs to the dining room on ten platters. A few minutes later, down came the platters almost untouched. In dismay, I asked what had gone wrong. The answer I received was that the rabbits were believed to be cats. As I think back, I should have gone upstairs to tell these engineers the trouble I had had finding the rabbits. (Also, I could have saved myself a lot of work and rejection if I had known at the time that the most popular and best-known rabbit dish was *civet de lapin,* a sort of stew, which I could have easily had cooked and the guests probably would have eaten with relish.)

We gave many dinner-dances at Thorland that were quite successful. People dressed for the occasion, which made a pretty sight. These paying balls (to benefit the Salesian Sisters) were for club members and their friends and friends of friends. I must say that these could not take place in today's world. Doors stayed open. Cars were parked every-where and usually not locked. We had watchmen, but most of the time they slept or played cards or dice, not at all doing what they had been hired for. Tables and chairs were stacked on a covered terrace. The dance floor was open to the breezes (or winds). (We did have canvas awnings that could be let down if it rained.) I do not remember a single theft, except for one, of a sum of money I had foolishly put on a kitchen shelf. I knew it had to have been an inside job, yet dared not investigate and accepted its loss. I did not wish in any way to alter my relationship with the cook, a heavy Chinese, nor with the six waiters who worked very hard and carried out their responsibilities quite well. It was up to me to be more careful.

* * *

Infection was always a worry, because the number of deaths caused by a mere scratch of a pimple was high. Even I found myself in grave danger once from an infection in my left thumb. Fortunately, I called the doctor, who said that if I did not take care of it immediately, it would go up my arm, and then it would be too late. I sat or lay with my thumb in a cup of the hottest water I could stand, which contained a disinfectant. Cup after cup of very hot water was brought up from the kitchen, and I myself went down to fetch it during the night. This routine went on for twenty-four hours, at which point the doctor pronounced the danger over. Later, the doctor's own young son died of an infected pimple on his face, as did a Norwegian living in Haiti.

* * *

In the spring of 1942, I had to go to Johns Hopkins in Baltimore, Maryland, because, as a result of my dysentery, I was getting thinner and thinner and occasionally had to stay in bed. Sometimes John would come to sit with me or beside me. He was so solemn. In the hospital, I was given belladonna to quiet the spasms, and then steaks and other foods to put on weight. In a month, I gained twelve pounds. All the women gathered around to see what I was eating because they were strictly on hospital food—purées, gelatins, and so on—and here I was having steak. I was asked if I minded being put in the same room with a young woman allergic to the bacteria in her throat. I said not at all, "just give me a sleeping pill," for it seemed she coughed all night. She had been there for several months, too weak to comb her waist-long hair. We became friends, and I combed her hair. She finally was told to go to Arizona. Her husband gave up his job, and off they went west, where she regained her health enough to do her own housework.

The hospital gave me a regimen to follow, and then I left for Ohio to see my parents for a few days. My brother Arthur was already in the army, and brother John would be off later that year. Even the doctor at Johns Hopkins was affected. He said I was his last patient since he had just received word that he had been accepted to go in as an army doctor.

While I was in the States, I bought a scooter for John which I sent to Haiti by boat. Unfortunately, the ship must have been sunk by German submarines because it never arrived in Port-au-Prince.

I was gone for two months, and luckily, my sister-in-law Renée had been able to stay with John. When I returned, it took him at least a half hour to recognize me. When I first came upstairs, he stood by his aunt and kept looking at me. I talked to Renée and Maurice, and finally he sidled up to me and sat down beside me.

* * *

John went to Furcy for the first time in the summer of 1941, when he was nine months old. We stayed from June to late September and had his first birthday there. Renée came up to stay part of the time, as did Fatboy. The next summer we went to Kenscoff; but in 1943, 1944, and 1945, we were back in Furcy.

On the day we left for Furcy from our house in Turgeau, I would get up at 4 am to greet twenty or so peasants, men and women who had come down from Furcy during the night and would be seated on the lawn. I had prepared packages the night before. The group's leader would decide who would carry what and for how much. By 5 am they were on the road, and sometimes we would find them at the shack in Furcy, having managed the narrow paths that led up the mountains. We ourselves drove by car to Kenscoff, where several horses awaited us that we rode up and over the hills and mountains.

When we arrived at the shack, the first thing I would do was to open it up and have a small table and chair brought out. I placed on the table a bag of money and a pistol Maurice had given me, and then I sat down. The leader stood beside the table and called up one porter after another, telling me the amount to give him or her. I insisted on paying each one separately because I was afraid the headman would cheat if I gave him the total to parcel out. He might have taken a percentage.

We never had a difference of opinion and never was anything missing. Most of the packs were clothes, bedding, pots and pans, and staples that would not spoil in the long walk in the sun. The perishable food was brought in the car to

Kenscoff, so it was exposed for less time during the rest of the trip to Furcy. If it was brought up by horseback, it could be done in half an hour; on foot, it took an hour and a half at minimum.

In the evening as the sun set, I fired the gun to show that it was loaded and that I knew how to use it. Not that I was a good shot; my only experience was that one discharge each visit. I never had to use it for we were never bothered, nor did I ever hear anyone treading around the shack. At times during the night, we heard voices of people going up or down the path not too far from us.

We had no running water in Furcy. In the morning, we took showers out back in a makeshift shower, built against the cut-out hill, via a sprinkling can held by Ti Tante (Little Aunt, the daughter of Exaïce [*pronounced 'X-ä-eese' as in 'geese'*], the guardian of our property), which she emptied little by little over our heads when we called out for more water once we had soaped ourselves. In the evening, just before bedtime, I would have a sponge bath in a basin and threw the used water out of the window. For John we put out a large washbasin filled with water early in the morning on the uncovered part of the terrace. By noon, it was quite warm and we bathed him there. On rainy days, we heated water, and he was bathed in the bedroom.

For drinking water, Ti Tante carried water from a distance. Our neighbor, Simone Dupuy, allowed us to use the spring on her property. (It was the only spring of clean water in the area, which we boiled for drinking and cooking.) Ti Tante made several trips a day with the five-gallon tin perched on her head.

There were two privies out back, one for us and one for the help. We all had chamber pots for the night, with each of us carrying out his/her own to the privy in the morning. After each use of the privy, a small shovel of lime was thrown in.

Maurice was so busy that he could get away only on weekends and then not always. We never knew at what time he would be coming, so we did not watch for him. However, we always sent a saddled horse to wait for him in Kenscoff. He had beautiful boots, several riding pants, a sort of riding helmet, and a short whip. When we heard the sound of horse's hooves, we'd run out or go up the hill to see him arrive. Whoever saw him first, galloping up the hill, shouted, *"Main li! Main li!"* (or *"Men li! Men li!,"* meaning "There he is! There he is!"). It was a pleasure to see his silhouette against the brightened cliffside. When he left Furcy, mostly on Sunday afternoons, we would watch to see if we could spot him on the last rise of the mountain before he turned out of sight on La Découverte. He rode very well, having learned when he was young. As an adolescent, he had had two horses, one of which was called Dodine, which in Creole means 'rocking chair.' It was Joseph Nadal who told me about Dodine and how generous Maurice had been to let him ride the horse. At that time, Joseph was very poor, since his father had died, and, like the Dartigues later on, his family had had very little money.

Friends would come up to spend the day or part of it with us. We only invited people for a meal when Maurice also came with extra food, and we usually sat under the pines or lay on blankets in the shade at the front of the shack. We occasionally had overnight guests, too, and a few times friends, especially women, stayed a week or so. The living room served as the guest room, with a single bed (a divan during the day) on either side of the door leading into the bedroom where we three slept.

I remember one night when our guest was David Hammond. We had all gone to bed when we heard a loud knocking at the front door. We hastily put on dressing gowns, lighted a kerosene lamp, and finally called out, "Who's there?" Two friends answered, "We have come from Kenscoff. We were told you were having a party." How they ever found us—we were at a bit of a distance from the main road, and they had never been there before—I'll never know. We let them in. David quickly tidied his bed, Maurice put out glasses for drinks, and I started a conversation. Then I noticed David trying to push the chamber pot out of sight under the bed as quietly and discreetly as possible. We could not put the men up, so after an hour or so they left. Somebody must have played a joke on them, a cruel one, since the night was black, with no stars or moon.

I also recall the ten days Paulette Paquin and Giselle Faubert (who I think worked in one of the ministries) spent with us. Giselle had become a friend when I had taken Spanish lessons with her. She asked Maurice if she could come up for a few days with Paulette, who had been in Europe but had returned because of the war and now wanted to get out of Port-au-Prince. Maurice explained the simple conditions in Furcy. (He had known the Paquin family for a long time because their house was up the street from his family's. I had met the parents, but I did not know Paulette and her brothers.) Their visit was fun. We took walks, played games, and read. *(Paulette would soon wed Clifford Brandt, the brother of Ghyslaine Liautaud].)*

During the first summer with John, there was a hurricane. The nursemaid and John slept right through it. Renée and I stayed up all night fearing the roof would be blown off. (As a result of that experience, Maurice and I decided to put the shack on a cement base and nail down the roof with cut trees whose ends were buried in the ground.) The next morning, we looked out into the fields of corn, which were bent far to the ground, and large tree branches were scattered about. Simone Dupuy came to see how we had fared. She said she had been up most of the night but that her husband Fritz had gone to bed, saying he would know soon enough if the roof blew away. I had never before been through a hurricane in Port-au-Prince; the city is encircled by mountains, except for the bay to the west, and most hurricanes came from the east. Though it had some protection, Furcy was high, with our hill facing toward the east and therefore far more exposed than Port-au-Prince. We were worried about the peasants near us. However, because they were farther down the mountain, they did not get the full force of the winds. It was the only hurricane I was subjected to during the fifteen years I lived in Haiti. There were episodes of winds and rains during the hurricane season, but other parts of Haiti were far more affected.

In the summer of 1942, I rented a small house in Kenscoff for a month because Maurice was going to Mexico and he thought that in Furcy we would be too far from Port-au-Prince in case of a problem. He was right, for John became ill, and I had to send for the doctor. The cause was not the house (which was drafty) nor Kenscoff itself (which never had the early morning sun and was damp and much steeper than Furcy—among the many reasons we never thought to buy land there). It was my fault. I felt that liver would be good for John, and I believed the cook would broil it. But in fact, she put flour on it and fried it, which disagreed with John's stomach. The doctor prescribed an antacid, which we were able to get and I changed John's diet.

Back in Furcy in the summer of 1943, I started going on walks in the hills with John because I wanted him with me. I had hired Antoine, a bachelor peasant who lived the closest to us and who had been in prison for petty theft. I told him I knew of his past so that if anything was missing from the grounds, he would be accused. I would use him for various jobs, such as going with us on walks and getting water from a source in the ravine below our shack for scrubbing floors or washing clothes. He also went about when we needed meat, to buy a young goat, or if a calf or cow had fallen down a mountain and had to be killed, to buy a piece of it for our needs. For our walks, I would put a clean shirt over Antoine's shoulders and head. John would be placed on his shoulders, and off we would go.

Once, on the hill across from ours (we were separated from the hill by a deep ravine with a waterfall at bottom where we would sometimes bathe), the head of a large family group died. It seemed that everyone in the surrounding area went to the wake, including Antoine, and we were kept up during the night by the wailing and the chanting.

We had been in the habit of asking the peasant women carrying baskets of produce on their heads up or down our hill if they had any eggs or vegetables we could buy. For four days, almost no one passed. At last, Antoine showed up, very tired. He said it was he who had gone down to Port-au-Prince once enough money had been collected to buy a coffin, and it was he who had carried the coffin up from town on his head. I listened, then told him to go quickly find a young goat to buy since John had not had meat for four days. Antoine went and, in half an hour or so, returned with a young goat. I told him to kill it immediately. He asked if he could sit on the ground to do it. I answered, "Stand, sit, or lie down if you want to, but kill it." Then he asked if he could drink the blood. I said, "Of course. All of it." So he found a receptacle, killed the animal, drank the blood, and then gave the liver, the heart, and the kidneys to be prepared for the noon meal. One leg was sent to Mme Mangonès, who often sent me gifts of food. The other leg was hung up to be cooked the next day. The rest was cut up to make *tasso*, a Haitian specialty. (Strips of raw meat are marinated in a brine made of vinegar, lemon, or sour orange juice, plus salt and various spices. This mixture is rubbed into the meat which is turned and stirred often in a large enamel basin. Then after two nights, the pieces are placed on the roof or hung on a line to dry in the sun. This would take several days and could only be done, obviously, if there were sunshine, since we had no refrigeration in Furcy.) When I served it to Maurice on his next visit up, he asked what it was since he did not like goat meat. Fortunately, it had been a young goat and had not as yet acquired the strong goat odor. The spices also helped to disguise the meat's color. I rarely lied to Maurice, but in this instance I did. I told him that a cow had fallen into a ravine and had to be killed, and we were lucky to have gotten a piece of it. He ate it without incident with fried plantains.

In the summer of 1944, John was old enough to be taken up to Furcy from Kenscoff on a *bête chargée*, a horse loaded-down with deep baskets on either side of the saddle, because John could clutch the saddle's horn. Exaïce held the rope and led the horse. We climbed up the hill to La Découverte, which has a flat top, and then began our descent toward Furcy, which is on the side of the rising sun. The view was beautiful, breathtaking, of the lower hills and valley, and opposite that the high range of Morne La Selle, which in the early morning light is pink and purple.

The narrow road was rocky and, in some places, worn deep by horses and rain-formed gullies. We had to be careful to have the horse's head held tight so it would not pitch and throw the rider. Just before reaching one of these gullies, my horse reared. Exaïce, thinking I was in danger, dropped the rope of John's horse which, taking fright, galloped off toward Furcy. Exaïce raced after it. I steadied my horse and watched John clutching the saddle, then beginning to slip off on one side while clinging to the bag pack, and finally falling to the ground. A peasant coming from the opposite direction managed to stop the riderless horse while I galloped toward John and jumped off. John was lying on the ground, crying and frightened. I said, "Don't touch John. Let us see if he can get up by himself." I was afraid. He did get up, and I took him close to me and asked, "Where do you hurt?" He answered, "My hands." What a miracle! He hadn't broken anything, the horse's hind legs had not kicked him, and he had fallen from the left side of the horse onto flat land, rather than from the right side which would have sent him off into a precipice. Fortunately, this incident did not stay with him, and he rode horses afterward.

* * *

The peasants were very superstitious. They put food in a *gourde* (gourd, in English), *calebasse* (calabash), or bowl on the graves of their dead or at crossroads so the ghosts would not come back to their homes. Exaïce would not tell us the real names of his daughters, whom we knew only as Ti Tante and Tite Soeur (Little Sister). We did know the son's name, Raphael, because Maurice was his godfather, and to this day he is given money annually *(until his death around 2006)*. We also gave Ti Tante sums, and each time we returned to Haiti, I would get to Furcy one way or another and seek them out. It was not easy, for they lived far down a valley. Once, with John on his shoulders, Exaïce took me around the hills and down to the level of a gushing source of water. I asked him why he lived so far down. He said in the winter it was much warmer. While we were in residence, he brought his family to live on a bit of land he had further down on our hill on an out-jutting. He also had a growing field on the setting-sun side of Furcy. Each year he would announce his absence of four or five days to go see a property at a day's walk from us, behind Morne La Selle. We never learned if he had another family there.

On the opposite side of our hill's footpath lived a peas-ant woman named Destina. She had two boys by a married peasant. She was hostile, as were her sons, because when we had planted trees, we had taken some of the flat land on which she had been accustomed to planting before we bought it. She had hoped to continue planting, but we said no. When she gave birth to a third child, I asked Exaïce what its name was. He said, "I don't know it, and if I did, I would not tell you, for if anything happens to the child, it would be said it was my fault because I'd told you its name."

One Saturday afternoon, Maurice and I strolled by a Protestant mission and greeted a peasant we knew who was attending the service. The next morning we walked in the other direction so Maurice could stop into church on the village square. There was the same peasant, coming out of the Catholic service. A few days later, we encountered him again. Maurice noticed that he was wearing a shirt with four stripes of several colors which indicated that he had made a vow to the voodoo religion. Maurice stopped him and asked what he was doing, wearing that special shirt. "Monsieur, I have been brought up believing in voodoo," he answered. "Then I was told to go to church [the Catholic one], and then the Protestants came and I joined that church. But I must not offend the voodoo gods, so during the week I wear this shirt." What could one say? I suppose if another religion were to install itself in Furcy, he would join it too.

* * *

Ti Tante had her First Communion at our shack. Monique, John's nursemaid, had prepared her. In order to make Mme Exaïce feel that she was participating, I asked her to provide

232

a chicken. Monique saw the scrawny thing and said it would never do, so I bought several more. Monique helped the cook marinate them. We prepared them in a stew and with it a huge cauldron of rice and beans. After the church service, the family returned to our shack, and Ti Tante broke bread and drank a small glass of wine. Then we served the family. As there was no fence and no gate, peasants sprang up from all directions and said they were family. We had to accept this, and at the end we were serving the chickens' feet, necks, and heads—which fortunately we had included in the stew, thinking Exaïce would take these home. We ran out of plates and served the food on banana leaves that one of the peasants had gone to fetch. I did not take part in the festivities, because I was too busy in the outdoor kitchen. We finally declared the reception over and asked Antoine to clean up the place. It was my turn to sit down. I don't know if Maurice ate, but I did not. From then on, we made no more celebrations in Furcy.

If peasants were caught in the rain, we offered them shelter and a drink of *tafia (tafya)*, a sort of cheap rum made from sugarcane. Before they would begin to drink it, they always let fall a few drops on the floor as a libation for the dead. After their departure, we had to scrub the floor so the marks would not become permanent. Besides, although they tried to scrape the mud from their feet at the cement edge of our terrace, they would track some in, which had to be cleaned up as well. Even on sunny days, peasants passing up or down the path would call out or come to sit a few minutes, especially the women.

When we bought produce or eggs from passing vendors, we had to be careful in the expressions we used. I recall particularly one concerning eggs. We could not say, "Do you have eggs?" For them that meant, "Are you pregnant?" Instead we had to say, "In your basket are you carrying eggs?"

For a while, I sold the peasants pieces of the long brown lengths of washing soap that they and we used. This was long before detergents, and it was the only soap available. It was a little more than an inch square and fifteen inches long. I bought it in town by the dozen, then cut up each one into four or eight pieces. The reason I did this was because I was shocked at the prices charged by the vendors who came to the small market by the church once a week: they collected the price of two or three bars for the one they'd cut up. But it ultimately became too much for me, and I did not continue.

In the summer of 1945, Exaïce came one day to announce that he was separating from his wife because she had "dropped" in the field an unborn child that was not his, and he would not have anything more to do with her. The next morning, his wife came to see me. Exaïce ordered her off the grounds. I called out, "Exaïce, this is my property. Madame is my guest. If you do not want to see her, you go down the hill." Mme Exaïce never asked me to intervene, and I never learned if he took her back.

John sometimes played with Raphael, who was about his age, when Exaïce would bring him around. John's other friends included the three children of Tigo Blanchet (Tigo was her nickname; I never knew her real first name *[it was Denise]*), Lucienne Mangonès' sister. Normally they lived in Les Cayes but came to be with their grandmother and great-grandmother in a large shack near the back of the Furcy church. The shack was even simpler than ours. I think it had a dirt floor.

We also saw the McConnells, who had three children about John's age. Reverend McConnell was one of a few who tried to put into writing the Creole language. Maurice included him in the Creole pilot project. He and his wife liked Furcy very much and had a small shack way below, at the far end of Furcy. It was a steep up-and-down incline. To come up, they used a horse on which they set the three children. We never went as far as their house nor they to ours. We met on the square between the church and the Grant cottage or at the end of the Furcy plateau. From here, there was a most beau-tiful view of the different valleys and the mountains, behind which the sun dipped in the evening, giving off a breathtak-ing glow. We often went to sit on a log someone had put there just at the edge to watch the sun go down, then hurry home before it was too dark to see our way.

One evening, however, we were too late leaving the pla-teau. Night came rapidly and a storm threatened. John was on Exaïce's shoulders. We cut across fields. I had a flashlight and turned it on, thinking to help Exaïce. He shouted, "Turn it off. My feet are sure. The light only disturbs me." It was true. He was sure-footed. I shut it off and stumbled after him among the upturned clods of earth.

Another day, Monique, John, and I went walking down our hill. The grasses and weeds were quite tall, and Monique and I could hardly see John. All at once, Monique saw a spider on his shirt sleeve. She took a leaf from a nearby plant and with it plucked the spider from his shirt. She said that luckily it had not bitten him, for it was poisonous.

From then on, we took our walks on the footpaths or played on the cut grass next to our shack. But still there were bees and wasps to contend with, and every once in a while, we had to have the latter smoked out. There were also scorpions and black widow spiders, both of which were dangerous since they could cause high fever and sometimes death. There were small harmless snakes but no other wild animals, except field rats, which sometimes gnawed their way into the shack. It was for this reason that, on leaving after every Furcy stay, we rolled up the mattresses and hung them from the ceiling, with barbed wire coiled around the ropes that held them. On arriving every summer, the first task after paying the porters was to put out chairs over which we unrolled the mattresses to air in the sun and inspect for scorpions and spiders. Fortunately, no one was ever bitten, for Exaïce insisted that the only remedy was human excrement.

We were on friendly terms with the Buchs, who had a large house on the main road just where our road turned off. We often stopped by in our comings and goings to and from the main part of Furcy. Our friends were the two young ladies of the house: Jeanne, the elder of the duo (*who married the Marquis de Veyrac, the architect of our house in Turgeau)*, and her sister Lucienne. Their mother Mme *[Luce]* Buch could neither walk nor ride a horse. She had rheumatism in her legs and was also much too heavy to get on or off the mountain horses (assuming an animal could have borne her weight). So to bring her up from Kenscoff, she would be placed in a makeshift sedan chair: a chair was tied to two poles about five feet long, which would then be hoisted up onto the shoulders of four men. Halfway up, another set of four men would take over. We knew when she was coming because we could hear and then see the men struggling down the hill. Sounds carried far in those quiet hills. Knowing she'd arrived, we would go to pay a visit.

Another older person we paid our respects to was Mme Roumain, the great-grandmother of Tigo Blanchet's children. She was lifted onto a packhorse in Kenscoff and led by a man on foot who kept the horse steady. One morning, as we were sitting under the arbor in front of our shack, Monique called out, "Madame, you are having visitors." On looking up, I saw plodding down the hill, using a broomstick for a cane, both Mme *[Clara]* Roumain and her daughter Mme *[Marie]* Mangonès. I was amazed and pleased. The former must have been around 82 and heavy. Walking was not easy, but she had taken the trouble to come all that distance from behind the church on the winding dirt road and then down our hill. It must have been an enormous effort, and I greatly appreciated it. I wondered at this visit. I had shocked the nuns in residence near the church by wearing shorts (the first woman to do so in Haiti), and perhaps Mme Roumain wished to show by this visit that I was an acceptable person despite the shorts.

When my sister-in-law Thérèse died and Maurice came up to fetch me, it was Tigo Blanchet who came over to stay with John. I had sent Exaïce to town in order to bring back clean sheets, but in the rush of things Maurice had forgotten to give them to him. Tigo had to sleep on my sheets, for which I was embarrassed. Mme Mangonès later said to me that she always kept a few sheets in readiness. I did, too, but this one time I was caught without any. Tigo must have told her mother what had happened. I stayed in town for only one night and returned with sheets.

* * *

Mme Mangonès and Mme Léger (a member of my mother's English conversation class, mentioned in Chapter Five) were Roumains and sisters. They were third cousins of Jacques Roumain and his sister Liliane Nadal. Mme Mangonès' husband Victor was the uncle of Gaston Mangonès, who would shortly become engaged to Ginette Rouzier, elder daughter of Georgette and Pierre Rouzier and a former pupil in my mother's school. Mme Léger's daughter Mi Ki had also been in my mother's school, while her son Ti Georges (Georges) and his wife Joujou (Raymonde) would be lifelong friends of my mother's. Pierre Rouzier was related to the Légers through his paternal aunt Louise, and his mother was a Nadal, making him a first cousin of Liliane's husband Joseph, Joseph's brother Robert, and their sisters Alice Villard and Marie Lavaud. In fact, the Rouziers seemed to be related to just about everybody.

* * *

Thérèse had been operated on for a hysterectomy. Instead of choosing a trained Haitian surgeon, she decided to have it done by a Viennese refugee who had not operated for some time since the Nazis had not permitted Jews to do so once the Germans took over Austria. So even if he was a surgeon, he was rusty. After the operation, Thérèse developed several embolisms. At the time, there were no blood thinners. It was a matter of luck if one survived. She did not. Nor were there painkillers and antibiotics as good as there are today. I was upset she had chosen the doctor she had, so I was not very sympathetic. After her death, I felt I should have stayed in town so that I could have gone to see her more than the one time John and I had visited her before going to Furcy. It was Renée who had devoted herself to Thérèse. Maurice had built a family tomb, in which he had laid to rest his father and two of his aunts. Thérèse was placed there, as was later their mother, who died in 1950.

Jehan Dartigue had been seeing Marguerite (nicknamed Margot) Salnave for quite a while, but although her great-grandfather had been president of Haiti, the Dartigue family disapproved of her for whatever reason. (If the Dartigue family had only known where I'd come from! So if they could accept me, then they should have accepted Margot.) Jehan had been employed at Damien in the 1930s, and Margot had been a secretary there. Many years later, Margot told me that Thérèse had telephoned her to say unpleasant things. In the year after my mother-in-law Régina died, Jehan and Margot married and went on to have four children: Marie-José, Robert, Jehan Henri, and Elizabeth (nicknamed Babou).

* * *

In January 1944, my mother was among seventy Haitians in the area of Port-au-Prince who, as part of a program insti-tuted the previous year by my father and the Ministry of Education, had sought to teach illiterates to read Creole (she had worked with ten students, which was more than the average) and to whom President Lescot now gave certificates of patriotic service at a ceremony at the Rex Theatre.

* * *

That fall, when John was four, I looked about for a school for him. I visited several, but they were so formal and dull. I did at last find a small one, quite informal. He only went mornings because the eating and toilet situations were primitive, and I thought it best for him to eat and rest at home. The chauffeur dropped him off at 8 am and picked him up at noon. John liked the school, and I liked the way he was taught to read. A motherly woman took each child one by one to her side, put her arm around him/her, and in a loving manner helped the child pick out the letters, then the sounds, then the words. John brought the book home each day, and we looked at it together. I read him stories and also sang to him and with him. He talked about the teacher, but I don't recall his talking about the children in class. He seemed more interested in the children with whom he played in the afternoon.

* * *

Effective October 1, 1945, President Lescot asked Maurice to give up the Ministry of Education and retain the Ministries of Agriculture and Labor because the president had prepared an ambitious five-year agricultural plan and said it would take all of Maurice's time to carry it through. André Liautaud, recalled from his post as ambassador to Washington, took over Education.

Marie Lavaud had warned me that opposition to Lescot was mounting because the blacks felt they did not have enough power in politics. The Army was miffed because the president had named his elder son Minister of Foreign Affairs and, more unwisely, appointed a younger son, who was in the army, head of the purchasing department, thus angering higher and more qualified officers. On January 7, 1946, on the heels of the government's shuttering of a youth-oriented newspaper, a student strike was launched, and calls for Lescot's resignation only grew from there. Despite attempted maneuverings, by January 11 Lescot had little option but to step down. If Maurice had any awareness, he never told me. We had been to a ball on New Year's Eve, to the reception at the presidential palace on the first of January, and to a recent dinner at the president's private home, so as far as I was concerned, things were as usual. On January 6, however, a photo of the president we had at home fell to the floor, the glass shattering. As I picked it up, I thought to myself, "Is he going to fall soon?"

Maurice was not liked by everybody. It was unusual for a minister to stay in office as long as he had, from the beginning to the end of a government in power. He had made enemies. Maurice expected discipline, seriousness, compe-tence. He was severe with those who did not measure up. Moreover, he disappointed many job seekers. In Haiti, those with any kind of education expected government positions. Maurice refused to hand out jobs, except when there was a need to be filled and if the person was qualified. (When I went to Damien in the mid-1980s, I was astounded to see rooms filled with desks, people sitting at them with nothing to do. I found the same at the Ministry of Education and at the Ministry of Finance—people just sitting around, five or six of them where there had been only one decades before. This happened even in the Bibliothèque Nationale, the National Library. When I first went there to work on Maurice's files, in 1983, there were eight workers; each year I returned, there were more and more, some doing absolutely nothing.) Furthermore, Maurice had to bring to justice two of the edu-cation staff who had sold the questions for the baccalaureate exam in Cape Haitian. (The students were made to take a second test.)

As Director of Rural Education, Maurice had fired sev-eral hundred so-called teachers who were constantly absent or were supposedly teaching in nonexistent schools or had hired substitutes to teach while they did something else. Of course, those who were then deprived of their sinecures hated Maurice, and he was threatened several times. Once when he stopped our car, he said, "Duck your head." He then slowly restarted the car and calmly drove on. I asked him why he had told me to duck. He answered, "A man on the opposite corner was aiming a gun this way, and I did not want you to be hurt."

When Lescot fell, telephone calls came in, some quite menacing. There was great turbulence in Port-au-Prince. The streets were not safe, and some homes were pillaged. Some of the calls we received warned of crowds coming up to Turgeau. This did not occur because we were so far up the hill, but it might well have happened. Maurice's life was threatened. Since 1941, he had always been given a special passport or official documents for his trips outside the country, so at present he had nothing with which to leave. What to do? I persuaded him to go to the home of the Cuban chargé d'affaires, a good friend of his, who was able to obtain from his government an invitation for Maurice to go to Cuba. Papers were made out for him, and he was taken to the airport in the Cuban's car. I can't imagine in what distress he must have been, having had one of the highest offices in the land for nearly five years and now having to seek safety and become a political refugee—this in recompense for his trying for twenty years to better the lives of his countrymen.

I was not too happy with the situation. John and I were alone in our house. John's godfather, André Liautaud, safe in the home of his father-in-law Oswald Brandt (who had become consul of a South American country), telephoned once to ask how we were. Mlle Vincent called after ten days, and I reproached her for not having sought out news of her godchild before that. She replied that she had been told that there were soldiers surrounding our house. I answered, "All the more reason to have come to fetch your godson," not that I would have let John go without me.

Franck Lavaud, who was head of the army, had thought to protect us by placing guards at our home to keep out marauders. After a day or two, I became very uncomfortable. The soldiers could not help making noise. They had to use the toilet in back of the kitchen. I did not know if I should feed them or offer them a drink. I did not know how often the men were changed. So I left with John.

First, we went to the home of the Cuban chargé d'affaires, but this proved unsatisfactory. Then, we were invited to stay a few days with Ginette and Frank Magloire, a newspaper publisher. Next, we stayed at my mother-in-law's, where the American minister's wife and a few of her friends made an official call, but not a friendly one. We even went to Mlle Vincent's for two days; but the guest room was uninviting, and it was difficult to get into the kitchen. So I decided we should go back to our own home since both John and I were suffering from not having the food we needed. I slept with the pistol I'd used in Furcy under my pillow and a machete under the bed, not that they would have done me any good if I had needed to use either. But I thought they might at least have a psychological effect on both me and any intruder.

After a few more days, with the political and social climate still unstable, I decided that John and I should join

Maurice in Havana. Fortunately, Margaretta and Fred Kroll were ready to rent our house. Frank Magloire bought the car. Bishop Voegeli, who had taken over Bishop Carson's house on the property adjacent to ours, bought my beauti- fully embroidered table linens and my paintings (save two that I still have *and that I now have*)). Most of the rest of our possessions I put up for sale. (I stored my two paintings at Bishop Voegeli's and confided my silverware and sewing machine to Renée.)

Finally, all was done. I don't remember who drove John and me to the airport, but it was barely dawn on January 29 when we got there. Little did I realize that I would never live in Haiti again on a permanent basis.

Chapter Eight

A Year On The Move:
Havana, Red Bank, Long Beach
(1946-1947)

The first stop the plane made in Cuba was Camaguey, at the eastern end of the island, and after that, I don't recall how many other stops there were before reaching Havana. It was a propeller plane, and it flew so low that the ride was very bumpy and caused John to throw up time and again. Finally, after arriving in Havana and retrieving our luggage, we both lay down on a wooden bench and just stayed there for a while before getting a taxi to the hotel (the Royal Palm) where Maurice was awaiting us.

We were together for just twenty-four hours because the next day Maurice was off to the States, having been granted a visa as a political refugee. John and I would spend a little over two months in Cuba before Maurice was able to get us visas. A Haitian woman who had a three-bedroom apartment rented out two of the bedrooms, but we had to provide our own food. For a week we were alone, and then a military man I vaguely knew arrived from Haiti with two of his daughters to take over the second bedroom.

John and I joined them a few times on Sunday afternoons to visit Havana. During the week, John attended an American school in the mornings, played outside with a few children in the afternoons and on weekends, and picked up Spanish quickly. I found a job substituting at the Ruston Academy, a primary and secondary school attended by Americans, Cubans, and other nationalities, and received an offer for a permanent position, which I declined.

What surprised me in Cuba were the Spanish hours. We finished supper by 8 pm and then sat on a covered porch two floors above the street to watch people coming and going from a private hospital across from us until closing time at 11. The vendor of tamales started his rounds around 8. He had a three-wheeled, covered, green box wagon from which he took the steaming food, and as he walked, he called, "*Hay tamales*" ("There are tamales"). They were really good: a hot corn-meal mush concoction wrapped in banana leaves or corn husks. In the early evening, we would go walking to a square not far from where we were staying. It was used as an open-air market during the day. Men would be cleaning up, but what struck me most were the huge ugly buzzards that swooped down to fight over scraps of one kind or another. It was their naked heads that seemed most repulsive.

International telephoning was very difficult. Most urgent messages were sent by telegram. One day, Maurice wired, "Found an apartment in Red Bank, New Jersey. Shall I take it?" I wired back, "Don't know where Red Bank is but take it." Shortly thereafter, John and I left Havana.

* * *

We arrived in Miami by plane on April 5 and took the overnight train to New York, then another train to Red Bank. I had written to Maurice the day and the time of arrival but had forgotten to mention the means. He thought it was by plane, and with our landlord, Wilson Hobson, he waited at Newark Airport. John and I had also waited for more than an hour at Penn Station when I decided that since there were trains to Red Bank, we would at least get that far. And so we did. I could not remember the address, but Maurice must have described in a letter the whereabouts: a very large house with an orchard, in back of which were railroad tracks. Fortunately, the taxi driver thought he knew and took us there, to Nut Swamp Road, and we installed ourselves.

I can imagine how worried Maurice must have been waiting for us at the airport. John and I had arrived around 5 pm, while he and Mr. Hobson returned just as night set in.

He must have been reassured when he saw the lights on. He was so glad to see us that there were no words of reproach. Since he had been in the apartment for several days, there was food in the refrigerator. We were lucky to arrive in April because we had no cold-weather clothes.

Allan Hulsizer had found this accommodation for us, asking around of relatives and friends. Allan had created the rural school in Haiti in Chatard in 1928 and had met Maurice a year later when the latter was placed in charge of it for eight months before returning to Teachers College. In the 1930s, Allan was working in the Bureau of Indian Affairs when TC recruited him to help in the instruction of Haitians sent by Maurice to the States to earn their master's and doctorates in Rural Education. Then in the 1940s, Maurice persuaded his friend to come to Haiti for two years to be a senior advisor at Damien, where he would bring modifications to the School of Agriculture and to the Normal School. Allan and his wife Polly would remain great friends, and we would see them years later in Paris and Washington, D.C.

Mr. Hobson had cleverly cut off a little apartment from the ground floor of his big residence. There was a small private entrance with a narrow hall, a tiny kitchen to the left, and a sort of bathroom to the right. Then came the living room, which was an extension of the main house, giving onto both the front garden and the back lawn where on weekends we often saw Mr. Hobson renovating furniture. He was a high school teacher somewhere and on weekends sometimes had young boys from his classes stay with him. He had an old black housekeeper who wanted nothing to do with us and must have been in pain since she moved around with difficulty. Our bedroom was really a glass-enclosed porch with three single beds. Outside, as spring advanced, flowers bloomed along the side of the house—daffodils, irises, crocuses. For John's first Easter in America, we had an Easter egg hunt among these flowers, to John's delight. Off in the distance at night, I often heard and listened to the hoot of the passing trains. To me this was comforting and a relief. I was so glad to be out of the uncertainty of Haiti and in better hands and climate.

Mr. Hobson's house had belonged to a well-known doctor. On his death, his widow Adeline Moffat had had to sell it. She had kept a part of the property near the main road and on it had built a cottage. Like us, she was in straitened circumstances, so we sympathized. Her mother lived there, as did her daughter Jean, who was just finishing high school, and a young helper named Henrietta. The cottage was so small that the bedrooms of the daughter and the helper were in the attic and could be reached only by a ladder. An old horse was also part of the family.

It was Adeline who came to see us a few days after our arrival and became a cherished friend. John often went visiting there since he did not go to school that spring. We were quite far from town. Adeline had a government job but was home weekends. She had a car and rendered us many services. I don't remember how we did our shopping. Perhaps it was done by Maurice and Mr. Hobson. We had to be very, very careful with our money because only $200 a month was coming in—$150 from the house in Turgeau and $50 from a smaller one (that Maurice had bought as an investment in late 1945 and where Jehan and Renée would later live). I had brought about $1,500 with me, but there were doctor bills, pharmacy charges, the rent, and Maurice's train fare for his job-hunting in New York City. In fact, we had so little money that Maurice and I ate a lot of canned mackerel, at 14 cents a can.

I saw an ad in the local paper for a person to sell Avon beauty products. The agent came to see me, and I paid a sum for a kit. I did sell a few items to a woman who had rented another part of the big house and to a few women I met through Adeline. But I was not a success, because first, I used little make-up myself; second, I could not leave John by himself; and third, I had no means of transportation.

We had a few visitors. Viola and Sidney Kantrowitz came by car from Croton-on-Hudson (in New York State) at the beginning of May. Later that month or in early June, my brother Arthur showed up one afternoon in his car. He said he had come to take us to Ohio. I had not seen my family since 1942. Of course, they knew about the sudden change in our circumstances, that we were in exile. My mother had sent us some blankets and sheets, and from time to time a freshly killed chicken would arrive by mail in a shoebox.

Arthur had been dispatched on the approximately 500-mile drive to take John and me to see them. (Maurice did not go). We packed and off we went. Arthur chose the quickest way through Pennsylvania and up through Ohio. We arrived in Auburn Corners at about 3 am. He got out of the car and shouted, "Here they are!" Lights went on in the darkened house and out came our parents to help us up the stairs to bed.

Uncle John Reithoffer told me that "the house had been built in the Western Reserve style in 1834 for $500." My parents had purchased it in 1934 for $925 with the proceeds from my late brother Otto's insurance policy. In a $25 secondhand convertible *("a 1924 four-door Hupmobile," John said, made by a company that was in business from 1909 through 1940),* Arthur and his friends moved the family and furniture from Cleveland. The house had had no electricity. *But, said John, Art and a friend put in the wiring the summer before the move-in, and running water was added within a few years; however, a proper furnace wasn't installed until the early Fifties.*

The barbershop was set up to the left as one entered, in the front parlor; right behind that was the living room with a sofa bed and it became our parents' bedroom at night. This room, which also contained a coal-burning, pot-bellied stove that gave off little heat, bled into a large kitchen that also served as a family gathering room. The kitchen at that time had two windows that faced the road, and at each of them was placed a comfortable chair, one for our mother and the other for our father, from which they looked out or worked or just chatted and received any visitors. To one side of the kitchen was a pantry, and in back were steps leading outside. One initially came to a woodshed, where washtubs, brooms, garden tools, and all sorts of things were stored, and beyond that was a henhouse. Originally, water was hand-pumped from a well in the backyard, which also contained a smokehouse (our father still made his sausages in winter) and farther back a sty, where our father raised pigs. Upstairs were four bedrooms, two large and two small. The large front bedroom was closed off in winter because it wasn't heated, but John and I could use it in June. My brother John was in the back bedroom. There was an attic and an expanded basement as well. The Hupmobile broke down for good soon after all the heavy moving was done. It had been placed at the side of the house and became for a few summers the family front porch.

John and I stayed for several days, just sitting around or being in the backyard. I recall my father picking John up one morning, taking him into the henhouse to see the chickens and their eggs, offering John to take an egg, and carrying him back out. Our greatest pleasure was watching a chipmunk that had become almost tame.

On Sunday, Arthur and his wife Annie, my sister Betty and her husband Lowell, and my sister Sue and her husband

Rob came over for a barbecue, joining our parents, my brother John, son John, and me. It was then that Betty said, "Esther, I can't invite you home, for if they see John they will burn crosses in front of my house." I answered, "It's all right, Betty. I understand. I cannot burden you with this. You have your life to live. What I have chosen to do with my life is my responsibility, not yours." *(Betty and Lowell lived in a town some fifteen miles away where the Ku Klux Klan was active—yes, that far north.)* On another day, John and I were sitting with his grandmother in the kitchen. We heard a knock on the front door. My mother said, "Esther, take John out to the backyard." I knew why. I took John quite far back so we would be out of sightline with the back windows.

John and I returned to New Jersey by train. I was glad we had made the trip because it gave my parents the chance to meet their grandson and vice versa, especially since they would never see each other again. My father died a year later, and my mother, in 1951.

The summer passed in Red Bank. In the fall, John was put into the first grade at a nearby school that he reached by walking through the fields. I found a job teaching French in a Catholic high school, Our Lady Star of the Sea Academy. It was at some distance (in Long Branch), and I had to use at least two buses each way. It was quite something getting John off to school and hurrying not to be late to work. My job was only in the mornings so that I could get back in time for John's return. Thankfully, he liked school, and the teacher liked him. When we left Red Bank, the teacher said she had lost her best pupil.

In an attempt to find work, Maurice wrote many letters to people he had met during his ministry, and he went into New York for a few interviews. But since no jobs were forthcoming, we decided that he should take a room at International House (where he could live inexpensively) in Manhattan and go out every day by train and then bus to Lake Success, on the north shore of Long Island, where the United Nations, which was just starting up, had been given housing by the Sperry-Rand Corporation, an engineering company. (To go from Red Bank would have taken him more than two-and-a-half hours each way.) I hoped that Maurice's going often and seeing anyone and everyone and being seen would eventually make someone give him a job. Finally, with the help of Ralph Bunche and others, he was offered a temporary (three-month) position as a documents clerk for the first General Assembly to be held in Flushing Meadows. (A shuttle bus took workers from Lake Success to Flushing Meadows and back.)

The job was in one of the lowest categories of the General Services as opposed to the various ranks of the Professional Staff. But Maurice had no choice. He had to take it because our savings were almost gone and the $200 a month from the house rentals in Haiti was just not enough. Our temporary visas were expiring, too. Several friends advised us to return to Haiti, but this was impossible since the political situation there was not favorable. Estimé, the current president, had, under President Vincent, been Minister of Education and Agriculture and therefore Maurice's boss when he was Director of Rural Education. Since Maurice had been adamantly opposed to political patronage in filling any position under his jurisdiction, he no doubt had angered those above and around him. When President Lescot appointed Maurice minister, the latter was essentially succeeding Estimé, who, during the next five years, could not have been unaware of the substantial reforms that Maurice was making in urban education, just as Maurice had in rural education the preceding ten years. Jehan Dartigue said much later that their sister Thérèse, had she lived, would have been too outspoken, as had been her custom, and might have caused great difficulties for the Dartigue family remaining in Haiti. As it was, Jehan, Renée, and their mother had to keep a very low profile during Estimé's presidency.

In 1947, the whole Lescot cabinet, including Maurice, was brought to trial in Haiti for the misuse of public funds (this really was just an excuse). Maurice was immediately exonerated since it was publicly known that never had any other minister adhered to his budget and never had money been so carefully and honestly administered and accounted for. I wonder what the reaction was when it was learned that he had slowly and painstakingly put aside a sum reaching $10,000 to buy land to create a university campus.

As it turned out, after his departure, the money was used for other things.

* * *

Mr. Hobson wanted our section of the house for a young married couple from his church, so, with Maurice in Manhattan, he gave John and me a room in the main house. I would go into the kitchen to prepare our meals and then carry them up on a tray to eat in the bedroom. We shared a bathroom with the old housekeeper, who was now even less happy with us since she had had it all to herself. When Maurice obtained his three-month appointment, he went to the UN housing unit to ask for quarters nearer to Lake Success than Red Bank, and something was found on the south shore of Long Island, in Long Beach (although that was not the easiest commute to the UN either).

* * *

We lived in Long Beach from November 1946 until May 1947. Housing was very tight after the war, and on Maurice's small salary, we could not afford rents nearer New York or in Lake Success. Moreover, we might not have been welcomed, given that we were a mixed family. The reason we could be in Long Beach was because it was a summer resort town and most houses would normally be closed for the winter. This one, on East Walnut Street, consisted of four apartments. We had a poorly furnished one on the ground floor. On the other side of us was a young government official with his wife and six-month-old daughter. Upstairs the two units were occupied by young army officers, just returned from Europe, and their families. I remember one of them, during the chats we had running into each other on the front sidewalk, saying, "We should have gone on and licked the Russians."

John was enrolled in a primary school not far from where we lived, which he got to by school bus. He made one friend, Norman, with whom he often played. He had another friend, a lady we never really met who gave John several books when we left Long Beach.

I recall a few people coming to visit us from New York: Irene Kent and her family, and Mama *[Maria]* Defly, who was a corset-maker in Port-au-Prince and had hand-made all my bras, since only a limited number of such items were sold in Haiti. I never dreamed she would want to spend the time and money to come out to Long Beach when she had traveled to New York for only a short stay.

I worked for six months as a substitute teacher in first grade for two days a week in John's school and also in high school French, English and Spanish classes. I was not very good at either level. I was unaccustomed to rough, loud, ill-mannered young people, so I could not control the situation in the classroom. Most of them were in school because they had to be and not because they wanted to be. But since we needed the money, I stuck it out. In the last class to which I was assigned, I told the class to study because it seemed of little use to try to do any teaching. (When we later got to Great Neck, I applied for a job at Kensington, John's elementary school, but was not hired. The teacher who applied at the same time was very good.)

In February 1947, Maurice was given a six-month contract. We were so happy! (We were very fortunate that he got any contract at all, since normally it was required that an individual have the support of his/her home government, which Maurice clearly did not enjoy.) He also told me that the UN had leased several apartment buildings in Great Neck, as well as semi-detached houses in Parkway Village. We chose Great Neck for several reasons. First, it was near Lake Success, about ten to fifteen minutes by car or bus, whereas Parkway Village was in Queens, closer to New York City. Second, Great Neck was an established town, while Parkway Village was a brand new area, with stores, schools, and post office yet to be built. Third, Viola Kantrowitz's cousins, Lena Five and Dorothy Lang, lived in Great Neck, and in fact the Langs were in an older non-UN building diagonally across the street from where we first found an apartment.

Chapter Nine

Great Neck (1947-1956)

(My mother stopped writing her own account when she got to 1947, and so material for this chapter is drawn from her narrative of my first fifteen years, in which she talked about some of the things she was doing, as well as from certain correspondence she kept and from my recollections and those of others. I have, as a result, inserted more of myself than before, and thus the reader will find a greater blend of normal typeface and italics.)

The original inhabitants of the area that came to be called Great Neck, a peninsula on the north shore of Long Island jutting out into the Sound, were the Matinecoc Indians (a branch of the Algonquin), who, in the 1600s, were dominated first by the Dutch and then the English. Between the American Revolution and the Civil War, the region was known primarily for its orchards and farms. In the latter part of the 19th century, Great Neck and other parts of Long Island attracted vacationers from New York City, and in time summer homes expanded into well-heeled estates, including those of Vanderbilts, Chryslers, Dodges, and Graces. Soon the town was said to rival Palm Beach and Grosse Pointe in its posh credentials. But little by little, estates were broken up, and although the new homes were smaller, they were still very comfortable. In the Twenties and Thirties, the area attracted a colony of vaudeville and stage performers, including W.C. Fields and the Marx Brothers, who were followed in the Forties by businessmen and professionals of some means. Although the town had gained a reputation for being a Jewish haven, a Catholic and Protestant presence still remained. This was the Great Neck we found when we arrived in May 1947, a quiet, largely residential town numbering in the thousands and consisting of nine incorporated villages, admirable public parks, and two elementary schools and one secondary school of excellent reputation. A main artery, Middle Neck Road, ran from Kings Point (home of the U.S. Merchant Marine Academy) in the north, through what is still referred to as the Old Village, into the "newer" sections farther south, past the railroad station (built as far away from the great estates as possible so as not to disturb their owners), and on to Northern Boulevard, after which it turned into Lakeville Road and continued to the village of

Lake Success and the Sperry-Rand Corporation—at the time,
Great Neck's one industry. (The other businesses served the
day-to-day needs of the community, which was essentially a
suburban bedroom.)

Our first home was a large L-shaped studio apartment on
the second floor of 46 Schenck Avenue, an offshoot of Middle
Neck Road in the village of Great Neck Plaza and a five-to-
ten-minute walk from the train station. Maurice and I slept in
what was meant to be the living room, while John's bed was
in the dining room/entry.

At least two other buildings in the immediate neighbor-
hood—one across the street, at 23 Schenck, and one on the next
block over, at 12 Welwyn Road—housed other United Nations
personnel as well. The families we met quite naturally formed
a mini-UN: they were from Austria (the Landaus), Belgium
(the Selbs), China (the Hos, the Wongs), Denmark (name
forgotten), Dutch Guiana (the Einaars), France (the Alperts,
the Dufours, the Richardots), Great Britain (the Langstons),
Haiti (the Rouziers), Holland (the Brandts), Hungary (the
De Hédervárys), Israel (the Jacoubovitches), Norway (the
Melsom-Andersens), Switzerland (the Lippetzes), and the U.S.
(the Lawsons), among those I remember.

Some had had very difficult times during the Second World
War. Klara de Héderváry, for example, had left Budapest a
widow to become Paris correspondent for several French and
Hungarian newspapers, while her daughter Claire enrolled at
the University of Louvain in Brussels. When war began, the

latter was evacuated to Paris, where through her mother's contacts she was able to obtain a fellowship in the U.S. for further study. Mme de Héderváry, most unfortunately, was seized by the Nazis and dispatched to a concentration camp.

Blanka and Fred Landau, sweethearts since high school, had fled from Vienna to Paris, where they lived until Fred was rounded up with other foreign Jews. By the time he was released, Blanka had already left for Spain. Fred was able to be reunited with her only after walking from Paris all the way to and over the Pyrenees *(roughly 500 miles, or 833 kilometers)* . Together they made their way to Lisbon, where they were put on a boat, first to England and then to America. They got themselves to Princeton, where Fred took a second doctorate.

The Brandts were from Amsterdam and had been in the Dutch East Indies *(soon to become Indonesia)*, where the father was manager for IBM. After the Japanese invasion, he was put in one prison camp in Batavia *(now Jakarta)*, while mother and daughter (Marianne) spent three years in another camp, which contained 11,000 women and children, and shared a room with twelve other people. The mother suffered beatings (in front of her daughter) for neglecting her assigned duties when tending to her sick child.

The Dufours had a singular background. He was born of a French father and Russian-Swedish mother in St. Petersburg and raised in the Orthodox Church, while she was Mexican, brought up in a convent. Their children—Adrienne and

Jean-Pierre (nicknamed Jumpy)—began life in Shanghai. Adrienne told me that in 1943, during the Japanese occupation of the city, her father, who was Director of Havas Presse (the French news agency that later became Agence France-Presse), was placed under house arrest, while her mother was able to flee the country with the children, using a Mexican passport, aboard a Swedish ship navigating through mined waters. The boat continued to Goa (then a Portuguese enclave on the Indian subcontinent), Port Elizabeth (South Africa), and Rio de Janeiro before docking in New York two months later. To survive, their mother went to work and was obliged to place the children in various care centers. It was very rough-going for all until their father was able to rejoin them in 1946.

That summer I took a six-week course in child psychology at Teachers College and left John each day with Grace Ho, a white American married to a Eurasian. They had a daughter Mei An (Mary Ann, as she was now called), born in Peiping *(known also in the West as Peking before it reverted to Beijing),* where the family had been interned for two and a half years after the Japanese invasion. They now lived on the first floor of our building, and Grace took care of several children whose mothers had to be absent during the day.

For this course, I did a study of transplanted children, based on my observations of, principally, John, Adrienne Dufour, Marianne Brandt, and Mary Ann Ho, plus subsequent interviews with their mothers. *My mother's conclusion was that, despite the tough experiences of those years for both child and parents, each child now functioned as normally as children born and raised in a stable environment in the U.S. during that same period. The paper earned her an A.*

In addition to another course that summer, my mother would take five more between 1949 and 1953—three at Teachers College (TC) and one each at New York University and the New School for Social Research, all in Manhattan. Most of this was the result of an exchange of letters in February and March 1947 with the Office of the Assistant Commissioner (of New York State) for Teacher Education. My mother had asked about the requirements for teaching in State public schools and was told, among other things, that for elementary-school teaching she would need to complete additional course work. After meeting with a member of the TC Education Department, she was informed that by her taking certain courses, it was likely that the New York State Department of Education would consider certifying her work. However, it seems that despite the post-graduate work she did do—twenty-two credits in all, including what she had taken at TC in 1935—certification became unnecessary because she proceeded to work exclusively in private schools (where such governmental approval wasn't required). In 1951, TC's Admissions Office wrote to her suggesting that, with all the credits she'd accumulated to date, she might want to formally declare for a PhD and get herself a doctoral thesis advisor. She never did. (A possible explanation is that she didn't think it a good idea to have a doctorate while my father had just a master's.)

* * *

In early 1950, for one of her TC courses, my mother com-pleted a term paper titled "Television and Little Children." She felt that the new medium had great potential for education and entertainment, but after observing its negative effect on the behavior of young children (five and under), she con-cluded that "where little children are concerned, Television viewing is an activity they can do without. It would be better for the under-fives to grow more slowly and to have the time now given to Television [going] towards the pursuits more in keeping with their age and development. "

She subsequently submitted the paper, now retitled "Television Hits the Nursery School," to Childhood Education *(described as "The Professional Magazine for Teachers of Children"). Its editor, Frances Mayfarth, liked the piece and was very interested in publishing it. However, Mrs. Mayfarth had just resigned, and her successor was not yet selected. Consequently, she asked if the magazine might retain the article for a while longer, and if her replacement vetoed its inclusion in* Childhood Education, *it might be right for a sister publication called* Portfolio on Audio-visual Materials, *to be issued later that summer. The piece may never have seen the light of day anywhere because there was no published version in my mother's files (as there were of some seven articles of hers that appeared between the late Fifties and early Seventies).*

* * *

John had hardly begun school at Kensington (in May 1947) when Jeanne Barron called to invite Maurice and me for drinks. Her daughter Barbara was in John's second-grade class, and the teacher may have announced that he was from Haiti. Jeanne and her husband Bill were going on vacation to Haiti, so we gave them my brother-in-law Jehan Dartigue's contact information, as well as that of some friends. On their return, the Barrons had us over for dinner, where we met friends of theirs, who in turn introduced us to other friends. It was through Jeanne and Bill that we met Helen and Hank Jaffe (both of whom smoked pipes), Becky and Morris Schwartz, Dorothy and Jesse Kuh (*who became our insurance agent*), Caroline and Joseph Farber (*who took me in during some of my college vacations, and later Joseph counseled me when I looked into buying a Manhattan co-op*), and several of their neighbors on Hutchinson Court—Mary and Phil Blume (*who became our dentist*), Hilda and Joe Liff, and Elise and Nat Feuerman (*whose younger daughter Ellin married the Jaffes' son Jimmy*). The Barrons also introduced us to Nathalie and Eddie Shavitz, through whom we met Eleanor and Milton Gould (*who much later put me in touch with several financial and legal advisors*). Through the Goulds we got to know Harriet and Lee Pomerance, and through them, Hannah and Ruda Schulhof. In addition to Lena and Helge Five, there were several others we saw regularly: Frances and Lester Velie, Shirley and George Marks, and Kay and John Fuchs. And, in 1954, we met Jean and Bob Benjamin. I believe these friends took an interest in us because we brought them something different.

When Maurice's professional situation became better and more stable, we moved in the fall across the street to a larger apartment, on the third floor of 23 Schenck, where John could have a bedroom while Maurice and I continued to be in the living room. John almost came down with meningitis that winter when, during several hours of outdoor play, his clothes got soaking wet. That evening he developed a very high fever, and I spent the night sponging him with alcohol to bring down the fever.

From the start of our living in Great Neck, my parents did a lot of entertaining, mixing local friends with those from the UN, visiting Haitians, and later a few from Mills College (where my mother taught for four years). They were lively and interesting gatherings. My mother might prepare a Haitian menu; my father might serve rum punch, made from five-star Barbancourt Haitian rum; and there was lots of conversation and occasionally dancing to records of the day, both Haitian and American.

As in most cases, the friendships were maintained through the women, and wonderful relationships they were, most lasting decades. Many of the women had artistic bents, as did some of the men. Jeanne Barron, Caroline Farber, and Harriet Pomerance were painters, as was Nathalie Shavitz, who went on to work in a number of other mediums. Jean Benjamin also painted and coauthored several books on Kandinsky. Mary Blume was a pianist; Dorothy Kuh, a sculptress; and Lester Velie, a writer. The Benjamins, Pomerances, Schulhofs, and Shavitzes were all art collectors, and Harriet and Lee Pomerance later underwrote an archaeological dig at Kato Zakro in Crete, which interested my mother greatly and to which she made small financial donations. (The dig, where the Pomerances spent one month each summer, ultimately led to the rediscovery of a Bronze Age palace.) Bob Benjamin was chairman of the movie company United Artists, while Eddie Shavitz, head of a business in Manhattan, starred in community-theater plays in Great Neck. And after retiring from the Campus Sweater Co. (once the country's largest manufacturer of sweaters and other casual menswear), Joseph Farber, who had studied with Edward Steichen, undertook a second career as an excellent photographer whose extensive work appeared in large-format books on Native Americans, Thomas Jefferson, Herodotus, and Palladio.

Jeanne and Bill Barron were very good to us. They had a lovely backyard where they had set up a barbecue and had put out a plain wooden table and benches and where we would have Sunday suppers with lots of iced tea, ice cream, salad, and rolls. Once George Simpson was with us after he had returned from Jamaica and the Rastafarians. Clifford Brandt also joined us there during a visit from Haiti. The Barrons were our closest friends among the Great Neck group. We often dined *en famille* at their home or at ours. *(My mother later told me of the pleasurable afternoons she would spend at Jeanne's stretched out on one living-room couch while Jeanne was on the other, talking over their thoughts and concerns.)*

* * *

In 1948, my mother became a founding member of the United Nations Women's Guild, along with Alice Lippetz and Klara de Héderváry, among others. The purpose of the organization was to lend a helping hand to children in need, largely in Europe. She remained active with the group until leaving for Paris in June 1956, and, as she wrote in a 1990 letter to Maria Angeles Mayor, president of a UNESCO service organization my mother belonged to, "I have [since leaving New York] kept in touch [with the Guild] and have followed its ups and downs." *That included New York visits in the early Sixties with Dorothy Cordier, who for many years had been head of the Guild (and whose husband Andrew had been, until his resignation in 1962, a powerful Undersecretary at the UN). In 1996, the Guild marked its forty-eighth anniversary and published* A Brief History of the United Nations Women's Guild 1948–1995. *Although my mother and Mme de Héderváry could be clearly seen in a photo of the founding members (none of whom were identified in the caption) attending the group's first-anniversary gathering in 1949, there was nary a mention of either of them in the text discussing the founding. My mother received a copy of the publication, and I could tell she was miffed. In 2010, as I started this book project, I decided to make her disappointment known and contacted the Guild, whose president offered to have this oversight corrected at some point in the future. (The future is still to come.)*

During the course of two summers, she also participated in the UN Volunteer Services program, acting as liaison to newcomers, their families, and their communities. The group's value to the United Nations was recognized at a luncheon in September 1953, honoring the two dozen women Volunteers. It was held at UN headquarters in Manhattan, with a welcoming address was by Secretary-General Dag Hammarskjold.

My mother had that time free to help out at the UN because I had gone off (on a partial scholarship) to a sleepaway camp in Madison, Connecticut, called Deer Lake, owned and operated by a wonderful couple, Elizabeth and Ralph Hill. Jeanne Barron had recommended it to us, since her son Tony, who was seven years older than I, and the Schwartzes' son Eric had previously gone there. It had a very relaxed atmosphere, some seventy boys divided up by age among seven or eight bunks, and I was able to attend three years in a row.

Additionally, my mother did volunteer work in Great Neck with the Red Cross, as a warden for the fire department, and as a collector for the local Community Chest.

* * *

I decided to consult the best doctor around for John's digestive problems, and that was Dr. John Mitchell Brush, at Columbia Presbyterian Hospital in Manhattan. Since the visit to Duke Hospital in 1943, John had subsisted largely on scraped lean beef, scraped apple, and ripe bananas because he couldn't digest milk or starches, and any vegetable gave him diarrhea. On Duke's advice, I had also been giving him daily injections of liver extract, but now his body had begun to rebel. Once, I had a hard time pulling out the needle. Another time, the needle bent, and I said, "This has got to stop. Let's see if something else can be done."

John was confined to the hospital for five days, and I went twice to see him. At the end of the stay, Dr. Brush said he thought John could eat anything except wheat and that each meal should be followed by a tablespoon of Kaopectate.

With Maurice, we went to a restaurant where we asked John what he would like to have. "A tomato salad," came the answer. And indeed he took Kaopectate for several years before he finally outgrew the need and folic acid became available in tablet form.

* * *

In August 1948, Maurice had the opportunity to go to Geneva for the UN Trusteeship Department for several weeks and then to Paris for the General Assembly being held at the Palais de Chaillot. I very much wished to go, too. I had learned so much about Paris and French literature from Haitian friends who had been to France, and I had read so many French authors that I wanted to see where they had lived. But what to do about John? I telephoned my sister Betty in Ohio, who was working as a lab technician for a dentist and had just returned from a two-week vacation. But she said she would come regardless of what her boss might say. Betty arrived by train the same day Maurice and I were leaving. Later, her husband Lowell came by car to spend two weeks and often took John fishing.

I had scraped together enough money for passage on the same ship (the *Queen Elizabeth*) as Maurice, and once in Europe, we lived on his per diem. After three weeks in Geneva, I went to Paris, where I was able to find a room for a dollar a night at the Hôtel du Louvre. I ate little but saw much. When Maurice joined me, we moved to better quarters. After a week together, I sailed home. What I had been unable to do in 1939 because of the impending war, I achieved in 1948. It was a wonderful six weeks.

* * *

In the fall, John fell and hit his head on cement attempting to jump from a park staircase onto a low-lying tree branch. (He had hit his head twice before in Haiti, and there would be a fourth incident, on the garage floor of 21 Schenck.) I had little sympathy for him (because I thought he shouldn't have been jumping like that) but told him to lie down. He also did this during the week when he came home from school since he kept complaining about his head. At the end of the week, I took him to the doctor, who said John had had an eye hemorrhage but it was too late to do anything about it. I felt awful for not taking him immediately, and I hoped nothing would happen in the future because of my neglect.

* * *

Adeline Moffat invited us to visit her in Red Bank during the 1948 Christmas school vacation. (Maurice chose to spend the time in New York.) It began to snow that after-noon, and it just kept on, eventually becoming The Blizzard of '48! We took the Long Island Railroad into Penn Station and changed to another train to New Jersey. It was snow-ing there even harder. By the time we got to Red Bank, the snow was so high that no taxi would take us out to Adeline's. I phoned her, and she said she would try to get a man who had a plow. He arrived, we got in with him, and he managed to get as far as a road somewhat near Adeline's property before the plow got stuck. John and I made it to a friend's who lived on the main road. I called Adeline again, and she said she would come for us on foot and lead us back. By this time, it was very dark. Her helper, Henrietta, went before her to push through the snow to make a path. For the return trip, Adeline was in front, followed by Henrietta, then John, and then me, dragging our two suitcases along the top of the snow which was waist-high.

We had no sooner got into the house than Maurice called. He had decided to return home but was now stranded in Flushing, halfway between Manhattan and Great Neck. He had gotten that far by subway, but the Long Island Railroad trains were not running to Great Neck. What should he do? I told him to go immediately to the nearest hotel to book a room (I was afraid rooms would fill up the longer he waited), then go out to buy a toothbrush and razor, get something to eat, read, and spend the night in Flushing. The next day the trains to Great Neck were up and running again. Some people, however, had not been so lucky. They had boarded trains in Manhattan that then encountered snow banks and were stranded for twelve to fifteen hours. We in Red Bank were obliged to stay indoors for two days until the plows succeeded in opening the roads.

* * *

The reason we moved to the ground floor of 23 Schenck was because John had been showing off in the third-floor hallway, and, very fortunately, I had seen him in time. He was playing Superman, trying to stand up on the staircase railing on the edge of a stairwell that plummeted uninterrupted all the way to the basement floor. I was dusting in John's bedroom and happened to look out the window that gave onto the hallway, where I could see Jumpy completely wide-eyed. After running to the apartment door, I walked slowly toward the staircase and without raising my voice said, "John, I need you." He got down. I told Jumpy to go home. We went back into the apartment, and I explained to John what I was about to do and why. Then I put him over my knees and spanked him for the first and only time that I can remember.

Once we were installed in the new apartment, which was another one-bedroom, this time with an eat-in kitchen, I told John he could climb in and out of his bedroom window whenever he wished, which he did a few times. Since we were now near the front entrance to the building, we ran into many more people than we had before, some of whom had young children. Consequently, we were able to exchange babysitting services, and this is how we became friends with the Richardots, for example, and the Wongs (who many, many years later would sublet the studio apartment across the hall from us in Paris). We refused to let John stay alone when we went out at night, and once I could afford a cleaning lady, she did not mind coming to sit.

John caught the measles and later chicken pox and had a bad case of each. He had high fevers, suffered delirium (imagining snakes and crawling creatures), and, in the case of the measles, had spots in his throat and esophagus. He was in bed for three or four weeks at a time, and I had a sitter for him since I couldn't get off work, for which he reproached me. I explained that I was sorry and asked that he understand that I needed to hold onto my job, first to help family finances and second I wanted to keep up my profession since our future was not assured. Moreover, I continued, once he was in high school and after, I could go on doing something useful. Fortunately, there was the example of a woman in the neighborhood whose son was a little younger than John, and she followed him everywhere. I remember saying to John, "Do you want me to be like her?"

* * *

One Saturday morning around 9 am, the doorbell rang. Luckily, I was dressed and the beds in the living room were made up and turned into divans for the day. I opened the door, saw two tall men in beige raincoats, and thought it was the FBI. Then I looked again and recognized Gustave Laraque and Gérard De Catalogne, whom we had not seen in four or five years. What a shock and surprise!

We would encounter many more Haitians, thanks in part to Georgette and Pierre Rouzier, who, with their four children—Ginette, Ghislaine, Pierrot, and Max—had also left Haiti and were now living just around the corner, at 12 Welwyn Road. They were a magnet for traveling Haitians, including some of their many relatives. Of the few I remember were Joseph Nadal, Dody (Georges) Wiener, Clifford Brandt, Giselle Faubert, and Marc Pasquet.

We had other visitors, too: Auguste Viatte and Mary and Joseph Bendler (the truant officer in Cleveland who had been so helpful to me).

* * *

My first job after we got to Great Neck was as a teacher in the UN's International Nursery School, which opened in mid-October 1947 in Lake Success, adjacent to UN headquarters at Sperry-Rand. I worked there mornings.

The print media took an interest in the school, with The New York Times, Time, Newsweek, *an unknown French publication (that ran a photo of my mother, though she went unidentified), and the* Journal of Home Economics *publishing articles. The last did identify her and said she was a Hungarian married to a Haitian. (*Time *described my mother in the same way but without giving her name.) Two UN house organs—*UN World *and* UN Secretariat News*—quite naturally also wrote about the school, with the latter running an unidentified photo of my mother teaching a class.*

I had expected to continue at the nursery school after my return from Paris in 1948 and was surprised to receive a letter saying that contrary to what I had been told, my services would not be needed.

Fortunately, I saw an ad in a local newspaper, placed by a Margaret Kibrig, an Englishwoman who owned a summer camp called Shelter Rock in the next town, Manhasset, and wished to use part of that property in the winter for a private nursery school. I was hired as director and head teacher. After busing the children to the nursery school she had in Great Neck, Mrs. Kibrig used her station wagon for the pickup out in Manhasset. I had to be ready by 9 am and was home by 3:30 pm. The short day suited me and our needs. The guardian of the camp was also the cook and cleaner; Mrs. Kibrig took care of the menus and shopping; and my job was the school program, contacts with parents and children, and supervision of two teachers. I enjoyed it, and it seems Mrs. Kibrig thought well of me, for she asked me to head her other nursery school, called Kibrig-Poulton, in Great Neck, for the following fall term. She also gave me an excellent reference which I sent to the placement bureau at Teachers College. That summer I worked at the camp, which John attended until he fell ill.

However, by December, I had had enough. I liked the work, and I liked the teachers and children. But I had reservations about matters affecting the children, and so just before Christmas I submitted my resignation.

I was, therefore, again looking for a job. We had acquired a car, a green two-door Plymouth. Maurice was in a car pool, so he needed it only once a week. I had learned to drive in Haiti before John was born. I contacted the Teachers College placement office and was advised of a possible position to supervise student teachers studying at Mills School in Manhattan, a nonprofit normal school for training teachers for nursery school and the first three grades of primary school. I was told I would have to go into New York City once or twice a week for faculty meetings and to talk with the students I supervised. (*One of my mother's former students, Annette Metis Gallagher, informed me that in 1950 [when she first enrolled], Mills was still affiliated with Adelphi College [later, University], and its academic degrees were issued by the latter. It was not until 1952 that Mills received its own accreditation and began calling itself Mills College of Education, with Amy Hostler as its president and Margaret Devine its dean.*)

In the meantime, my mother received an offer to be Summer Director of the Great Neck Cooperative [Nursery] School, which she was obliged to decline because of me. I spent that summer and the next as the chauffeur for John and his friends, taking them to different parks or swimming beaches, packing sandwiches and drinks. It was often very hot; the temperature could go to 110 degrees Fahrenheit. It was better to be in a park or on a beach than to sit in a hot apartment. Stepping Stone Park, very near Kings Point, was a great retreat. We went there often, and at the time, we were allowed to swim in Long Island Sound. There were trees, and there was a breeze.

I got the job at Mills and started in the fall of 1950, thanks to having the car, since cross-island travel was difficult. *(There was bus service, but it took a long time to get from Great Neck to Hempstead, Mineola, or beyond.)* The work gave me nightmares. For instance, I would dream that my eight students were sleeping at our apartment, and I would wake up with a start to find that only Maurice and John were there. The next year, I was given a full load of sixteen student teachers, which required me to supervise in Brooklyn, The Bronx, Queens, Harlem, Greenwich Village (Bank Street), and Central Park West (Ethical Culture), in addition to the responsibilities at Mills itself, which included conducting a course called "Activities for Young Children." Since the subway commutes and the walking were difficult on my feet, I had a pair of "space shoes," as they were called, made for me. They were ugly, my feet looked like gunboats, but they did give me a measure of relief.

Mills was in the habit of taking third-year students on a trip. *Annette's year, it was to Europe, she said.* Another time, it was to Amish country. Those who did not go I took to the United Nations and, to my surprise, was reproached for making the tour too interesting!

During her days at Mills, my mother made lasting friend-ships with Annette, Amy Hostler, Louise Mitchell, Myrtle Searles, Margaret Devine, and especially Doris Bock.

I shall always be grateful to Doris and her husband Charles, a kind, shy, brilliant physics engineer, for inviting us to their weekend home on twenty-eight wooded acres in Southbury, Connecticut, on Kettletown Road. Charles was building the house himself, section by section, and there wasn't a right angle anywhere, he told us.

Other than going to Adeline Moffat's or the Bocks', we as a family did not travel or go away weekends because we were afraid we would be turned away. We might go for a day trip, as we did to see the Kantrowitzes in Croton-on-Hudson, but that, too, was an exception. In the United States, a man could be well educated, well bred, and well dressed, but only his color counted. If he was dark-skinned, no other quality mattered. The sentiment was evident and even more so for a mixed couple. *All of this naturally upset my parents. My mother once told me that in restaurants she could sense a chill and felt that people were talking about them.* Maurice and I spoke only French in all public places—buses, trains, restaurants. *Some people were patronizing, she sensed, including some of her colleagues at Mills. When my parents attended mass at the Catholic church in Great Neck, she believed they were barely tolerated.*

My mother remembered two incidents involving me: a young girl said her journalist father had told her she couldn't play with me because I was colored, while the daughter of good friends said that I would have to get up to give her my seat for the same reason. There were occasions when the word 'nigger' was shouted out by a child on the street. (It was also uttered by adults behind my father's back or mine, though we still heard it.)

Maurice was under great stress at work. There were very, very few professional nonwhites, and the whites felt superior and were of the opinion that nonwhites could not measure up. So Maurice had to prove constantly that he was as good as or even better than some of those in the higher ranks in his section. In time, he would rise to the position of Senior Specialist in Education in the Trusteeship Department.

My mother told me that she had once consulted a psychiatrist to discuss both the stress and distress she and my father experienced. The doctor's frank advice was that nothing was going to change very quickly, if at all, and the only option for them was to leave the country.

The first play I took John to see on Broadway was *Porgy and Bess.* It was the only nonwhite stage production I was aware of, and I wanted him to know that there were blacks in the acting profession. That is also why I brought back from my trip to Paris in 1948 a copy of the Gauguin painting *Tahitian Women on the Beach,* to show him that nonwhites were worthy of being in art. I was concerned as to how John felt about himself. (*This may be the reason why my mother bought two 78 rpm record albums: one by Katherine Dunham and the other by Marian Anderson, a collection of spirituals. It's possible, however, that her purchases had nothing to do with me since she and my father had met Dunham in Haiti, which the latter visited to study voodoo, and since my mother had long been a fan of Anderson's. She was a great fan, too, of Lily Pons, several of whose albums we had [and whom Beverly Sills credited with bringing to the public that "extraordinary repertoire" (Sills' words) with her pure coloratura, long before the bel canto revival attributed to Maria Callas].*)

After a number of years, Maurice and I decided we had enough savings to put a downpayment on a house in Great Neck and began looking about. Jeanne Barron, always realistic, discouraged us, saying that even Great Neck was not ready to accept a black buying a house. Later, we found out that Ralph Bunche had wanted to buy there, too, but even someone as eminent as he had to settle for a home on Union Turnpike near Parkway Village, where nonwhites had begun to be accepted, or at least not resisted.

Jeanne helped us to get into a swimming club, and one day John invited Max Rouzier and another friend to swim.

Max appeared to be showing off, made noise, and attracted attention. The manager told Jeanne that it would be best if in the future John didn't invite any friends and suggested that he be as discreet as possible. We never went back there *(and only this year did I learn from Barbara Barron DiPierre that her parents were so horrified by what the manager said that they immediately resigned from the club.)*

Doris, who was made of equally strong stuff, dared take John and me (Maurice only went once to Connecticut) to restaurants in and on the way to Southbury, where people stared at us, just as they did at Maurice and me in Manhattan. But I was so happy to be out of the city and in a garden (Doris grew both flowers and vegetables), to hear the birds, walk in the woods, and have Doris' wonderful breakfasts, that it tended to erase the experience of the public situations. *(Did Doris' garden and surrounding land ever remind my mother of her high-school weekends at Miss Hastings' country cottage?)*

* * *

In the summer of 1951, my mother died of lumbar pneumonia. My brother John came East to pick up me and son John and take us back to Ohio. My brother drove nonstop through seven rainstorms!

One afternoon, my mother and I played at golf in my uncle's backyard. Instead of standing behind me when it was my turn to tee off, she stood at a distance but directly in front of me. I hit the ball, and it went flying, hitting her left temple and knocking her down. She was dazed, and I was very frightened. She made her way into the house, lay down with a cold compress, and remained on the bed for several hours. Neither Uncle John nor I remember her calling him to ask for a doctor's number, and fortunately, by the next morning she was on her feet again.

We spent a number of days in Auburn Corners, during which time I got to see Mary and Joe Bendler again. We returned by train to Great Neck.

Uncle John came to see us on two other occasions. The first was around 1949 when we were at 23 Schenck. The next was probably in 1954 with Aunt Sue, whose first trip to New York it was and who was pregnant with her second daughter Becky.

While John and I were in Ohio with my brother, Maurice was on a UN mission to Ruanda-Urundi, the trust territory administered by Belgium (and today known as two separate countries, Rwanda and Burundi). Sometime after his return from Africa (with vacation stops in Mombasa, Addis Ababa, and Cairo), he decided to have a party for the UN delegates with whom he'd traveled, to which we added a variety of other people. In the early hours of the morning, around 2 or 3 am, after the guests had gone, Maurice felt unwell and tried to get from his bed to the bathroom. But as he approached the door, he threw up quasi-black blood and fell to the floor. I immediately called our doctor, who insisted it must be an upset stomach. I insisted right back that all that black blood must indicate something far more serious. So he finally consented to come. When he saw Maurice's state and the bloody mess in the room (which by now had begun to stink), he called for an ambulance, and off Maurice went. We learned that he had a duodenal ulcer caused by overwork and also by the aspirin he took every morning about which he had never said a word. He said he had taken it because it gave him a lift.

When I went to see him at Manhasset Hospital (North Shore Hospital had not yet been built), I was appalled by the conditions. But since it was the only hospital in the area, he had to stay there. At the time, the usual remedy for ulcers was rest, a bland diet, and fresh cream and milk. Maurice spent three weeks in the hospital, then three more at home, finally returning to work in New York with permission to rest for two hours every day in the infirmary. I packed white meat of chicken and baked custard for weeks. He was very good about eating these. I think the illness had frightened him.

Three years later, it was my mother's turn to be hospitalized, for a hysterectomy. She mentioned it only parenthetically in her account of my life, saying that her operation was done at North Shore Hospital. My mother never talked about her ills, and I wasn't very good about asking. My only memory is of her friends delivering casseroles of food for my father and me, since neither of us could do more than boil water.

* * *

In late 1951, we moved around the corner to 12 Welwyn Road, to a two-bedroom apartment. Maurice and I could finally have a room of our own. This is where we saw a great deal more of the Rouziers, who lived right across the hall. Georgette and Pierre both worked at the UN, their son Max was in John's grade at school, *and their daughters Ginette and Ghislaine had each occasionally been my babysitter.*

In 2012, I managed to find Ghislaine in New York, and she said that we were considered not just friends but family, that she felt much closer to us than to some of her relatives. She'd been told that as a young man in Haiti, my father was in the habit of coming over to her maternal grandmother's quite often. In the late Forties/early Fifties, he, whom she thought of as very reserved, would visit with them roughly two Saturday afternoons a month, and they would have a wonderful time chatting, telling jokes, and laughing. In 1961, my mother saw Georgette and Ghislaine back in Haiti, where they lived for the next seven years, after which they returned to the States, where my mother caught up with them in New York. Ghislaine and her daughter Brigitte came to visit my mother in Paris in 2001, the day of the attack on the Twin Towers in Manhattan.

The move also allowed us to become much better acquainted with Alice (from the United Nations Women's Guild) and Jacques Lippetz (John already knew their son Eric very well from their playing together), Sophie and Paul Alpert, and May Dammond, an African-American *(whose husband, the few times I saw him, struck me as being a scientist or an engineer).* It was through May that I met Jean and Bob Benjamin. In 1954, Hurricane Hazel had ravaged Haiti. Maurice, with some of his countrymen and others, organized a lottery at the UN and gave me tickets to sell in Great Neck. May told me to go see Jean. She was sure she would buy some tickets, which she did, an entire book of ten! (It was Lena Five who won one of the prizes, a painting by Haitian artist J.E. Gourgue, one of whose works we have.) My friendship with Jean began with this. Shortly thereafter, both her daughter Meg and her son Jon were in the Great Neck Community School, the nursery school where I became director. When Maurice and I let it be known that we would be leaving for Paris, Jean and Bob were extremely generous and arranged a wonderful going-away party for us.

The Benjamins, who were big boosters of Brandeis University, encouraged me to apply there for college (which I did and was accepted with a scholarship). A few years later, after I'd written to Bob recommending a number of movies I'd seen in Paris during two successive summer vacations, including Black Orpheus *and* Never On Sunday *(which, in my naiveté about the movie business, I was unaware United Artists had already acquired for distribution under their subsidiary, Lopert Pictures), Bob invited me to come see him for a job after graduation. I didn't then but rather waited until I'd completed my master's at Columbia in early 1965. True to his word, Bob saw me and then turned me over to David Picker, the head of production, who found me a spot, first as a reader in the Story Department (which I wasn't very good at) and then as a trainee in the Foreign Advertising and Publicity Department (of which my Brandeis friend Ashley Boone was Director).*

When I heard this, I telephoned Jean and said, "If John does not measure up, throw him out!"

* * *

The presidency of Dumarsais Estimé in Haiti came to an abrupt end in May 1950. This had two important consequences for us. The United Nations could now offer my father a permanent contract and professional status, which allowed my parents to breathe a sigh of relief. And we would be able to return to Haiti for a visit for the first time in five years, which we did during the Christmas holidays.

The new president was Paul Magloire, whom Maurice had first known when the former was an army major and chief of the palace guard during the presidency of Elie Lescot. Magloire would serve as part of the military juntas that followed the ousters of Lescot and Estimé. When we visited Haiti that December, Maurice formally paid his respects to the new president, and later, in 1952, when Magloire and his wife were on an official visit to the United States and a formal luncheon was given in their honor by Secretary-General Trygve Lie at UN headquarters, we were included.

In Port-au-Prince, we stayed with Oncle Jehan and Tante Renée in a simplified version of a gingerbread-style house. (My grandmother had died earlier that year, and Jehan and Renée were observing a year of mourning.) I remember little about this trip other than our going up to Furcy for the day, Renée showing me how she made buttons on a hand-operated device, buying mahogany serving pieces chez Paquin (the store owned by Paulette Brandt's parents), and the complete transformation of the waterfront slums into the International Exposition, a pet project of Estimé's.

When we had left Haiti in 1946, it was to Renée I had confided the silverware and the sewing machine. She had taken good care of them, and upon my return in 1950, I sold the latter and most of the silverware, giving her half the money and the other half to Sister Joan, an Episcopalian nun who had founded St. Vincent de Paul School for the physically handicapped. Sister Joan was remarkable. She started in a simple church with two handicapped children. Then she developed the school to house more than one hundred, and now there were also more than two hundred fifty nonboarders who received a noon meal. Years later, she agreed to make room for a certain number of abandoned nursery-aged children and installed a workshop for making limbs and crutches. Dr. Gérard Léon (Rulx Léon's son) helped run and worked in the clinic for many years. Someone else created a secondhand or antique-furniture shop, as well as a workshop where these could be repaired. Homage must be paid to Sister Joan, who retired in 1993, and to all those who helped in this extraordinary under-taking. It is to this group that I gave our dining room furniture when in 1984 I sold the house we owned in Pétionville.

On the way to Haiti in 1950, my mother and I stopped off in Puerto Rico for a few days, staying at the Condado Beach Hotel in San Juan.

I foolishly asked for a room on the beach side, which at that time of year was cold and dark, and the waves, instead of making a soothing sound, were so high and hit the rocks with such force that the noise was unnerving. We toured the sights of the port and the city's monuments. We also took a cross-island bus that wound through hills covered with beautiful woods and arrived in Ponce, a very Spanish-looking town. Here we had lunch in a tavern and saw a group of horsemen dressed as they might have been in Spain or Argentina: sombrero, riding boots, spurs, whips, kerchief around the neck, and so on.

We visited Haiti again during the winter of 1952, staying this time in a rented house on the Place Boyer in Pétionville. Renée joined us for part of the time. We went to Furcy for the day, of course, and on another occasion went sightseeing with Paulette Brandt in her car. Because we were thirsty, we stopped at a vendor selling green coconuts. When the coconut is green, it is slashed to make a hole through which one can drink the liquid. Evidently the coconut John was given was not good for he developed diarrhea, and I don't think he has ever had green coconut juice again. (*I haven't.*)

On leaving Haiti, John and I spent a few days in Jamaica, which was still a British colony and where the native Jamaicans did not like whites. We stayed at a hotel on the outskirts of Kingston and were told not to go off the grounds on foot. But we did. People looked at us, but we were left alone. Once, we took a bus into Kingston and back. In it we were pushed and squeezed. I wondered if it was done on purpose, rather than because the bus was crowded. In the local papers, what attracted my attention were the articles on arrests and imprisonments for the theft of an apple or a loaf of bread. One could sense the tension between the colonizers and the colonized.

In the summer of 1955, on our last trip to Haiti before moving to Paris, we opened up the shack in Furcy and spent an idyllic month there. Since my parents wanted me to see the Citadel, we drove from Port-au-Prince to Cape Haitian and then made our way to the top on horseback, just as they had done more than twenty years before.

* * *

When John was 13, Maurice and I decided he was ready for his First Communion, as well as his Confirmation. I had promised to bring up any children we had in the Catholic faith, and had we stayed in Haiti, John probably would have done his communion earlier. But we had jumped around so much from 1946 to 1947—during which time he had attended five different schools—that we felt he needed a breather from any other demands. For two years, he and I joined Ethical Culture because it did not refer to heaven or hell or the hereafter, which was much more to my liking. But I was troubled about this, and although Maurice did not oppose what I was doing, I felt guilty.

Then I read *The Seven-Story Mountain,* written by a monk who was in a monastery of the strictest order. One of the reasons he had joined was that in his youth he had had no religious upbringing. I decided that John should have a religion and that later on he could stay with it or leave it. Renée had been after us for some time to have John go through both rites. His junior high school allowed him to skip seventh period once a week so he could attend catechism classes at St. Aloysius, which was a short walk from school. Thus in June of that year, John took communion one morning and was confirmed the same afternoon.

* * *

We never had to tell John to study. He did his homework and was always a good student. However, he was too well-behaved, and I worried about this. In the sixth grade, his teacher called me in to tell me that his behavior had changed and that he had started to throw spitballs like some of the other boys. I said, "Hurrah!" She was quite surprised. In the seventh grade, his homeroom teacher phoned to say that for the first time, he was misbehaving. Again I said, "Hurrah!" But neither of these periods lasted long, and neither teacher contacted me again.

My mother was employed at Mills College for four years, from 1950 to 1954. I don't recall why she decided to stop, but I'm going to guess she was worn out from the day-in, day-out traveling. She then became director of two parent-cooperative nursery schools in succession. The first was possibly (I couldn't find confirmation of the name) the Great Neck Cooperative School, during the academic year 1954–1955, while the second was the Great Neck Community School the following year.

In October 1955, during the course of a four-day biennial conference of the National Association for Nursery Education, held at the Statler Hotel in Boston, my mother participated as a "discussant" (i.e., panelist) in a Section Meeting titled "Present Status and Concerns of Teacher Education," presided over by Amy Hostler, her friend and president of Mills, who I imagine had recruited her. (Amy was also the organization's current Assembly Chairman and its former President.)

Another "discussant" was Frances Mayfarth, former editor of Childhood Education, *who five years earlier had so liked my mother's article on television and young children and who was now president of Wheelock College in Boston.*

* * *

My father was offered a new job, at UNESCO in Paris, and my parents felt this would be a good opportunity for us all for the next two years. He accepted the position and, in early June 1956, left to assume his post and to find us lodgings. My mother finished out her school year, waited for mine to be over, packed us up, and closed down the apartment. She and I set sail on June 30 aboard the ocean liner Ile de France, *traveling for the first (and last) time in unaccustomed style, first class (courtesy of the United Nations).*

Chapter Ten

Paris, Part I (1956-1966)

(There is almost no record of my mother's activities for the years 1956 through 1961, except for her passports, an article she wrote for an education magazine, and a sheet of general information that I will call the Errant Page, possibly written for her 1988 unpublished manuscript or one of the two books she issued in the 1990s (more on those later) but never used anywhere. So I've had to rely on my recollections and those of others, as well as notes I made during the year I lived in Paris and annual visits that followed. Beginning in 1962, my mother held on to almost all her monthly calendars, on which she jotted down a word or two, sometimes more, about what she'd done and whom she'd seen. These notations, the talks she gave, and a few of her letters to me and others provide the basis for later

parts of this chapter and subsequent chapters. Her remarks appear in normal typeface between quotes. [Titles of books, plays, magazines, operas, films and ballets appear in normal typeface.] From this point on, the text is largely in italics because I have taken over the narrative, and the reader will come upon a density of detail that is meant to camouflage the absence, alas, of a first-person account.)

The accommodations my father found for us for the first three months in Paris were part of a larger apartment at 51 Avenue George V, one block in from the Champs-Elysées, in the 8th arrondissement. We shared a common entryway with the owners (who must have been experiencing financial difficulties). One large room served as our dining room, living room, and my bedroom, while my parents slept in a small antechamber. There was a bathroom nearby, but an antiquated kitchen, used by our landlords as well, stood at the end of a very, very long corridor; my mother said she would do well to get herself a pair of roller skates to cover the distance.

No sooner had we arrived than we were off to Lutry, on Lake Geneva in Switzerland, to enroll me in a peculiar six-week summer camp. (There were three hours of French every weekday morning, and afternoons were spent at lakeside when no other activity was planned for us, which was often.)

* * *

I don't know if my mother had thought about what kind of work she might do in France. (Since she wasn't a French citizen, many avenues were closed to her.) But barely two months after arriving, she received an offer to become Director of the United Nations Nursery School (Jardin d'Enfants des Nations Unies), which she accepted, starting in just a few weeks' time. It would be her longest post of employment: she remained in it for ten years. And although it was not her goal, she became recognized as a spokesperson for and specialist in the field of early childhood education in a bilingual and international setting. She also contributed articles to education publications, was befriended by a leading figure in French education, and was invited to speak at a number of education conferences.

The UN Nursery School was founded in 1951 by UNESCO employees. (The American Community School of Paris, which opened right after the Second World War, did not go below the elementary-school level, and the Ecole Bilingue [the Bilingual School] had not yet come into being.) Because of limited space, the UN school could accommodate a maximum of fifty-eight children at a time. By 1962, nearly eight hundred had passed through its doors, representing forty-six different countries. The kids attended either the morning session or the afternoon. There were four teachers (the three-year-olds had two instructors; the fours and fives, one each), who were bilingual since both French and English were used in the classroom.

As director, my mother oversaw the teachers; provided additional training to them when necessary; dealt with individual parents, the PTA, and the Board, as well as with new children, troubled children, or those needing a lot of attention; and participated in fundraising activities (since money was always of critical concern to the school).

As she later said in a talk she gave (that I've excerpted and translated) at a French national conference of OMEP (Organisation Mondiale pour l'Education Préscolaire, or World Organization for Early Childhood Education), held in Nice in 1962 (and that appeared simultaneously under the title "Les Ecoles Internationales" [International Schools] in the conference publication Journées Internationales*), the UN Nursery School was* "for children [aged three to six] who are temporarily or permanently outside their home countries as well as for children of the host countries where parents may be attracted by the idea of an international school... [one of whose goals] is to increase mutual understanding and respect.

"We do our best to maintain a program based on the methods of active education and on the latest information about child development. Each year our program varies as to the details, depending on the needs and aptitudes of our children.

"Students of different nationalities, different formations and talents, some coming, others going, during the course of the year [some stay only a few months, others for two or three years]—not only do they have to make an adaptation to the school but also linguistic, social, and psychological adjustments as well. To deal with the needs of such a group of children, one requires a staff that is understanding, with special training. Parents [also] play a very active role in the school.

"Our principal goal is to have the child feel at ease and happy by discreetly giving him directions to aid him to develop his talents and possibilities and self-discipline, for his full physical, social, mental, and emotional blooming. [Most children adapt quickly to our environment], but inevitably there are some who've been jostled about in their customary lives and feel it deeply and who come to us rather troubled. Our program and our activities are tailored especially for these children. We have lots of free play with a variety of equipment and discreet direction that gives them encouragement.

"We do not insist children learn a new language, be it English or French. The child hears both in class and retains what he needs and what interests him. We find that time and a feeling of security are important factors at this age for a child to learn a new language.

"French-speaking children leave us the year of their fifth birthday; children who will segue into an American or British school stay with us for kindergarten where we prepare them for reading [and here we use only English]."

Eighteen months after she'd begun at the school, Child Study, *an American quarterly magazine founded in 1888 and devoted to parent education, was planning its Winter 1958–1959 issue, in which it would include articles about nursery-school education, as well as child-rearing and family life in different cultures. My mother was contacted by the editor, who had consulted with Amy Hostler of Mills College for leads on possible writers. This would be my mother's first published piece as far as I know, and in it she outlined the school's approach (along the lines described above), adding that it was at the time the world's only completely bilingual nursery school and also one of the most informal (which initially could shock some of the non-American parents). She also addressed, in contrast, the experiences of a French child at home and in the local school system.*

She would write about bilingualism and international schools several more times. A piece in the UNESCO magazine Opinion *titled "Back To School" appeared in 1964 and may have been intended as a way of letting new UNESCO employees with young children know about the school (just as two articles in* The New York Times International Edition— *"East Meets West at P.-T.A. Party at the Burmese Embassy in Paris" [April 24, 1961] and "Nursery in Paris Charms Children" [October 20, 1965]—served to publicize the school to a wider audience).*

The year 1965 would see the publication, in the January-February issue of ISA Bulletin *(organ of the International Schools Association), of "Rapport de Mme Esther Dartigue: Notre expérience au Jardin d'Enfants de l'ONU à Paris en ce qui concerne le bilinguisme"* ("*Mrs. Dartigue's Report: Our Experience at the United Nations Nursery School in Paris as Concerns Bilingualism"*).

In February 1966, The French Review, *the magazine of the American Association of the Teachers of French, published an article of hers titled "Bilingualism in the Nursery School." Here the focus was on how French was "taught" at the school, which was essentially by osmosis (i.e., whatever the child picked up on his/her own). And later that year, in July, there appeared a piece in German that summarized either the* ISA Bulletin *article or a talk she'd given at the New Education Fellowship Conference in Paris in 1965. It was called "Der Bilinguismus beim Kleinkind" (roughly, "Bilingualism in Nursery School Children") and ran in* Mitteilungsblatt, *newsletter of Arbeitsgemeinschaft für Mädchen- und Frauenbildung e.V. (the Association for Girls' and Women's Education), in Germany.*

* * *

S. (for Suzanne) Herbinière-Lebert was a pre-eminent and charismatic force in French education. She was Inspector General of Public Instruction, a founding president of OMEP, and president of the Comité français de l'OMEP (the French Committee of OMEP), a national organization that was under the protective wing of one of the French ministries.

She was present at the birth of the United Nations Nursery School in her then-capacity representing the Direction de l'Enseignement de la Seine (roughly, the Office for Education in the Seine Region) and continued her interest in and sup-port for the school, as well as a friendship with Amy Hostler that had begun in 1951 and had been fostered by their mutual involvement in OMEP. Whether it was the school or Amy that brought my mother to Mme Herbinière-Lebert's attention, I don't know. In any event, my mother joined the French Committee of OMEP (and by extension the world organization), and in 1962, she was asked to address the national conference mentioned earlier, a convention of some fifteen hundred French nursery-school teachers, directors, and inspectors, plus forty-four delegates of national com-mittees of OMEP worldwide, which was held in Nice in July. (Her friendship with Mme Herbinière-Lebert would continue for quite a few years, and I wonder if it ever reminded my mother of her relationship with Mlle Vincent in Haiti, though the gap in years was far less: fifteen in the case of the for-mer, thirty-seven in the latter.)

The subject of her talk in 1962, as mentioned previously, was "a brief look at international schools and some consid-erations on bilingualism." *She noted that* "before 1940 the International School in Geneva was the rare such school; by 1962 there were 60 international schools around the world." *(The remaining high points I've already quoted in the first pages of this chapter.)*

Paris, Part I (1956-1966)

I was in Paris that summer and planning to accompany my mother to Nice when we invited Sylvia Washington (later Bâ) to join us. I'd met Sylvia in New York earlier that spring through mutual International House friends, and she, too, was in town for three months. She was a French literature major who developed her PhD thesis into a scholarly treatise on Senegal's poet-president, The Concept of Negritude in the Poetry of Léopold Sédar Senghor, *published by Princeton University Press in 1973, and who then for thirty years was a Professor of Francophone African Literature and of Comparative Literature at the University of Dakar. She spent the rest of 1962 and most of 1963 in Paris at Cité Universitaire, during which time my mother was able to make a number of invaluable contributions to Sylvia's research for her book. "Your mother arranged some most helpful and significant meetings and interviews for me," Sylvia said. The two saw a great deal of each other. (For example, my mother wrote on her calendar,* "Sylvia took me to a Chinese luncheon for Mother's Day and then we went to Saint-Germain to gaze." *On another occasion,* "I took Sylvia to the Drugstore" *[which had recently opened]* "so she could see it." *) Subsequently, Sylvia would pass through Paris every few years. She was game for the trip to Nice, so off the three of us went, my mother behind the wheel.*

The first morning of the convention, my mother found the bulletin-board display for the UN Nursery School either unacceptable or absent. She quickly phoned to have Sylvia and me rush over to help her mount a proper exhibit.

Sylvia and I spent the daytime hours on our own and met up with my mother for dinner. One evening, we went to the Negresco (the five-star hotel on the Promenade des Anglais), where my mother informed the waiter that she'd attended the conference luncheon there earlier in the day, had enjoyed an exceptional "loup au fenouil" (sea bass with fennel), and was certain there was still some left in the kitchen that she'd like "les jeunes" (the youngsters, meaning Sylvia and me) to have. Although the waiter probably found this request outlandish—something a French man or woman would never dream of making—he bowed, consulted with the maitre d', and in time returned with the loup, which was indeed delicious.

(Sylvia would be ensnared in several of my mother's restaurant outings during her stay in Paris. That fall, for instance, my mother felt Sylvia should experience the pressed duck at and the view of Notre Dame from the Tour d'Argent, but since the establishment was notoriously expensive, she had devised a plan. Once seated, she informed the waiter that "Mademoiselle est au régime" ["the young lady is on a diet"] and therefore they would be ordering one duck to be divided between them. The waiter probably became bug-eyed at the outrageousness of the declaration [for there was no such thing as a split order!], but since he must have sensed he was up against an immovable object, the half portions were produced. Sylvia had undoubtedly wanted to evaporate during the exchange while managing to suppress her laughter.)

My mother had instructed Sylvia to share her hotel room in Nice so as to save Sylvia money. This meant that when she and I returned late the first night from a discotheque, Sylvia wanted to avoid disturbing my mother, who was already in bed and presumed asleep. As she recounted it to me the next day, she had removed her heels and was try-ing to enter the room as quietly as possible when she was suddenly greeted by "Stop that pussyfooting around!" Sylvia didn't know whether to burst out laughing or be terrified as she scurried to get herself into bed.

My mother decided that on our return to Paris, we would stop off at one of France's great restaurants (and one of her favorites), the Hôtel de la Côte d'Or, in the town of Saulieu, on whose celebrated chef, Alexandre Dumaine, the Guide Michelin had bestowed its coveted three stars. It was going to be a long drive under the best of circumstances—682 km (about 423 miles)—but it became even longer after we encountered a detour on the auto-route that caused us to be on surface streets for some time. As the afternoon sun beat down on my mother's sleeveless left arm, she sought relief by asking Sylvia, who was seated behind her, to apply eau de cologne to cool off her skin. Sylvia, I imagine, felt awkward, given that she had met my mother only the week before, but proceeded nonetheless to tend to this task for the next few hours.

The deadline for seating in the restaurant was 8:30 pm. By 7 pm chances of our making it were looking slim. My mother stopped long enough to place a quick call to say we were on our way, and from that point on, our wheels seemed barely to touch the surface of the road, so determined was she to arrive in time. And we did—and had a remarkable meal. My mother asked M. (short for Monsieur) Dumaine if he would kindly autograph a menu next to the listing for one of the specialties we'd had, "timbale de quenelle de brochet eminence" (finely chopped pike, shaped into several roughly four-inch oblongs, poached and served in a cream sauce containing bits of sole, crayfish, mushroom, and truffle—crudely put, highly refined gefilte fish); that menu sits framed in my dining area to this day. (The following summer my mother would offer to drive Sylvia, two friends of ours [Laurel Frank and Everett Jacobs], and me to Saulieu for lunch. We feasted, Sylvia reminded me, on another house specialty, "poularde vapeur à la Lucien Tendret," which had to be ordered a day in advance.)

A week after our return to Paris, my mother was off to the OMEP World Conference in London, where she attended a number of lectures, including one by Anna Freud, and visited nursery schools and playgrounds. She also took in several plays and the Tate Gallery and invited Amy Hostler and Mme Herbinière-Lebert to dinner at Simpson's.

In 1964, the OMEP World Conference was held in Stockholm, where, my mother noted, she heard "excellent speeches from Lady Marjory Allen of the UK and Alva Myrdal of Sweden," cofounders (along with Mme Herbinière-Lebert) of OMEP. (Mrs. Myrdal had also been among the founders of the UN Nursery School in Paris.) Five months later, when Lady Allen and Amy Hostler came to the French capital, the three went to dinner, and after dropping off the former at the Gare du Nord for her train, my mother drove the latter around to see Paris by night and then to Le Drugstore (at that time a novelty, based on the old American model) at the top of the Champs-Elysées so that Amy could make some purchases. On her calendar my mother wrote that the evening had been "a lot of fun."

My mother participated in several more educational conferences—in Milan in 1963, in Paris (for the International Schools Association) in 1964, and in Zurich (ISA again), Sèvres (just outside Paris), Bourges (in central France), and Paris (the New Education Fellowship Conference, held at the Institut National de Pédagogie), all in 1965. She gave talks on bilingualism and international schools at the last three. (During the ISA gathering in Paris, she hosted a lunch at the apartment for twenty-three conference attendees. A year later in Zurich, not a reciprocal finger was lifted.)

* * *

In February 1963, in response to a questionnaire mailed out by the International Schools Association, of which the UN Nursery School was a member, my mother elaborated on a point she had noted before but which she now felt needed emphasis: the importance of diversity at any age, but most certainly at an early age, to help people better understand and respect one another.

To begin with, her letter took issue with the questionnaire's title, "East-West Project," which, she said, was immediately divisive. She suggested that a more appropriate, inclusive title might have been, say, "Cultural Exchange" or "Cultural Understanding" or "Intercultural Understanding."

She continued by stating that the questionnaire focused on primary and secondary international schools as the foundations for creating understanding between cultures and people but completely ignored the contribution nursery schools could make. "We are convinced," *she wrote,* "that the nursery school level has as much to offer in international understanding and cooperative interests as any other branch of the [international] school system.... [A]ttitudes are formed and often fixed at an early age. Therefore, International Nursery Schools have a vital and important role to play in the child's life in regard to his feelings about himself and his attitudes towards others.... Thus, whenever possible, every nursery school should have children from as many different nationalities as possible, so that as a child's awareness grows, he is conscious of familiar differences in himself and others as a part of his natural and normal daily life. In this way it is easier for a child to accept others who are not quite like himself or his family group for whatever reason, and yet not feel an isolate in any group because of differences."

She went on to give examples of remarks children make that might hurt others and how teachers need to handle these situations with sensitivity and discretion. In each case the role of the teacher was *paramount in easing the effect of comments made about differences so that* "the child accepted the answer in a matter of fact way" *and the other child did not sense he or she was different.* "We feel that *how* we say something is as important as *what* we say. The child does not lose his own identity by recognizing differences, but instead accepts the wide varieties of individual identities marked by the differences in himself and in others.... Such an opportunity for mutual respect and understanding must be undertaken by teachers whose own attitudes and methods surmount national, racial or religious prejudices of any kind. We seek qualified bilingual nursery school teachers, no matter what their nationality, but they need to have the desire and ability to be with children from any background and help in promoting mutual self-respect.

"The lessons we teach are not only the planned ones, but the ones we evolve from the opportunities which present themselves.... We scrutinize our stories, games, and records carefully before we use them. There are quite a few that unconsciously or not belittle or ridicule or hurt. ....[T]hough [our] nursery school and kindergarten cannot perhaps have the same kind of content 'lessons' as the primary and secondary grades, it can be and is a vital learning place for being accepted as oneself and accepting others in like manner, for being a friend and having friends, for 'belonging.' This is not a lesson taught, but lived.

"Badly managed, an international school can create more prejudices than it eliminates. But the challenge and the opportunity at the nursery school level are such that a child, armed at this age with the emotional security which a good nursery school can offer and the acceptable and wider horizon which a good international nursery school can present, will, hopefully, never feel himself an isolate or a stranger in any group, nor will others be strange to him.

"International nursery schools are fundamental to international understanding; understanding is fundamental to knowledge and progress; and the young child can be a valuable ally in the implementation of these."

I don't know what kind of response, if any, she got from ISA and whether her remarks influenced future questionnaires. Hopefully they heard her.

* * *

As we know from her days in Haiti and Great Neck, my mother had a facility for chatting with people and making friends. The French, on the other hand, were notoriously difficult to know, and she had the typical experience of any foreigner, although my parents did have a few good friends among the French, such as Edmée and Jacques Tézé. And their old pal Auguste Viatte, who was Swiss-born, now made Paris his permanent home. "We learned," *she said in the* Errant Page, *"that the French were less open, less outgoing, less encouraging, more self-centered than Americans.*

"However," *she continued,* "we came to have a large acquaintance and made some good friends through Maurice's work." *Luckily, too, a number of Haitians were living in or visiting Paris. In fact, the first social call my parents paid was to Marie and Franck Lavaud, whom they had last seen in Haiti ten years earlier and who now resided on the Rue de Bassano, just a few blocks away from where we were living on George V. After serving as part of the military junta that had temporarily ruled Haiti after the fall of President Lescot and again after the unseating of Lescot's successor, Dumarsais Estimé, Franck had been appointed ambassador to France. A few years later, he was offered the post of ambassador to the United Nations in New York but declined because he wanted to remain in Paris for the benefit of his children's continuing education. (All three would stay on in France after graduating and wed French citizens.)*

My parents would see a great deal of the Lavauds and their daughter Marie-Alice in the years to come, as they did of another couple they hadn't seen in quite a while, Marie's brother Joseph Nadal and his wife Liliane, who had an apartment on the Avenue Raphaël in the 16th and who split their time between it and their home in Haiti (and later a house in Plascassier, a hamlet a few miles from Grasse [the perfume capital of France], to which in the Seventies and Eighties the Nadals would invite my parents each year).

Eliane Laraque was another great friend from Haiti who, after her husband Gustave's death, in 1963, installed herself in Paris for some thirty years (with the exception of a short spell in Mexico with one of her daughters). Gustave had served as ambassador in a number of foreign capitals, including Lima and Washington; his last assignment was in Rome, where my mother and I visited the Laraques in 1957.

Ghyslaine and Pierre Liautaud, Yvonne and Max Rigaud, and Nelly and Marcel Dupuy traveled from Haiti to Paris from time to time, for all three couples had sons in boarding schools in the area. My parents acted as what the French call "correspondants," a family who has students over for Sunday lunch (and most of that afternoon) as a way for the boys to have a change of scenery and a bit of home environment as well. Approximately once a month for three or four years my parents received Ghyslaine's Claude-Hervé and Zoupite, the Rigauds' Philippe, and the Dupuys' Edmond, Ronald, and James. There were times when they were all at the house at once, but when there might be just one or two, my parents might take them out to a restaurant and possibly to a movie or play. Claude-Hervé wrote to me, "Your mother was for my brother and me a very important person during our development at a key age for a young person advancing towards maturity."

There was a steady stream of other travelers—Americans my parents had known in Haiti, many from Great Neck, and a few from Mills College and Wooster College.

As a result, my mother entertained a great deal at home, dined out often, and attended foreign embassy receptions (through my father's position at UNESCO). She traveled a lot and was able to indulge her great love of the arts by frequently going to the theatre, ballet, opera, concerts, art exhibitions, and some movies. For my mother, Paris was a veritable cultural candy store.

* * *

Our living quarters on the Avenue George V were meant to be only temporary, and in September, thanks to Hannah Schulhof and a cousin of hers living in Paris, we rented an apartment in a new building in the adjacent suburb of Neuilly, a block or two from the western edge of the Bois de Boulogne and the gardens of the Bagatelle (which, for the rest of her life, was one of the spots my mother loved most to visit, especially when the daffodils and roses were in bloom). It was on a street fronting the river, formerly called the Boulevard de la Seine but recently changed to the Boulevard du Général Koenig (in honor of a French hero of

World War II who fought Rommel in North Africa). My parents kindly gave me the one bedroom, while they once again were relegated to sleeping in the living room.

Our weekday morning routine involved my father taking us in the small, bright-blue, British-made Anglia he'd gotten; dropping me off at the American Community School of Paris (the word 'Community' was later eliminated), where I was a senior, situated on the Boulevard d'Auteuil, yards into the suburb of Boulogne-sur-Seine; and then taking my mother to her school on the Rue Louis David in the 16th arrondissement, before reaching his office at UNESCO, which at the time was housed on the Avenue Kléber, halfway between the Trocadéro and the Etoile (which is how the French refer to the site of the Arch of Triumph and where twelve avenues converge for a driver's nightmare).

It was not the time, unfortunately, to be in a new, oil-heated building (as opposed to an old one fueled by coal). The Suez Crisis erupted at the end of October, and we and so many others spent a very cold winter without heat or hot water and with rationed gasoline. Bathwater was boiled on the kitchen stove (which, luckily, used natural gas), and my parents bought several space heaters (one of which, almost fifty years later, I spotted on display, surprisingly, at the Pompidou Museum).

We thought to escape some of the winter by spending a Christmas holiday week in the south of France, but the weather was unseasonably cold there, too. We saw the sights in various cities, and in St. Paul de Vence, my mother bought a half-dozen Picasso ceramics inexpensively, one of which she gave to Jeanne Barron, another to Doris Bock.

* * *

In the summer of 1959, my parents received a letter from my father's first cousin Agnes (daughter of his paternal aunt Carmen and her German husband Carl Heinrich Voigt). Although she had left Haiti very, very young, Agnes had formed an attachment to her roots and early on initiated a lengthy correspondence with Tante Renée (with whom she became particularly close) and an intermittent one with our family and with Oncle Jehan's. Sadly, tragedy befell the Voigts: Agnes' Haitian-born siblings Bertha and Heinrich died—Bertha in 1912 after surgery in Hamburg and Heinrich in 1918 as a soldier in the Kaiser's army in Belgium during the First World War. Then another brother, the German-born Carl Jr., would contract malaria during a stay in Haiti in the early 1920s. He died in 1930.

Agnes had survived the Hitler regime, my mother thought, because she had become a medical doctor (and looked typically German). (The real explanation is that although Carmen and her two daughters were asked to submit proof of their being Aryan and did, there was, blessedly, never any follow-up [possibly, I'm told, because the Gestapo was so obsessed with uncovering and exposing Jews that they let other matters slide.] Nonetheless, I can imagine the family lived for years under a great deal of tension and fear. [The filed papers, incidentally, claimed that Carmen was from an important French family, with some—ahem!—Arab blood mixed in.]) In the post-WWII period, my parents sent the family CARE packages since the Voigts were far worse off than we were in our first years in the U.S. While her sister Gertrud (Agnes' last remaining sibling, born in Germany in 1904 shortly after the family's arrival in Uetersen, just outside Hamburg) had married, Agnes had not, until 1953 when, at age 51, she wed a former Nazi lieutenant colonel! Her letter to my parents announced that she and her husband were planning a trip to France and wanted to see us. My mother was aghast at the notion of a Nazi (even a former one) in her home and very plainly told Agnes no; she said that she would be welcome but not her spouse. So Agnes came to visit us while her husband went off to the region of France where he'd been a commandant during the war— which my mother found equally appalling.

Agnes would travel to Paris to see my parents once more ten years later. After her death in 1977, the two branches of the family lost touch until 2012 when, through the miracle of the internet, I was able to locate Gertrud's son/Agnes' nephew/my second cousin Lorenz Schwegler, a successful attorney heading his eponymous law firm, with offices in Dusseldorf, Frankfurt, Berlin, and Cologne. It was a truly

lucky find because Lorenz provided me with correct informa-
tion about the Voigts in Haiti during the first quarter of the
last century and in Germany up through 1945.

* * *

It had been my parents' intention to spend just two years in Paris; however, when UNESCO offered my father an extension of his contract, it gave them pause. Despite a few frustrations, they were both doing more interesting work than they had in the States; culturally, Paris in particular and Europe in general had so much to offer; and racially, they were much happier in France. "Maurice," *my mother wrote in the Errant Page,* "felt he had a real contribution to make at work, while as director of my nursery school I experienced all the satisfactions (and problems) that such a position could give. UNESCO salaries at the time, compared to those of the French, were quite high so that Maurice and the other employees considered themselves privileged. Maurice, too, was assimilated into the international Diplomatic Corps, which also helped in various ways. (But he was very careful never to take advantage of his position.) Furthermore, we were comfortably at home with the French language and French culture, and we enjoyed living in Paris and being able to travel around freely in Europe, whether on business or as tourists. Most importantly, the problems of discrimination

and restrictions that we had encountered in the U.S. completely disappeared in France. We could live wherever we
wanted to and we bought an apartment without any difficulty." *Consequently, my father accepted the contract extension, and my parents decided to put down stakes.*

*My mother said she must have visited nearly one hundred
apartments, but my father always found something wrong
with each of them. Finally, she declared she would look no
further and he would just have to choose from among those
she'd already seen. So, with a certain reluctance, he opted
for 3 rue Cognacq-Jay, which he financed through savings, a
UNESCO loan, and the very kind assistance of Joseph Nadal.*

*Although the apartment had three negatives that my
mother had vowed she would never want in a residence (it
was on the ground floor; faced north, allowing little or no
light into the rooms not directly on the street; and was cold),
its location couldn't have been more ideal. It was on a quiet
street in a quiet neighborhood in a quiet arrondissement (the
7th). The Seine was two short blocks away, and within easy
walking distance (ten to twenty minutes) were various landmarks (it was situated, for instance, halfway between the Eiffel
Tower and the Hôtel des Invalides), several museums, the
Avenue Montaigne, and the Champs-Elysées. In the way of
public transportation, we were very well served: six bus lines,
two subway (métro) lines, and the Little Train (as it was then
called, now part of the RER express system) to Versailles, all
within a five-to-ten-minute walk from the house. My mother*

could now take the 63 bus to reach her school, while my father, if he wanted to, could take two buses (the 92 and 49), but he preferred to drive the ten minutes to UNESCO, now installed in a spanking-new, ultra-modern building, designed by the troika of France's Bernard Zehrfuss, Italy's Pier Luigi Nervi, and the naturalized American Marcel Breuer (Bauhaus alumnus and creator of Manhattan's Whitney Museum and the Breuer chair). It sits right behind the Ecole Militaire, on the Place de Fontenoy (which commemorates a major French victory in 1745 during the War of the Austrian Succession).

It was nice to finally be in town after more than three years in the "sticks" (although Neuilly is essentially an extension of Paris, unlike such suburbs as, say, Le Vésinet or Saint-Germain-en-Laye). Soon after my parents moved in, in January 1960, they held a housewarming party. At some point the doorbell rang; my mother answered it to find a momentarily startled woman who proceeded to say, "Oh, it's you! I couldn't remember who you were, but the address was good, so I decided to come." (It was the attorney Maître Misard, whom my mother would get to know well.) In France, too, it can be all about location.

The apartment was furnished mostly with our secondhand pieces from Great Neck (bought at Ye Olde Trading Post in the Old Village) and others like them purchased in Paris, while my mother made her own slipcovers and cushions for the divan and armchairs. (She would redo them several times more, the last being when she was nearly 80. She would also do so in my father's apartment in Dakar during her first visit there and would recover two armchairs for her sister Betty.)

However, my parents did allow themselves a few "extravagances." In addition to finally living in a home they owned for the first time in almost fifteen years, they traded in the little Anglia for a dark-blue Mercedes and bought crystal stemware from Baccarat, Luneville everyday dishes (that my mother loved and were relatively inexpensive at the time, but today are quite pricey—she called them her legacy to me), and Limoges formal dinnerware (although many years later a saleswoman at the department store Galeries Lafayette was eager to point out that it wasn't real Limoges because, although it had been made from material originating in Limoges, the porcelain had actually been manufactured in another town, Châtres-sur-Cher). But the purchases were less indulgent than they might appear because there was a healthy discount on each, courtesy of my father's UNESCO tie.

My mother made a few changes to herself, as well. She had started turning gray in the 1940s and had been dyeing her hair a dark brown for about fifteen years. Once she got to Paris, a coiffeur suggested she try ash blond, which she did with great success. And like any parisienne who was neither too rich nor too poor, she found herself a little dressmaker and had several suits, blouses, and coats made.

* * *

In the summer of 1960, my parents were in the Netherlands on their way to Denmark when I called to say UNESCO was urgently trying to reach my father. It concerned, I learned later, the unfolding Congo Crisis. Belgium had reluctantly granted independence to its prize colony but in revenge had withdrawn all its trained personnel, including teachers, plunging the new nation into a state of chaos since Brussels had educated very few Congolese—there were only fourteen university graduates in the entire country—to assume the responsibilities of government. The United Nations, UNESCO, and many other UN agencies rushed to the rescue, and initially my father was appointed Chief Consultant in Education to the Head of United Nations Civilian Operations in the Congo, before being promoted shortly thereafter to Chief of the UNESCO Mission in the Congo. It was as though he'd been preparing for this role his whole life: his twenty-year career in Haiti, his work at the UN with the African trust and other non-self-governing territories, and his four years at UNESCO in Paris all came together to produce the right man at the right time for the right job, for, as my mother wrote in the Errant Page, "Maurice was to have a very important role in the reconstruction of the system of education of that newly freed State."

During the ensuing year, my father came back to Paris several times for meetings, which gave my parents the chance to reunite briefly. Given the mortal danger throughout the Congo and the people's suspicion of and outright hostility toward whites, spouses were initially not allowed to travel there. (My mother wrote in her book about my father's career, An Outstanding Haitian, Maurice Dartigue, *that in November 1960, for example, "There was rioting in Leopoldville.... [Then] fighting broke out between the UN troops and the national army.... [A]t least 12 UN personnel were savagely beaten by Congolese soldiers.") When travel permission for families was granted, she, the intrepid soul she was, flew to Brazzaville (capital of the former French Congo) in April 1961 and crossed the river into Leopoldville (capital of the former Belgian Congo and now of the new Congo) to be with my father for a few weeks.*

* * *

When one first comes to Paris, it can seem like para-dise—the food, wine, culture, history, art, fashion, nightlife, jazz, the cafés, boîtes and bistros, the architecture, the wide tree-lined avenues and boulevards, and those expansive squares—all contributing so much to the splendor of the City of Light.

But in this post-war period, there was also a spiritual darkness that had begun with the generations of men dev-astatingly lost in the two quasi-back-to-back world wars. (The disabled veterans, known as "mutilés de guerre," and the seats specifically reserved for them on every bus and subway car were daily reminders of those conflicts, if in fact one needed a reminder.) There were also the ghosts that were the result of that terrible secret—the collaboration by a certain number of the French, both civilian and governmental, in the deportation and murder of their Jewish countrymen during the second war. (It would take until 1995 for these crimes to be officially acknowledged.) In 1954 came more spectres, from the deaths and humiliation of Dien Bien Phu and France's ouster from Indochina, the start of the dissolution of the country's vast colonial empire. That same year an even blacker storm gathered— the outbreak of the Algerian War, which would become a political and psychological nightmare, tearing at the nation's soul. Where India had been the jewel in the British crown, Algeria was seen as an integral part of metropolitan France; to sever ties was to sever limbs, inexplicable and unthinkable.

The Algerian Crisis became particularly tense and bitter between 1958 and 1962. The FLN (the Algerian liberation movement) was setting off bombs in Paris; the right-wingers who wanted to keep Algeria French were plotting mayhem of their own, including an assassination attempt on President Charles de Gaulle by the OAS (the secret organization comprised of disaffected members of the French military); and in what was called the Paris Massacre, the French police killed some two hundred among the thousands of Algerian demonstrators.

Thus my father worried about my mother in Paris, my mother worried about my father in the Congo, and they worried together after my father's return to the French capital. (One day, my parents were coming back to the Rue Cognacq-Jay by car when army personnel guarding the entrance to the street [at the time France's national TV was housed on Cognacq-Jay and there was a real concern that either the FLN or the OAS would try a takeover] told my father to stop and asked for his papers. [My father could sometimes be mistaken for Moroccan, say, or Egyptian.] Always prudent, he very slowly reached into his breast pocket. Had his movements been sudden, he might easily have become a statistic. The car was waved on.)

* * *

UNESCO had a mandatory retirement age of 60, which my father attained in March 1963. During the next eight years, UNESCO and other UN-associated agencies and programs hired him for short-term and longer-term missions in Africa, which had become his specialty and which opened up the African continent to my mother. When he spent two years (1963–1965) in Dakar, in Senegal, she visited twice and saw, among many things, Saint-Louis (former capital of the former French colony from 1673 to 1960) and the island of Gorée, where slaves had been loaded and shipped *into the nightmare of the Middle Passage, winding up—those that survived the horror—in the New World, including, of course, Haiti. (She also noted on her second stay in Dakar that "many people in the streets are reading Arabic books and wearing Arabic-style clothes," which hadn't been the case on her previous trip. Islam was already further on the march there.)*

When, during those same two years, my father organized courses (the first of their kind for future African teachers) in Cairo, it provided an opportunity for my mother to take in the great wonders of the city and the Nile Valley (she jotted down such words as "fantastic," "beautiful," and "stupendous" to describe what she saw, especially the massive twin temples, monuments to the Pharaoh Ramses II and Queen Nefertari built in the 13th century BCE at Abu Simbel. She viewed them at sunrise in their original setting; this was just as the tremendous world rescue mission had begun that would relocate them above the Aswan High Dam.) She spent twenty-one months with my father in Bujumbura, Burundi, which allowed her access to parts of that country, the eastern edge of the Democratic Republic of Congo, Rwanda, Uganda, and Kenya, including wildlife preserves. When my father was briefly in Tunis for a UNESCO-sponsored meeting, she visited that city and Carthage. Later, she made two trips to Morocco, the first on her own to Rabat (where Margaretta and Fred Kroll, her American friends from Haiti, were now based), Casablanca, Marrakech, and Fes (or Fez), which she described as "extraordinary", and the second with my father to Tangier (where Peggy and Bill Krauss, another American couple from Haiti, were also vacationing).

One of the great advantages of being on the European continent is the proximity of destinations—everything is about an hour or two away by plane, within a day or two's drive by car—and so my mother traveled a lot through Western Europe and extensively in France. She also crossed the Atlantic. Twice she went to Haiti, in 1957 (with my father and me) and in 1961 (my father was in the Congo at the time), after which there came an eleven-year hiatus because the reign of François Duvalier ("Papa Doc") had become far too dangerous. She made stops in Manhattan and Great Neck at either end of these trips to see all the friends who had come to Paris and all who hadn't, and to take in a few plays each time. She also saw family in Florida and Ohio. In 1961, Doris and Charles Bock drove her from New York to Waltham, Massachusetts, and back so she could attend my college graduation.

* * *

As it was for so many, the death of Franklin Roosevelt in 1945 was jolting. My mother and I were upstairs in our house in Haiti, she sewing and I coloring, with the radio on, when the broadcast was interrupted for the announcement.

My mother was incredulous, got to her feet, threw open the window behind her, and yelled out to her American neighbor Nelly to learn if it was true. Nearly twenty years later, Sylvia Washington Bâ told me, she was at a Thanksgiving celebration at my mother's Paris nursery school when "someone burst in with the shocking news of John Kennedy's assassination. Great consternation and confusion ensued, what with parents arriving, getting the kids taken care of, people wanting to get home." That night my mother wrote in her calendar, "I could not believe it!" and on the first anniversary of the president's death, she noted, "A year ago a terrible date!"

* * *

The British and the Germans have long been drawn to the shores of Spain, and one can find colonies of vacationers almost year-round. There was, as a result, high-rise after high-rise dotting beach communities, and in some (or perhaps in many) the building's management would rent out an apartment when an owner was not in residence. In October 1965, my parents went to the area with a budget in mind to look at possibilities for an investment. They settled on something in Torremolinos, near Malaga, on the Costa del Sol, more expensive than they'd intended, but the building was well-constructed, in the middle of town, with a nice view from their floor, the ninth. Their first stay there was in April 1966, but essentially their timing of the purchase was off because at the end of that month, my father would begin his more-than-two-year stay in Burundi. But the deal had been made, and it inspired my mother to brush up on her Spanish at Berlitz (where she had sometime earlier taken a year of Italian, although I don't believe she ever felt she had mastered the language and found some of the instructors lacking). They vacationed in Torremolinos several times between their return from Burundi in 1968 and their decision to sell in late 1972.

* * *

My father's acceptance of the post in Burundi prompted my mother to retire from the UN Nursery School so she could accompany him on what was initially to be a six-month assignment. (I think the two-year separation while my father worked in Dakar had been sufficiently instructive.) A going-away gathering for her was held in late May 1966, attended by some of the Board of Trustees members and by her teachers. Her friend Ruth Métraux, who was board vice president, gave a short speech of thanks and appreciation before presenting her with a memento for her years of service, an engraved silver plate.

My mother's earlier reference in the Errant Page to problems at school *and additional remarks Ruth now made indicated that all had not been smooth sailing during the ten years, that some of my mother's efforts had gone unappreciated. She had undoubtedly given more to the school than anyone had expected or acknowledged, and she may have made suggestions that were rejected. She had often had to fill in for absent teachers, sometimes for weeks at a time, and to cope with the school's limitations, both physical (the quarters were cramped) and financial. My mother also kept up the school's physical plant when necessary, spending her own time during some weekends and holidays varnishing furniture, for instance, or repainting walls, boats, and the playground jungle gym, to save the school money on labor. She shopped for school materials, advanced money for bills, hosted some of the monthly Board meetings (which included preparing and serving dinner), and visited many different bilingual nursery schools during her travels to see if there were pointers to be picked up—in New York, Washington, Puerto Rico, London, Copenhagen, Stockholm, and Nice, as well as a number of schools in and around Paris. She had, furthermore, sought to raise the school's profile by attending educational conferences, giving her talks, and writing her articles. Yes, these endeavors had brought her professional recognition, but it was really for the school she'd done them. All this was in addition to her regular responsibilities mentioned at the start of this chapter, and I imagine there may have been even more that I'm just not aware of. She'd really given a great deal of herself.*

But she could take pleasure and pride in all that she had accomplished, and she'd made significant impressions on teachers, parents, and children. She would enjoy long friendships with some of those she'd met. Of the few whose names I remember were the teachers Alice Daifuku, Kathy Kessler, Martine de Lavernette, and Maguy Duchesne. She had had them over for an occasional dinner as a group (I suspect it was to create a feeling of solidarity that benefited them all as well as the school) and saw them individually and collectively long after her retirement. She would also continue to see parents Rae Gronich, Barbara Pleskow, and Mary Carter and would even occasionally hear from some of her former students, including Daphne Gronich and Drew Boatner.

Through the resources of the internet, I was able to locate Drew Boatner, in Louisiana, and he sent me a wonderful account that is both moving and chilling:

"You know, whenever I read someone's reminiscence about why a particular teacher played a key role in shaping his life or future, I think about your mother, whom I remember as 'Madame Dartigue.' Granted, I can list at least a dozen teachers or administrators who played key roles in my development from school to college. Your mother will, however, always be first on my list.

"I was four years old in your mother's nursery school. My parents knew that I wasn't developing the way Dr. Spock said I should. Being in Paris without access to competent pediatricians, they were at a loss as to why. They did take

me to several French doctors who told my parents that I was retarded. They suggested that my parents should go ahead and commit me to a facility. Believe me, at age 54, I still shudder every time I think about that!

"It was your mother who, after observing me for a while at school, insisted with characteristically firm conviction that I was hard of hearing. Afterward, my dad made an appointment with a traveling Army pediatrician passing through Paris. The doctor 'confirmed' this diagnosis as soon as he saw me enter the room. (I've never figured out what the doctor saw; maybe he watched my eyes?) A hearing test officially confirmed this a few days later. Because of this early diagnosis, I wear hearing aids and otherwise function normally.

"While I was attending college in Strasbourg (1978–1979), I wrote to Madame Dartigue. She invited me up for a weekend and I stayed in your parents' apartment. I remember your dad Maurice. I found both of them fascinating as they regaled me of their separate and joint lives. We had lunch at UNESCO. Your mother was absolutely thrilled to see how I had turned out as she had long wondered what became of me. She will always have a special place in my heart."

* * *

My mother's decision to leave her job to be with my father couldn't have come at a more opportune time, although for an unfortunate reason. In August 1966, my father was diagnosed with prostate cancer and underwent surgery at Manhattan's New York Hospital. He recuperated for a month at the Gramercy Park Hotel (where their room was burglar-ized!), and they returned to France by ship. The doctors advised my mother that for the sake of his morale, my father should return to work as quickly as possible (but initially spend only half days in the office). So after four more weeks at home, they left in early November for Burundi.

* * *

For those of you who may want more specifics about who was part of my mother's life during this period, the area she moved to in 1960, the places she traveled to, the things she saw and bits of their history, you may wish to read on. If not, skim along.

Among my parents' closest UNESCO friends were Ricardo and Choncha Diez-Hochleitner (from Spain), Carlos and Lily Cueto (from Peru), and Herbert and Jo Abraham (he was British, she American). Two others my mother came to know were Ted (formally, E.R. [for Edward Ricardo]) Braithwaite, the British Guiana-born diplomat, writer, teacher, social worker, and education consultant and lecturer for UNESCO, best-known for his 1959 autobiographical novel, To Sir, with Love, *that in 1967 became the Sidney Poitier film; and Ginette*

Eboué-Fontaine, a colleague of my father's who focused on national-liberation and anti-apartheid movements in Africa and who was the first wife of Senegalese president Léopold Senghor and the daughter of Félix Eboué, the French Guiana-born first black colonial governor of Guadeloupe who, during the Second World War, was largely responsible for steering Chad (where he was stationed at the time) and in turn French Equatorial Africa to supporting Charles De Gaulle and the Free French against the Nazis.

In addition to Marie and Franck Lavaud and Liliane and Joseph Nadal, Haitians who put down roots in and around Paris included Yolande and Pierre Wiener, Agnès and Pierre Pouget, Simone and Serge Defly (Mama Defly's sister-in-law and brother), former President Lescot and his family, and a few years later, Eliane Laraque and Jacqueline Delannoy and her French husband Robert. There were visits by others, such as Paulette Brandt, Grette Cameron, Tite Soeur (Renée) Mangonès, Jacques Antoine, Alice Villard (Marie Lavaud's sister), Cito (Léonce) Bonnefil, Lucien Léger, and Félix Morisseau-Leroy, who had successfully championed the writing of Creole and writing in Creole.

Some of the American friends my parents had first met in Haiti came to live in Paris for various periods of time such as Margaretta and Fred Kroll, Peggy and Bill Krauss, and Vashti and Mercer Cook, while Eleanor and George Simpson and Polly and Allan Hulsizer paid short visits.

337

Other travelers—some of whom came on more than one occasion—included, from the Great Neck contingent, Jeanne Barron (after her husband Bill's death), Jeanne's daughter and son-in-law Barbara and Joe DiPierre, Jean and Bob Benjamin and their daughter Meg, Mary and Phil Blume and their son Jim, Eleanor and Milton Gould, their daughter Patricia, Hilda (Milton's cousin) and Joe Liff, Harriet and Lee Pomerance, Hannah and Ruda Schulhof, Helen and Hank Jaffe, Joan Farber, Jesse Kuh (following his wife Dorothy's death), Lena and Helge Five, their cousins Viola and Sidney Kantrowitz, and Nathalie and Eddie Shavitz and their elder son Ingram (who would become the Burt of Burt's Bees, Burt being his nickname, a sound-alike adaptation of his given middle name, Berg, Patricia Gould Booth told me).

From the UN: Blanka and Fred Landau, Sophie and Paul Alpert, Alice and Jacques Lippetz, the Richardots, the Lawsons, Victor Hoo and his daughter Mona, as well as Hungarian-born Steve Lazlo and Vietnamese-born André (Too Kim) Hai and his American wife Ruth, who had lived farther out on the North Shore (the Hais on a houseboat) when we were in Great Neck. From Mills College: Amy Hostler, Annette Metis, and Doris and Charles Bock. And from Wooster College: my mother's roommate Mildred Meeker Grant and their classmates Frances and Margaret Guille. (Frances at first had written about Victor Hugo and then turned her attention to his tragic daughter Adèle in Les Lettres d'Adèle Hugo, *which some ten years later became the movie* L'Histoire d'Adèle*

H. [The Story of Adele H.], *directed by François Truffaut. Frances collaborated on the screenplay, which the New York Film Critics Circle named the best of 1975. Its star, Isabelle Adjani, received an Oscar nomination for best actress.)*

A few friends of mine whom my mother had gotten to know well passed through Paris while I was there or not: Sylvia Washington and her parents, Sallie and Sidney Washington; Laurel Frank (later Brake) from Brandeis and her then-beau Everett Jacobs; and Ashley Boone, whom I'd also met at Brandeis and whom Bob Benjamin later invited to come work at United Artists.

* * *

The Rue Cognacq-Jay, where my parents bought their apartment, had got its name from the street's previous private owners, Théodore-Ernest Cognacq and his wife Marie-Louise Jay, founders in 1869 of the huge and hugely successful Paris department store La Samaritaine. After their deaths, at different times in the 1920s, the property was deeded to the City of Paris on condition that an approximately seven-foot swath of greenery be maintained in perpetuity along both sides of the street. There was thus a buffer between our building (constructed in 1930) and the sidewalk, discouraging passersby from peering into ground-floor windows.

The street runs just a block, is one-way, and meets another street that is one-way in the opposite direction, minimizing traffic considerably. It was lined with cobble-stones, which, my mother felt, added a great deal of charm. (She was furious when much later the city removed the cobblestones because it had become a nuisance to replace them individually.)

A short block north is the Quai d'Orsay and beyond that the embankment (the Left Bank, although what is popularly known as the Left Bank, the Latin Quarter, lies farther downriver), from which you can look down onto the Seine.

The Rue Cognacq-Jay falls within the 7th arrondissement, which is shaped like a wide wedge of pie. The Eiffel Tower is at one end of the "crust" that continues along the Seine, past the National Assembly (France's equivalent of the House of Representatives) and the Impressionists at the Musée d'Orsay (which for a long time had been an abandoned railway station, the Gare d'Orsay), to the other end of the "crust," the Pont du Carrousel (the bridge leading across to the front of the Louvre). Midway between these two points is the gilded Pont Alexandre III, Paris' most beautiful bridge, dedicated to the Russian tsar, and if you travel straight back from there, past Napoleon's Tomb and the Rodin Museum, you will come to the tip of the pie wedge, the Place de Breteuil with its monument to Louis Pasteur.

The 7th is said to be the home to old money (blatantly untrue in our case) that prefers its quiet to the higher profile of the newer rich in the better-known 16th arrondissement. Some of its neighborhoods, including Cognacq-Jay, are the most expensive in Paris. It is largely residential, although behind a number of the old façades are foreign embassies and French government offices. (Eight national ministries are housed in the district, including the Ministry of Foreign Affairs, which the media often refer to as the Quai d'Orsay.)

The Pont de l'Alma is one of the many bridges connecting the city's Left and Right Banks. It begins at the northern edge of the Place de la Résistance (the square at the west end of our street) and terminates at the southern edge of another square, the Place de l'Alma, where many avenues converge (and which is the site of the makeshift memorial to Princess Diana). (The bridge and the square commemorate the Anglo-French victory over Russia in the first battle of the Crimean War, at the River Alma, in 1854.) In the Sixties (and still today), if you crossed the bridge and proceeded to stroll down the Avenue Montaigne, you would find yourself passing the Théâtre des Champs-Elysées, where Stravinsky had stunned and outraged "le tout Paris" when he debuted The Rite of Spring; *the "grande dame" of Parisian hotels, the Plaza-Athénée; and the fashion house of Christian Dior and the jeweler Harry Winston (which over the years would be joined by Nina Ricci, Chanel, Chloé, Prada, Pucci, Fendi, Armani, Bulgari, Valentino, Ferragamo, Dolce & Gabbana, Bottega Veneta, and Louis Vuitton, among others, in a veritable luxury row)—before you reached the Rond Point des Champs-Elysées, the halfway mark between the Place de la Concorde and the Etoile.*

If you chose instead the Avenue George V, you would amble past Givenchy and Balenciaga, the Crazy Horse Saloon, and the well-heeled George V and Prince de Galles (Prince of Wales) hotels, before coming to the Champs-Elysées and Fouquet's, the pricey, starry café and restaurant that began in 1899 as a humble coachman's bistro.

Or if you wandered up the Avenue du Président Wilson, you would encounter the Museum of Modern Art in the Palais de Tokyo, the Musée Guimet (one of the largest collections of Asiatic art outside the Far East), and ultimately the Palais de Chaillot, housing (at the time) the Cinémathèque française and the Musée de l'Homme (the anthropological museum and descendant of the Musée d'ethnographie du Trocadéro, whose exhibits of African art bowled over Picasso and thus changed the face of Western art).

Each avenue takes about ten to fifteen minutes to walk. And walk these streets my mother did, here and all through entire sections of Paris. She loved walking and as a result got to know many neighborhoods of the city like the back of her hand.

* * *

My mother's first travels within France began in the winter of 1956 with the cities and towns of Marseille, Nice, Menton (known as the Pearl of France for the luxury hotels and other buildings erected by Russian and British aristocrats), and Eze (which offers a panoramic view of the Riviera), as well as Vence, with its Matisse chapel.

During the next ten years, she went on to visit many other spots, such as, in the southwest, the great walled city of Carcassonne, Toulouse (site of one of Europe's oldest universities, founded in 1229), Cahors (whose Valentré Bridge is one of the legendary medieval Devil's Bridges of Europe), and the wine capital Bordeaux (from which many a Haitian's French ancestor sailed).

In Provence, she toured Avignon, Arles, Nîmes, Aix-en-Provence, and Saint-Rémy-de-Provence (where Van Gogh painted The Starry Night)*; in the Dordogne, the underground caves of the Gouffre (i.e., abyss) de Padirac, the remarkable Paleolithic cave paintings of Lascaux at Les Eyzies (five years before the caves were closed to the public), and Rocamadour (location of one of Europe's Black Madonnas); and farther south, Saint-Cirq-Lapopie, voted year after year France's favorite village, perched on a sheer rock cliff.*

In the middle of the country, she saw Tours (capital of France under Louis XI), Poitiers (in the vicinity of which the French infantry defeated a Muslim invasion in 732 in the conflict variously known as the Battle of Poitiers or the Battle of Tours), and the grand chateaus of the Loire Valley.

In the north, she visited Giverny (Monet's home), Honfleur (a postcard-perfect town), Caen (burial site of William The Conqueror), Deauville, Trouville, Mont St. Michel, WWII's

Omaha and Utah beaches, and Rouen (the history-rich capital of Normandy), as well as Rennes, Saint Malo (the walled port city on the English channel that served as a notorious pirate base), and other parts of Brittany.

To the east, there were Compiègne (where Joan of Arc was captured), Reims (with its very important collection of historic buildings), the Champagne town of Epernay (where her good friend Jacqueline Bouvet had her country home), Troyes (with its high density of splendid old churches), Nancy (capital of Lorraine), Strasbourg (capital of Alsace, where the Marseillaise was composed), and Vittel (where on several occasions she and my father took the curative waters).

Farther south, she explored Dijon (a treasure-trove of 12th-to-15th-century buildings), Lyon (France's gastronomic capital and birthplace of film via the breakthrough of the Lumière brothers), and Courchevel, a ski resort in the French Alps.

And in the Ile-de-France region surrounding Paris, she toured the 13th-century cathedral of Chartres, the medieval town of Provins, the royal palace of Fontainebleau, the grand palace of Versailles, the restored park of Marly-le-Roi (where another Louis XIV residence once stood, destroyed after the Revolution), the forest and chateau of Louis XVI's Rambouillet (which Marie-Antoinette hated and called a toadhouse), and Malmaison, home of the Empress Josephine, Napoleon's first wife.

My mother's travels outside France during this time took her to Greece, Lisbon, Copenhagen, Stockholm, Vienna, Istanbul, Dubrovnik, and Andorra once each; Holland twice;

Italy, Belgium and Monaco three times; Switzerland and England each four times; and Spain six times. It was in Spain that she met in 1959 Gladys Cumming, an Englishwoman who over the next forty years would often visit her in Paris and whom my mother would see in London or Torquay. On one of these trips to England, my mother made a point of going to the Lake District, which was particularly meaning-ful to her because it was the setting for some of her favor-ite poems, including Wordsworth's "I Wandered Lonely as a Cloud," which she would recite to me as a child.

In 1963, she went to Puerto Rico, where she visited the Spanish-born painter Angel Botello-Barros (and his Haitian wife), whom she'd known in Haiti and whose canvas sug-gestive of the style of Gauguin was the first she'd ever bought (and which I have today); to Washington, D.C., to see the Carters (former parents at her Paris school), the Diez-Hochleitners (my father's UNESCO colleague), and the Washingtons (Sylvia's parents); and to Florida to spend a few days with her sister Betty and brother-in-law Lowell.

That same year, in addition to catching up with all her regulars in Manhattan and Great Neck, she took Ruth Bunche to lunch and to the theater. She would see her and her hus-band Ralph together for the last time six years later, at lunch at the United Nations; Mr. Bunche would die in 1971.

* * *

Highlights of plays, dance troupes, operas, and concerts my mother attended included, in London, Flora Robson in The House by the Lake, The Mousetrap *(then in only its fourth year),* Beyond The Fringe, *and Peter Ustinov in* Photo Finish; *and in New York, Anne Bancroft in* Mother Courage and Her Children, *Geraldine Page in* Strange Interlude, *Maureen Stapleton in* The Glass Menagerie, *Uta Hagen in* Who's Afraid of Virginia Woolf?, *Barbra Streisand in* Funny Girl, *and Zero Mostel in* A Funny Thing Happened on the Way to the Forum *and* Fiddler on the Roof *(though she thought Mostel over-acted in the latter, which he did).*

In Paris, she saw James Baldwin's The Amen Corner, Black Nativity, *Mostel in* Ulysses in Nighttown, *Cyril Cusack in a double-bill of Shaw's* Arms and the Man *and Beckett's* Krapp's Last Tape, *Simone Signoret in a French adaptation of* The Little Foxes, *classics at the Comédie-Française (including a highly touted* Cyrano de Bergerac), *Josephine Baker at the Olympia, Rudolf Nureyev and Margot Fonteyn (who "danced as they have never danced before in* Giselle—*beautiful, exquisite—such empathy, such technique," she noted on her calendar), Yvette Chauviré (prima ballerina of the Paris Opera Ballet, "the best dancer in Paris," she said), various dance companies (Alvin Ailey, Paul Taylor, Merce Cunningham, the Harkness, and the National Dance Company of Cameroon), Elisabeth Schwarzkopf in* Der Rosenkavalier, *Franco Corelli with Régine Crespin in* Tosca *and with Maria Callas in what she didn't say (but noted that his singing was excellent while her upper register was not*—"if she were not Callas, she would be thrown out," *she wrote),* Wozzeck *done in concert form (*"exciting music," *she noted),* Lucia di Lammermoor, *Claudio Arrau, Arthur Rubinstein, Van Cliburn, and the Cleveland Symphony Orchestra under George Szell (which she described as* "excellent—nothing like it in France").

Although she missed seeing Baldwin's Blues For Mr. Charlie *on Broadway (because she didn't go to the States that year), she read it in published form as she did other early and middle Baldwin:* Go Tell it on the Mountain, Notes from a Native Son, Giovanni's Room, Another Country, *and, of course, the explosive* The Fire Next Time.

On October 24, 1965, my mother heard Martin Luther King speak twice: in the morning at the American Church (on the Quai d'Orsay, two blocks from her apartment) and that evening in a crowd of five thousand at the art-deco Maison de la Mutualité, to which Dr. King had been invited by the Fédération Protestante de France (the Protestant Federation of France).

RED BANK. A rare moment of levity amidst difficult times, in Mr. Hobson's apple orchard (1946)

GREAT NECK. With John, Georgette Rouzier, and two visitors from Haiti: Dody Wiener (far left) and Joseph Nadal (ca.1948)

GREAT NECK. Teaching at the UN International School in Lake Success (1947–1948)

GREAT NECK. With Maurice in our apartment at 12 Welwyn Road (1956)

WALTHAM, MA. John's graduation from Brandeis, with Doris and Charles Bock
(June 1961)

THEBES. On one of her many, many trips (1962)

PARIS. Outside our building at 3, rue Cognacq-Jay (ca.1963)

PARIS. Inside our apartment at 3, rue Cognacq-Jay (1965)

PLASCASSIER. With Maurice at
Liliane and Joseph Nadal's in the
South of France (1970s)

PARIS. 1990s

PARIS. With UCA friends (left to right) Shari Rajah, Pamela Barabas, Jeanette
Verhoog, Nieves Claxton, Uma Rao, and Austin Atherley (1990s)

Chapter Eleven

Bujumbura (1966-1968)

(My mother spent less than two years in Burundi, and the calendar pages from the last seven months of her stay are lost. Therefore, this chapter is short and spotty. But after looking at the material, I felt it was best to have it stand on its own rather than integrated into the previous or following chapter.)

Burundi is a land-locked, dime-sized nation, a bit bigger than West Virginia, located in East Africa and surrounded by Rwanda, Tanzania, and the Democratic Republic of Congo. The farthest points in the Nile's headwaters are here, and the country lies in the path of the Rift Valley, which stretches from Mozambique to Syria. The capital, Bujumbura, sits on the northeastern shore of Lake Tanganyika.

Burundi has existed as a political entity since the 16th century. After the Tutsis invaded, they established dominance over the native Hutus and expanded their territory. They brought cattle to the country and formed the warrior class; the Hutus served them as herders and farmers. By the 1850s, Burundi was ruled by a Tutsi "mwami," or king; but in the late 1880s, it was absorbed into German East Africa, though the "mwami" refused to pay the Germans much mind and was generally left alone. After Berlin's defeat in the First World War, Burundi was shorn of its eastern regions: the League of Nations gave them to Tanganyika, another former German colony. The League then yoked Burundi together with Rwanda in a union known as Ruanda-Urundi and turned over its administration to Belgium (which already controlled the vast and vastly rich Congo). After the Second World War, the two became a trust territory, still under Brussels' thumb but also under the watchful eye of the United Nations. In the wake of the independence movement that swept through Africa in the late Fifties and early Sixties, the separate sovereign nations of Rwanda and Burundi were re-established in 1962.

When my father was in the UN's Trusteeship Department in New York, some of his work naturally had to do with Ruanda-Urundi, including a mission there in 1951, in the company of Assistant Secretary General Victor Hoo. My father authored the mission's report (albeit uncredited, in keeping with UN staff policy). During his years at UNESCO,

*he was again concerned with Rwanda and Burundi, espe-
cially as Chief of the Africa Division. So, as in the case of
the Congo Crisis, though far less critically, my father was, in
1966, well prepared to be director of the newly established
university-level normal school (Ecole Normale Supérieure)
to train secondary-school teachers in Bujumbura. He was
also appointed chief consultant to the government in educational matters.*

*He went to Burundi at the end of April 1966 to begin
his work and held meetings with ministers and functionaries. In July, the nation's king was deposed by his son and
sent into exile. Four months later, the son was booted by
the Hutu prime minister who proclaimed himself president
and Burundi a republic and brought in yet another round
of government officials. An evening curfew was imposed,
creating jitteriness in the international community and
even more tribal tension (which would continue for years
to come).*

*After his three-month medical absence, my father returned
to Bujumbura on November 5, accompanied by my mother,
and they were met at the airport by Nelly and Marcel Dupuy,
a Haitian couple they knew who were already stationed
there. (The Dupuys' sons had been among the boarding-
school students my parents had received for Sunday lunches
in Paris over the course of several years, and so the Dupuys,
I imagine, were eager to repay the kindness.) They offered
to take my mother on errands and on sightseeing rides to*

various parts of the city and into the countryside and invited her often for lunch or dinner.

My mother found the furnished apartment that had been arranged to be "a horrible, dreadful place," *according to her calendar. The street was heavily trafficked and thus* "noisy," *and because of its proximity to the market, it was also* "smelly." *Apparently, the lease couldn't be broken, but since my father's stay was only to be for six months, she thought she could endure it. In March, however, she learned that his contract was being extended to August, and then in July my father announced he was now to stay on until March 1968. When that March came 'round, the departure date was pushed back yet again, to July, which is when they finally did leave.*

Hal Fuller, who was in Bujumbura with his wife Pat for two *years (overlapping a portion of my parents' stay), said that my mother's dislike for her apartment was hardly unique.* "I don't think anyone liked the apartments in Burundi," *he told me.* "We had the same experience."

The apartment was not the only negative. She had no job to engage her mind and energy, and she was dependent on others to get around for any travel beyond the center of town. ("I walked," my mother wrote, "when almost no one else in the foreign community did. Everyone recognized me because of that and the fact that, at a time when ladies no longer wore hats, I was the only one who did, to protect me from the sun.")

Bujumbura (1966-1968)

But she adapted as best she could and began to attend to some immediate needs for the apartment: making bedspreads, drapes, cushions, and a divan cover, and buying a new stove, floor lamp, and bed lamp. She purchased a book on Swahili but must have realized fairly quickly that, despite the proximity of the former British colonies where it was the lingua franca, very few in Burundi spoke Swahili other than for the purposes of commerce. The subject was never mentioned again in her calendar.

Benoît, the young man who served in the apartment, was good at his job, my mother thought, and he spoke French. However, he was not problem-free: my mother had to bail him out of jail once (for reasons unknown) and had to lend him 1,500 Burundi francs (roughly $150) so that he could repay his daughter's dowry or else face another jail sentence.

In early 1967, she and other Haitian women in the international community "formed a sewing group to sew for the handicapped boys in a missionary school and for a home *(an orphanage)* for very young children," *she would later write in* An Outstanding Haitian, Maurice Dartigue. *(The missionary school was named St. Kizito, in memory of the youngest of the child martyrs executed by the king of Uganda in the early 1890s.) After buying sixty yards of material at a time, she would spend hours and days making sheets, mattress covers, shirts, short pants, and dresses.* "These kept us busy," *she noted. She also bought mattresses, made almost weekly gifts of meat and eggs (on the first day,* "the children crowded

357

around and hugged my knees," she noted), and occasionally baked cakes. I imagine all this may have reminded her of her work in Haiti for the public maternity hospital and for Mlle Vincent's girls' school, just as, she said, the marketplace she frequented in Bujumbura recalled Croix des Bossales in Port-au-Prince, while the cities of Kitega, almost five thousand feet above sea level, and Bugarama, where the Dupuys took her to buy vegetables, brought back, she said, memories of Kenscoff.

* * *

My mother mentioned in her calendar some seventy surnames of people with whom she and my father socialized, most of them couples, but the number was always in flux as folks arrived and left over the course of the nearly two years. (I suspect there were more than the seventy since seven months of her notes are missing.) The small community banded together and saw a great deal of each other at home or at a few receptions. ("The international group from the various agencies and embassies [apart from the Russians] mingled socially, but [we were] rarely joined by the Barundi" *(as the country's people are known), she said in her book about my father.* ("Most entertaining was done at home," *Hal Fuller wrote me.* "There were only four restaurants in town that were frequented by the diplomatic corps,

European businessmen, and Barundi officials. But for a gathering of any size, you entertained at home.")

* * *

In July 1967, there were great troubles in Bukavu, a city on the other side of the border, in the Democratic Republic of Congo, and UN personnel stationed there were evacuated to Burundi. At first, it seemed as though my mother's circle would be taking in families, but enough vacant accommodations were found. However, the foreign community, including my mother, did provide meals to refugees. About two weeks later, a friend returning from Bukavu informed her that the city had been plundered.

Eight months after her arrival in Burundi, she finally saw the exquisite "Tutsi dancers in leopard skins with drummers," *she wrote,* "as well as twirlers from the South in grass skirts."

By August, my parents had settled into a different residence—a house this time—that my mother liked. ("Gardens," wrote Hal Fuller, "were one of the pleasures available.") However, the young man in service there spoke no French which initially caused her certain difficulties. She set about once again to sew new bedspreads, drapes, and cushions.

She attended several short courses and lectures in such subjects as Burundi's German era, aspects of African vegetation, art, and geography (Pat Fuller joined her in these last two) and served as a substitute teacher in a university English class. She was asked to give a speech to a group of women teachers but found they were quite uninterested in it.

Her reading was devoted largely to African subjects and included a history of Burundi, Serengeti Shall Not Die, The Blue Nile, The Lonely African, The Masai, Timbuktu, L'Ame des Barundi (*The Soul of the Barundi*), Uhuru, *and a biography of Sylvanus Olympio, who had led Togo to independence in 1960 and was assassinated three years later. (In the early 1950s, my mother had seen Olympio plead before the United Nations for the reunification of the Ewe people, whose lands, once part of German Togoland, had been arbitrarily hacked up by Britain and France after World War I. Olympio's entreaty was rejected because the two European nations, although exhausted by World War II, still clung to their fantasies of being world powers, ignored the sensitivities and aspirations of their African colonies, and exercised their vetoes. Of course, within a mere decade, they would lose their empires on that continent to independence.) In the mid-1980s at UNESCO in Paris, my mother would happen to meet and become good friends with Olympio's daughter, Rosita Armerding.*

During her stay in Burundi, my mother was able to get away from time to time: two weeks in the States; a week in Tunisia; two trips to Paris, one of ten days, the other of three weeks; five days in the Serengeti (where, she noted, she saw "lions, elephants, birds, buffalo, a rhino, a hippo and a leopard with babies"), *preceded by visits to parts of Uganda (Kampala and Murchison Falls [a significant waterfall on the Nile]); short excursions into neighboring Rwanda and Congo; and a week in Kenya during which she visited Nairobi, the Rift Valley, and the wildlife preserves of Naivasha (known for its birds and hippos), Nakuru (famous for its hordes of flamingo), and Samburu (where Elsa the lioness of* Born Free *had in part been raised).*

* * *

Though I don't know what transpired from January through July 1968, there does remain the transcript of a talk my mother gave that spring to young teachers (not the same group mentioned earlier) "in the mountain region," *says a notation; it is titled (and I am translating here and farther along)* "The Role of the Teacher in Promoting Social, Cultural and Economic Improvement." *She acknowledged that she* "was not very familiar with the particular problems teachers in Burundi face in their daily work but felt that because there are certain aspects of education that have points in common in all developing nations," *she would recount her experiences in rural education in Haiti, which came from what she'd seen when she'd accompanied my father on field trips, what she'd heard him say, and the reports and monographs he'd written.*

She stated that teachers in rural communities were in a position to serve as leaders, to reach students and through them their parents, and to be a point of stimulation and encouragement to effect progress. In addition to the tra-ditional program of reading and learning (for those aged five to fourteen), a teacher could introduce new elements unknown to both children and their parents; they could show that in-school education could reveal agricultural and craft techniques helpful in the adults' day-to-day lives outside of school. Nor was a teacher meant to work in a vacuum; he/ she could try to involve an agricultural agent and in some cases a public-health worker and thereby possibly gain access to some financial disbursement available from these other governmental departments.

"Adults could be invited to come to the school in groups or individually," *where they could be given plants and seeds, courtesy of the agricultural agent, and receive advice about their use and cultivation.* "A teacher might help adults to organize a cooperative of their vegetables for sale in the next town.... Night classes for illiterate parents could be arranged and a teacher could visit homes (if people lived relatively close by) to encourage adults to decorate those homes, using plants," *for example. Older children and adults could be introduced to cottage industries, such as* "mak-ing soap, extracting oil from certain plants, tanning ani-mal skins, weaving, and basketry" *(encouraging both new types of industry and new designs), and teachers should be on the lookout for local materials for use in craft projects. Additionally, a teacher could make recommendations* "in the area of hygiene and comfort by instructing parents, for example, how to build latrines…. At girls' schools, not only would the students be taught sewing and embroidery but also be introduced to child care, housekeeping, nutritional cooking and canning," *all of which would have an impact on the community at large. None of these ideas, she said, were part of a planned, fixed curriculum. They were opportunities that a teacher might notice and act upon that in practical ways would benefit the community; he/she should be on the alert and be prepared to take initiatives that would have helpful consequences. And reaching adults as well as children would build, in time, a sense of community and also civic pride.*

These were all simple ideas, logical, practical ones that required only a willingness and an ability to look beyond the traditional approach to teaching, to take the initiative and thereby achieve useful results.

* * *

My parents left Burundi in July 1968, and my mother would never return to sub-Saharan Africa again. In her book, An Outstanding Haitian, Maurice Dartigue, *issued some twenty-five years later, she would write,* "We enjoyed our stay in Burundi despite the drawbacks and some incon-veniences. ....[It] was a very interesting experience." *For years she remained in close touch, largely through cor-respondence, with a number of the friends she'd made in Bujumbura, especially the Dupuys, the Fullers, and Ena and Jim Murdock. She would see the Dupuys sometimes in Paris but most often in Haiti. She and the Fullers rendezvoused in various cities: New York, Washington, Boston, Paris, and Brussels. And the Murdocks lived in Paris for a while before returning to their native Scotland.*

Chapter Twelve

Paris, Part II (1968-1983)

When my mother returned from Burundi in July 1968, she found herself without a job in Paris for the first time since the summer of 1956. So she filled her time by joining and/or volunteering with several organizations.

She was invited to become a member of the Board of Directors of the UN Nursery School, her former professional stomping ground; but by the end of October 1969, she'd submitted a letter of resignation and noted a few days later on her calendar that Ruth Métraux, her friend and fellow Board member, had called to discuss her decision. There is no indication in her notes as to her reason(s) for leaving, but she did not change her mind after the call. (However, it did lead to a rift in her relationship with Ruth.)

At the beginning of that year, she had hosted a supper for thirteen visiting Mills College students and arranged for a former colleague of my father's, Francis L. Bartels, the Ghanaian educator, to speak to the young women.

Soon after, she became a member of the Association Française des Femmes Diplômées des Universités (AFFDU), national chapter of the International Federation of University Women, to which her friend Jacqueline Bouvet and several others she knew belonged. She also helped out occasionally in the office. Founded in 1919, the organization advocates for the rights of women and girls to be educated, to have equal footing with men and boys, and to develop their skills and move into leadership roles both in public and in private.

She also volunteered her time with a charity for the handicapped, which I believe was the Association Point [sic] Carré [sic] Handicap, founded in 1958 under the name Club des Loisirs et d'Entraide (Club of Leisure Activities and Mutual Aid) and affiliated with the well-known hospital for the handicapped Hôpital Raymond Poincaré in Garches (a Paris suburb). Her interest may have been prompted by the work she'd done in Burundi for the St. Kizito boys, as well as her long-standing admiration for and support of Sister Joan's activities at St. Vincent de Paul in Port-au-Prince. She wrote that she accompanied a group to the Jardin d'Acclimatation, the zoological park on the northern edge of the Bois de Boulogne inaugurated in 1860 by Napoleon III, and on *another occasion to Truffaut, a chain store specializing in indoor and outdoor plants, as well as flowers, fish, and birds.*

It may have been due to Amy Hostler and Lady Marjory Allen that my mother offered her services to Valia (Mme Claude) Tanon, president of the International Playground Association (IPA), which, founded in 1961, sees a child's right to play as a fundamental human right and seeks to protect and advance this right (which accords with Article 31 of the UN Convention on the Rights of the Child). Amy, Lady Allen, and Mme Tanon had long been interested in the subject, and Amy and my mother had visited two London playgrounds during the 1962 OMEP world conference (which is where the latter met Mme Tanon). My mother wrote her last education article for the IPA's Newsletter *(Volume IV, No. 4, September 1970), titled "[A Few Observations on] Free Play and Language in the U[nited] N[ations] Nursery School [and Kindergarten of], Paris"/ "[Quelques Observations sur] Le Jeu et le Langage au Jardin d'Enfants des Nations Unies à Paris." (The bracketed sections complete the full title headlining the actual piece; the nonbracketed sections indicate how the article was listed in the Table of Contents.) My mother believed that for a child under the age of six, free play is one of the most important considerations. Without it, the child is unlikely to realize his potential; a part of him will not mature if such activity is denied. He needs to go through the experiences of experimentation, exploration, and discovery, derived from creative activity and learning by doing, because free play will allow the child to better develop physically, emotionally, and socially.*

* * *

My mother had for many years been involved with the Association France-Haïti when she had the time. The organization's aim was to foster and maintain friendly relations between the two countries in the realms of culture, science, and economics, as well as to offer a welcome center for Haitians visiting Paris and for any French man or woman traveling to Port-au-Prince. It came into being in 1954, on the occasion of Haiti's 150th anniversary of independence from France, through the efforts of, among others, two of my parents' close friends, Auguste Viatte and Franck Lavaud. My mother's calendar notations from 1962 and beyond indicate that she was occasionally able to attend their meetings. During the 1980s, she was listed in the organization's annual Bulletin, *along with her friend Jacqueline Delannoy, as a member of the Advisory Board. (The name of another Haitian chum, Lily [Aliette] Vieux, the niece of Lina and Dadal [Randall] Assad and the aunt of my mother's niece/my cousin (by marriage) Martine Baussan Dartigue, appeared in the minutes of a 1980 meeting as also being on the Advisory Board.) My mother continued with the Association into the 1990s, at one point serving as vice president.*

In October 1980, her longtime friend Dr. Yvonne Sylvain, vice president and a founder of FHASE (Fondation haïtienne pour la santé et l'éducation [Haitian Foundation for Health and Education]) came to Paris to ask the Association to form a special committee to help seek funding in France and among the Haitian diaspora for a hospital she wanted to see constructed in Frères, a ten-minute drive from Pétionville, to serve a community of over 100,000 people without medical access. Auguste Viatte (in the position of Secretary-General), Raymonde MBow (Jeanne Sylvain's goddaughter [according to Yvonne's daughter] as Coordinator), my mother (as Adjunct Coordinator), and Jacqueline Delannoy and Lily Vieux (as Advisors) all agreed to join the committee, which proceeded to draft a letter to the Association's members and to the Friends of Haiti informing them of the fund drive and asking for donations, however small. An approach was also made to Jacques Chirac, then-mayor of Paris (and later president of France), who was willing to have City Hall help financially and to solicit contributions from the capital's twenty district town halls.

My mother further supported Yvonne by writing an article for the organization's 1981 annual Bulletin *and another for the 1984* Bulletin *concerning the progress of the hospital's construction (based on on-site visits she made with Yvonne during her trips to Haiti). She produced a third article, on Yvonne and her three sisters, in the 1985* Bulletin, *titled "Le Féminisme en Haïti: 'Il était une fois quatre soeurs…'"*

("Feminism in Haiti: 'Once upon a time there were four sisters...'"). (My mother mentions the Sylvains in Chapter Six of the present book.)

France-Haïti cofounder Auguste Viatte's was a very prominent voice in France's attempt to maintain French as the world's pre-eminent language (a losing battle, as it turned out), and he was the driving force behind such other francophone organizations as France-Louisiane, France-Amérique, and France-Québec. (My mother mentioned going to several meetings of the last two groups.) In 1971, in his additional capacity as president of the Association Culture Française, he wrote a strong letter to then-president Georges Pompidou, decrying Britain's entry into the Common Market, foreseeing a threat to the French language. In 1987, he was received into the French Legion of Honor.

* * *

My mother did take a job, albeit a temporary one, as did my father, as college professors. Herbert Abraham, a former UNESCO colleague of my father's, encouraged my parents to spend part of a summer teaching in the U.S. After Abraham retired, he had joined the faculty of Moorhead State College in Moorhead, Minnesota. (In 2000, the institution underwent a name change to Minnesota State University Moorhead.) The school had received a grant to make short-term hires of people with interesting backgrounds and experiences, and he suggested my parents apply to teach two courses each for four weeks during the 1970 summer session. (My mother was to lecture on Problems of Elementary School Teachers and Curriculum for Elementary Schools, while my father's subjects were to be Research and Foundations of Education.) They agreed, the school agreed, and some months later contracts were signed.

My mother began her preparations by compiling a reading list at the American Library in Paris and by asking Amy Hostler and Myrtle Searles (of Mills College) for input. She also borrowed and read a number of books on education, including Francis Keppel's The Necessary Revolution in American Education *and Carl F. Hansen's* The Amidon Elementary School. *By late March, she had completed planning the curriculum for her two courses.*

My parents arrived in Fargo, North Dakota, in early June and were taken across the state line to Moorhead and to their rooms in a dormitory they found to be hot, far from things, and accessible to little food. Luckily, a professor they met was willing to rent his apartment which they had visited and liked.

"As the first [classes] were held at 7:30 am, it was a challenge to keep the students awake," *my mother wrote in her book,* An Outstanding Haitian, Maurice Dartigue. "Most were teachers and directors profiting from the facility given them to take the courses for an increase in salary, better status, and the latest knowledge of educational trends and interests or 'modes.' Maurice's two courses were for administrators and directors of primary schools, and my two were for primary school teachers. As our assignments were changed from those first given to us, we had to spend most of our time outside of class studying, writing, or in the library to be ahead of our students...."

There were, fortunately, a few outside distractions. My parents socialized with other faculty members and were taken to the North Dakota Badlands and Itasca State Park, whose 32,000 acres contain the placid headwaters of the Mississippi River.

Back in Paris later that year, she did an interview with a Mlle Ballanche on the subject of bilingualism and young children, but her notes do not indicate for what outlet.

* * *

My mother was then contacted for a position at UNESCO, the nature of which she did not say, and was in fact hired. However, in July, she wrote on her calendar that she had gone to see a M. Lema to tell him she couldn't take on the job, again for reasons unknown. But it shortly became evident that she would have a full-time job, though not one she had envisaged: looking after my father for the next twelve years as his professional assignments ended (his last mission was

*in June/July 1971 to Equatorial Guinea [now Guinea Bissau])
and his medical issues increased. So that he would have
reason to get up and dressed each day and have diversions
during the course of the day, my mother scheduled some
breakfasts out, walks in the morning and/or afternoon, and
lots of visitors in for lunch and dinner, as well as accepting
outside invitations. (She also continued to do her own washing [at home and at the neighborhood laundromat, since
neither she nor the building had a washer or dryer], ironing,
shopping, and housecleaning [which at times took on hercu-
lean proportions, such as scrubbing down walls, floors, the
large front windows, and outside metal shutters, and which
I believe later took their toll or contributed to that toll when
she developed increasing back and shoulder pain].)*

*There was an ample source of lunch and dinner guests
because many old Haitian friends (and some new) were
now spending more and more time in Paris; consequently,
there was a constant round of get-togethers, conversations on current events, and enjoyable reminiscences—and
probably a good dose of gossip. And when Claudette and
Jean Fouchard came to live part-time in the French capital
beginning in 1971, the social activity seemed to accelerate
even more, but that may have been coincidental. (In 1973,
Fouchard, who'd written several books about early Haitian
history, called to say he'd won the Prix littéraire des Caraïbes
[Caribbean Literary Prize] for his* Les Marrons de la liberté
from the Association des Écrivains de Langue Française

[Association of French-language Writers], an award given to a writer from the French Antilles for his/her exceptional prose. The book was later published in English under the title The Haitian Maroons: Liberty or Death. *['Marron' and 'maroon' mean in French and English, respectively, a runaway slave.])*

Residents and visitors (many of whom my parents would also see during their stays in Haiti beginning in 1972) included the Fouchards' daughters Claudinette Fischl and Edwidge Kenn de Balentazy (who was married to a Hungarian, which she said gave her and my mother a further connection), Yvonne Sylvain and her sister Suzanne Comhaire, Raymonde MBow (whose Senegalese husband was the first black to be Director-General of UNESCO [from 1974 to 1987]), Simone Dupuy and her daughter and son-in-law Anne-Marie and Franck Laraque (who was Gustave Laraque's third cousin once removed), Didine Maximilien, Céline and Claude Préval, Rachel Artaud (who had worked for my father in Haiti and with whom we shared a kinship [her mother was the half-sister of my father's aunt Amalia]), Marie Bourand (whose husband Ludovic had been in the Congo with my father), Max Fombrun and his sister Jeanine, Tite Soeur Mangonès and her daughter Gila (Gisela), Nelly and Marcel Dupuy, Fatboy (Ghislaine Stecher) and her daughters Carola and Nana (Anne-Marlène), Joujou and Ti Georges Léger, Ti Robert Nadal, Lina Assad, Muriel Lamothe, Lily Vieux, Suzanne Déjoie, Paulette and Clifford Brandt and their daughter Sibylle, Grette Cameron,

Pierre Montas, Jean Salès, Amélie and Raoul Séjourné and their daughter Nicole (who had been in my mother's school in Haiti). These were in addition to the "old timers" who had lived in Paris for a while: Franck Lavaud (Marie, sadly, died in 1973) and his daughter Marie-Alice and her French husband Bernard Gatbois, Eliane Laraque, Liliane and Joseph Nadal and their daughter Jacqueline, Jacqueline and Robert Delannoy, Agnès and Pierre Pouget, Simone and Serge Defly (before they moved to Cannes), Ginette (Geneviève) Gardère (Lina Assad's niece), and a passel of Wieners—Yolande and Pierre, Pierre's sister-in-law and brother Andrée and Dody, and Liliane Moravia, who was the sister of Amélie Séjourné and the Wiener brothers (all of whom were Lina Assad's second cousins).

(Haitian family connections have always fascinated me, perhaps because for half my life I thought our family in Haiti consisted only of the three of us, plus Tante Renée, Oncle Jehan, Tante Margot, and my four cousins. (I didn't know until I was past 35 about the relatives mentioned in Chapter Five.) Everyone else had these seemingly wonderful extended families, and I marveled that so many of my parents' friends all appeared to be interrelated, some more heavily than others. This was possible because Haiti is a small country with a minuscule upper class whose members tended to frequent only each other, although there was the occasional interjection of an outsider, such as my mother; Grette De Catalogne [later Cameron], who was Swedish; Eliane Laraque, who was

French; and Altagrâce Denis [Carola Stecher Denis' mother-in-law and a neighbor of ours in Furcy], who was Lebanese. Families of that generation and earlier were large, with the average minimum number of children being four and the average maximum eleven. The marriage of my father's nephew/my first cousin Robert to Martine Baussan in July 1980 brought us into the orbit of these families. Martine's great-grandmother, for instance, was Louise Rouzier, and her grand-uncle was Dadal Assad, Lina's husband. And then in 2012, I discovered our family had been part of the cir-cle all along, ever since the second half of the 19th century, because of our connection—double, as it turned out—to the Légers, first through the Léons [Ti Georges' paternal grand-mother Rose Marie Catherine Léon Léger was the half sister of my father's paternal aunt Amalia Léon Bermingham] and second through the Durets [Ti Georges' father was the first cousin of Jules Duret, the son-in-law of my father's maternal aunt Carmen Duperval Durand]. Thus through the Légers, we had a familial connection, for example, to the Rouziers, who, as I mentioned in Chapter Seven, were related to prac-tically everybody. All this, I know, conjures up an image of a street urchin with his nose pressed to the store window, at which one has to smile.)

"Every Haitian living in Paris, or just visiting," Jacqueline Delannoy wrote in an e-mail, "had opportunities of meeting other Haitians at your parents'. Your mother had memo-rable afternoon teas and warm, delicious dinners. Do you

know that her 'chiquetaille de morue' [a Haitian dish made from dried mackerel, oil, vinegar and spices] was the only authentic and best one I ever had in my whole life? In her later years [when her back pains limited how long she could stand and how much else she could do], your mother still received people but would warn us that everything came from the frozen-food company Picard. These occasions were always so interesting that Robert and I went with joy, trying to be on time. Esther was always punctilious. Four o'clock, for example, meant 4 pm, and not 4:15! Earlier, during our two sons' adolescence, we invited your parents to the house so that our boys could have contact with friends whose openness of mind, moral rigor, culture, and great kindness we admired. I always include your parents, whom Robert and I liked very much, in my prayers, for they marked me as much as my own parents, in-laws, and very dear friends."

Some relatives also passed through town: Tante Margot, her elder daughter/my first cousin Marie-José (who pursued her studies, got married [to Félix N'Zengou-Tayo, from the Central African Republic], and lived in France for some thirteen years), and their cousin (and ours by extension) Maryse and her French husband Raymond Lachenal. David Reithoffer, the son of my mother's first cousin Bill, made his initial visit to France at age 17 and then in 1974 spent his college junior year at the University of Caen. He returned often to Paris over the next thirty years or so and between

1996 and 2006 came every April to promote the Chicago Marathon at the Paris Marathon.

Of those U.S. residents who had visited in droves in the 1960s, their number as travelers had now substantially dwindled. Of the Great Neck group, Hannah Schulhof still came almost every year, while Jean Benjamin made the journey to Paris periodically (up through 1997), usually in connection with her Kandinsky books and often in the company of her coauthor, Hans Roethel. Jeanne Barron visited several times, once with Caroline and Joseph Farber; their ten-day stay prompted my mother to comment on her calendar that it had been "a happy reunion."

There was an array of locally based women in my mother's life: Jacqueline Bouvet (later Marchand), Maître Misard (whose first name I never knew—'maître' being an honorific given to a member of the French legal profession), Irja Spira (from Finland), Ida Subaran (from Jamaica, of East Indian descent), Betty Thompson and Phyllis Haas Picard (both from Australia), Rose Khin Wan Thi (from Burma), Ida Hark, Barrie Black, Susan Dowling, and Mimi Rommeden. My mother also befriended three American couples who lived in Paris for a time: Vivian and Weir Brown, Barbara and Bob Green, and Maggie and Leonard Amster. (Weir Brown was extraordinarily helpful to my mother in navigating the National Archives in Washington, D.C., in 1991. He spent three successive days there on his own, locating files from the U.S. Departments of State, Defense, and Agriculture;

the U.S. Office of Education; and the American Embassy in Haiti, that contained some of my father's correspondence and U.S. government papers concerning him. When my mother in turn went to the National Archives, she noted on her calendar that "without Weir's preparation, I could not have done my research. What time and patience it took to ferret all this out.")

She stayed in touch with Mme Herbinière-Lebert. They occasionally shared a meal at the house (she even came once for Thanksgiving) or went to UNESCO (which had a restaurant with an excellent view) or elsewhere, either together or with others, such as Amy Hostler or various school inspectors. From time to time, my mother accompanied her to, for example, the Ecole Bilingue, to AFFDU (the University Women's organization), and to the ORTF (Office de Radio-Télévision Diffusion Française, the national agency for public broadcasting). After the conference at the Institut National Pédagogique in 1965, they had a beer together, after which my mother noted on her calendar, "Boy, did she let her hair down!" When Amy Hostler retired from Mills College the following year, Mme Herbinière-Lebert wrote a testimonial, which my mother translated into English and forwarded to New York. In 1974, during her annual trip to Port-au-Prince, my mother was asked by a group of women educators, members of OMEP-Haïti, if she would deliver a letter to Mme Herbinière-Lebert, who they hoped would represent them (though I don't know about what). Apparently, the latter accepted because a few months later, a Simone Audant of the group came to Paris. My mother brought her to meet Mme Herbinière-Lebert, who had first gone to Haiti in 1969, shortly after the founding of OMEP-Haïti, and again in 1975. (Mme Herbienière-Lebert was indefatigable in her travels throughout the world on behalf of OMEP, and her interest in Haiti extended beyond her visits. In 1977, she wrote an article for Conjonction, *a publication of the Institut Français d'Haïti (which my father had helped set up in the 1940s), titled "L'Education préscolaire en pays francophone: l'apprentissage du français dans les pays francophones dont la langue n'est pas le français" [that is, the learning of French by preschoolers in former French colonies where French is not the first language].)*

* * *

Somehow my mother did manage time for herself. She took three courses in French civilization at the Sorbonne, for which she was awarded a certificate in early 1971. Two years later, she began to study Hungarian on her own, though I don't believe she got very far. Some years after that, she enrolled in several more Sorbonne courses, including one on health, for she had begun to experience a certain discom-fort in her back and knees, which prompted her to take up swimming twice a week, enroll in a weekly tai chi class a few years later, and have at-home physical therapy (starting in 1982). She also tried acupuncture for a while.

She carried on a voluminous correspondence, mostly with friends in the States and in Haiti, but also with some as close as London and others as far away as Australia. She received as many as four or five letters a day and had a tendency to respond almost immediately.

She attended weekly (sometimes twice-weekly) concerts (under the baton of such conductors as Oistrakh, von Karajan, Osawa, Solti, Bernstein, Menuhin, Rostropovich, Zukerman, and Mehta), generally at the nearby Théâtre des Champs-Elysées, where she usually ran into her former nursery-school teachers, Kathy Kessler and Martine de Lavernette and occasionally Alice Daifuku, along with Kathy's husband Rudy and Martine's friend Helen Robb. My mother often had them all over for lunch or dinner following a morning performance or preceding an evening one, or else they treated her in a neighborhood restaurant.

She got to many art exhibitions: Cézanne, Matisse, Chagall, Picasso, Monet, Miró, Kandinsky, Klee, Magritte, Degas, Goya, Dali, Delacroix, Rubens, Jackson Pollock, Fernand Léger, Francis Bacon, Edvard Munch, and Juan Gris. She continued to enjoy the theater, including the performances of two legendary actresses of the French stage: Madeleine Renaud (in an adaptation of Harold and Maude*) and Edwige Feuillère (in an adaptation of* A Lion in Winter*).*

She read on a wide variety of subjects, especially Africa, Arabia, Haiti, and French politics; loved the murder mysteries of Agatha Christie and Ngaio Marsh; and over the course of several years plowed through a flock of English classics of a certain period: George Eliot's Adam Bede, Middlemarch, The Mill on the Floss, Silas Marner; *Jane Austen's* Pride and Prejudice, Mansfield Park, Emma, The Watsons, Northanger Abbey, Persuasion; *Charlotte Brontë's* Jane Eyre, The Professor; *Anne Brontë's* Agnes Grey; *Elizabeth Gaskell's* Cranford; *Frances Burney's* Evelina; *Thomas Hardy's* Far from the Madding Crowd, Jude the Obscure, Tess of the d'Urbervilles, The Return of the Native, Under the Greenwood Tree, The Woodlanders, The Mayor of Casterbridge; *Laurence Sterne's* A Sentimental Journey through France and Italy, ...Tristram Shandy....; *Anthony Trollope's* The Warden, Barchester Towers, The Last Chronicle of Barset, Can You Forgive Her?, The Way We Live Now; *Thackeray's* The History of Henry Esmond, Vanity Fair....; *and Dickens'* Bleak House, David Copperfield, The Old Curiosity Shop, Great Expectations, A Tale of Two Cities, The Pickwick Papers, Little Dorrit, Oliver Twist, Nicholas Nickleby, Martin Chuzzlewit, The Mystery of Edwin Drood, Dombey and Son. *(In 1972, she read a biography of Dickens and also visited his home during a trip to London.) Subsequently, she moved on to Virginia Woolf, including* Jacob's Room, Orlando, *and* Mrs. Dalloway *and in 1991 in New York saw Eileen Atkins as Woolf in the one-woman show* A Room of One's Own.

She attended lectures, including one by John Kenneth Galbraith on "Youth and Organizations" at the Salle Adyar. The theater, about a fifteen-minute walk from her apartment, was packed, she said, and Galbraith displayed "sly sarcasm" throughout his talk. The next day she heard Raymond Aron, the eminent French philosopher, journalist, and strong anti-Communist, speak on the subject of "Youth and Community."

She made two short trips each to Morocco and England and one to Portugal (that included the Rock of Gibraltar, which she had no doubt first seen in 1914 on her way from Hungary to the U.S.), as well as a few visits of a week or two to Spain and longer annual stays with the Nadals in Plascassier, in the south of France (initially two months but quickly reduced by half, and by 1979, my father could manage no more than two or so weeks at a time). There were also day trips to Epernay and Verrières (both with Jacqueline Bouvet), Chartres (with Frances Guille), Rouen (to see Gladys Cumming), Versailles (with the Lopers, my father's former UNESCO boss), and Saint-Germain-en-Laye (with Maître Misard, by way of the RER, the then-brand-new express subway system), in addition to several days in Dijon, Beaune (the wine capital of Burgundy), and Illiers (Proust country, which she saw with my father and the Krausses).

With the death of François Duvalier ("Papa Doc") in 1971 and the sense after a year that his son's reign was going to be less awful, another travel door opened: my parents began in

1972 to make yearly trips to Haiti, staying with Oncle Jehan, Tante Margot, and their children in the Pétionville house my father had bought for them to occupy.

That first visit, made after an eleven-year (for my mother) and fifteen-year (for my father) absence, was certainly a homecoming. It started wonderfully well as they ran into, visited with, and received visits from friend after friend after friend. It could be said to be like the old days, but without the pressures of job, official engagements, and other commitments.

But the joy was cut short when my father fell painfully ill, had to be hospitalized, and was advised by a cousin, Dr. Gérard Léon (the son of Dr. Rulx Léon), to seek further medical counsel and treatment in New York. He believed there was a metastasized malignant tumor at or near his spine, for which he recommended radiation. (And to think, the doctors in Paris had been treating him for rheumatism during months and months of his complaints about back pain!) The doctors in New York were in agreement, and he began treatment at Sloan Kettering, where one day my father happened to encounter Harriet Pomerance, whose cancer had recurred (and who would, sadly, succumb a month later).

Also halted was the idea my parents had entertained of retiring to Haiti. The medical attention my father would need from this point on could best be gotten in either New York or Paris. In addition to the treatment he received in 1972, he was operated on again in 1976 and in 1982. Fortunately, my parents did choose to stay on in France because a medication that was beneficial to my father but banned in the U.S. was available in Europe. (It could be shipped into France from Switzerland, once an annual prescription was presented in person.)

During their visits to Haiti, my mother regularly saw, among others, Liliane and Joseph Nadal and their twin daughters Jacqueline and Marie-José (plus the latter's then-husband Yves Gardère), the Nadals' daughter-in-law Bibou (whose real first name was coincidentally the same as her mother-in-law's, although written Lyliane), Liliane's sister and brother-in-law Suzanne and Edouard Mathon, Ed's first cousin Alix Mathon, Muriel and Willy Lamothe, Fatboy, Paulette and Clifford Brandt, Simone Dupuy and her brother-in-law Valério Canez (my father's best friend in his youth), Mama Defly, Grette Cameron, Lina and Dadal Assad, Nelly and Marcel Dupuy, Yvonne Sylvain, Raymonde MBow (who had temporarily returned to Haiti after her father's death), Céline and Claude Préval, the Liautauds (before Pierre's death and then it was just Ghyslaine), Claudette and Jean Fouchard and their daughters Claudinette and Edwidge, Claudette's sister Nonotte (Fernande), Amélie and Nicole Séjourné, Amélie's brother-in-law Max, Joujou and Ti Georges Léger, the Lescots (who had moved back to Haiti, before the former president's death in 1974), Jacqueline and Carlos Pereira, and the Fombruns, as well as the American contingent of Margaretta and Fred Kroll, Peggy and Bill Krauss, the

Breretons, and Gordana Ashton. She also saw occasionally Lina Assad's sister Olga, Max Mangonès, Pierre Montas, and Louis Moravia, and she always took time to visit the Salesian Sisters in Thorland and Sister Joan at St. Vincent de Paul.

* * *

In 1973, my mother was able to go up to Furcy for the first time in twelve years (my father's illness the year before had prevented her from doing so then), and she made a point of spending the day there at least once during every visit to Haiti thereafter. In her account of my early years, she wrote, "Long ago we had given $150 to help make a road. At first, only Jeeps could make it safely. Now it is good enough and wide enough to go in regular cars if great care is taken to avoid bumps and puddles." She continued, "Fatboy and all her family loved Furcy. She herself had bought a house built at the edge of the plateau toward the setting sun and promised it to her elder son Jimmy [James]. (On one of my trips to Haiti after Maurice's death, I spent a few days there with Fatboy. It was much more comfortable than ours, much larger, but still very simple.) Tonton [Clive], her younger son, has their grandmother's house across from the church. Her daughter Foufoune [Shirley] bought a house below the road just at the entrance to Furcy before one gets to the *gendarmerie*. And her daughter Carola and Carola's husband Maurice Denis wanted a place of their own and were interested in what was left of our land. (We had already sold the much smaller hill to Marie-José Nadal Gardère.)

"We had paid Exaïce for years to continue as guardian of our property. But then he was jailed for inadvertent murder. He thought he was an herb doctor, and in prescribing things to cure a woman, he killed her instead. We managed to obtain another guardian, who used the woodless part of our land below the house to grow vegetables, which he took to either Kenscoff or Pétionville to sell, but he was not too satisfactory.

"We were told that a fence had to be put up all around the property. This we did, with poles and barbed wire, but parts of the fence were often stolen and had to be replaced. Not only that, but the pitch pine trees on the footpath were constantly slashed as the sticks containing sap could be used to start charcoal kitchen fires and were sold in small bundles in the markets. Additionally, squatters were increasingly taking land if the owners were far away or unable to get up to Furcy.

"And so in 1979, we decided to sell to Carola and Maurice Denis. They started to build immediately. They used our shack as a depot and built around it. Maurice Denis had two boats that ply the Caribbean, and he was able to bring back from Guatemala pine lumber with which he constructed three bedrooms, two bathrooms, living room, dining area, pantry, and kitchen. The living room is the cement cover of a large reservoir. He also put up a system for catching rainwater. Once the walls and roof of the new house were finished, he demolished our shack and used what he could for the servants' quarters. They were able to make use of some of our old furniture as well. Two bedrooms, including Carola and Maurice's, and one bath are upstairs and are actually where our shack used to be. When I saw the whole thing for the first time, I was very happy. The property is still referred to as the Dartigues'.

"It is so good to know that Carola and Maurice really like to go up to Furcy, and although they lived in Miami for a long time, the whole family kept going to Furcy at every vacation time, no matter what the political situation. They have improved the grounds, too. What's more, they held the marriage of Stéphanie, their eldest daughter, there two or so years ago. The ceremony took place in the Furcy church. There were over one hundred guests. A caterer brought up everything—dishes, chairs, tables, food, and wait staff. Fortunately, the day turned out to be beautiful. (Stéphanie wrote to me the other day to say that for her parents, Furcy was home.)"

* * *

After their annual stays in Haiti, my parents would stop for a month or so in New York to catch up with old friends in Manhattan and on Long Island. They were invited on several occasions to spend the weekend with Eleanor and Milton Gould in their country home in Warren, Connecticut. In 1972, wanting to see Milton in action (he was one half of the powerhouse law firm Shea & Gould), my mother trooped down with Eleanor one morning to a Foley Square courtroom for a federal case involving, Patricia Gould Booth told me, justice-elect Seymour Thaler, accused of fencing stolen U.S. Treasury bills. Despite Milton's best efforts, which were usually formidable, the trial did not end well for His Honor.

Milton loved to tell the story of my mother driving on a Paris sidewalk. He and Eleanor were in the back seat of the car when my mother encountered an obstacle in the street. Short of turning around and going on a lengthy detour, she saw one other option: to pull onto the sidewalk for a stretch before regaining the street, and that's precisely what she did, to Milton's amazement and amusement.

During this same trip, the Goulds took my mother and me (my father was in Dakar) to the tony three-star restaurant Lasserre. At one point, waiters advanced on the table and began to remove empty plates. My mother asked what they thought they were doing and told them to put the dishes right back down and wait until everyone had finished eating. There was a certain amount of perplexed and strained apologies (the French hate to admit they're wrong). "Ah, Madame," said a waiter, "we heard English being spoken and we know how much Americans dislike sitting with empty plates in front of them" "Well, go away," my mother said, and the waiters sheepishly withdrew.

During each New York stay, my mother always took in about a half-dozen plays, on and off Broadway, which included, in 1980, The Elephant Man, *written by Harriet and Lee Pomerance's elder son Bernard. She called Lee the next day to say how much she had liked it.*

She would make a point, too, of seeing Haitian friends who had established residence in and around Manhattan or who were just passing through: Paulette Brandt's young-est son Billy (William), Yvonne and Max Rigaud, Georgette Rouzier, Ghislaine Rouzier Ruas, Anne Marie and Franck Laraque, Didine Maximilien, Tite Soeur Mangonès, Max Mangonès, Marie Bourand, Jacques Antoine, Marc Pasquet, and Pierre Montas.

She also kept up with family and friends elsewhere in the States, going to Florida, Ohio, Boston, Chicago, and Washington, D.C. And Uncle John Reithoffer came to see her in New York a number of times.

* * *

My mother usually didn't cry when someone she knew and liked passed away. She found it sad certainly and felt for the family; but dying was part of life, and one just had to go on. But Marie Lavaud's death in 1973 affected her differently, and she noted on her calendar that that evening she "listened to Vladimir Ashkenazy to soothe me." Four days later, when visiting Franck Lavaud, she noted, "I can't keep back tears." The funeral was held on the fifth day at St. Pierre de Chaillot and again she wrote, "I can't hold back tears; Franck breaks down; I go to the cemetery with the Krausses." Her reaction may have been for a combination of reasons: this was someone she'd known for some thirty-five years and whom my father had known since adolescence; Marie's may have been the first death among my parents' close Haitian contemporaries since André Liautaud's (in 1951) and thus was disquieting in its implications; Marie had helped my mother acclimate to Paris; and my mother was very much concerned for Franck, now on his own, and for their daughter Marie-Alice, who had had such a strong bond with her mother. In the ensuing years, my mother invited Franck often for lunch or dinner and sought to be supportive of Marie-Alice. I think Marie-Alice was grateful for both these gestures, for after my father died, Marie-Alice, of whom my mother was very fond, was in turn very considerate to my mother, and very caring.

* * *

My mother had several operations and mishaps during this period. In January 1973 in New York, she had a lump removed from her left breast, and fortunately, it was deemed benign. A month later, she broke a rib slipping on the staircase of the house in Pétionville, the same exact spot where my father had fallen the previous year (and which was to have been repaired in the interim). "It hurt like hell," she wrote. In 1981 in Paris, she had an encounter with a motorcyclist on the Champs-Elysées, and her left leg was broken in several places. (My father tended to get anxious whenever my mother wasn't home at the time she said she would be. In this case, the coiffeur had been late in getting her through her appointment, and then she had stopped at the Maison du Danemark [a Danish shop selling a variety of excellent smoked fish]. She was rushing to cross the avenue as the light was beginning to change, the motorcyclist jumped the light, and they collided. She was taken to the American Hospital, steel rods were inserted, and the leg was placed in a cast. The hospital allowed my father to occupy the other bed in my mother's room for the several days she was there, relieving her of the worry of how to care for him.) The surgeon saw a hammer toe on her right foot and said he could correct it. Since it had been giving her trouble, she decided to have the operation a year or so later. Unfortunately, the surgeon was not a foot specialist, and as a result, over time my mother's foot expanded. This caused her no end of discomfort and outright pain for the rest of her life because she had to squeeze that foot into a shoe that was the proper size for the left foot but too small for the right.

* * *

During this period, my mother renewed an old friendship that had been moribund for years, deepened another, and made a number of new ones that became very important to her.

The rekindled relationship was with her old pal Tamara Baussan. The two women resumed their closeness, seeing each other during Tamara's occasional visits to Paris and during my mother's annual visits to Haiti in the Seventies and Eighties. (They might meet at Ibo Lélé, the Baussans' highly successful hotel above Pétionville, or at Ibo Beach, a noncontiguous extension of the hotel.)

Paulette Brandt and my mother had known each other since 1941, when the former had stayed with her in Furcy. Paulette began coming to Paris every year from 1970 on, during which time she dined often at the house and went to the theater and art exhibitions with my mother. They also saw a great deal of each other during my mother's visits to Haiti.

Sibylle Brandt, Paulette's only daughter, spent part of her first solo visit to France in 1971 bunked down at my parents'. The next time she came through town, in 1977, she was married to a French-Canadian in the diplomatic service. She'd already had one baby, and a year later gave birth to another. "Your mother," Sybille wrote in an e-mail, "followed my pregnancy with great interest and affection and accompanied me to various clinics so that I could make a choice for the birth." They also went together to the Bon Marché department store, where Sybille looked at baby carriages. During the eighteen months Sibylle was in Paris, my mother became very close with her and the two girls. "She was very much involved in my daily life during that time," Sybille continued. They might go for a stroll or to the Jardin des Poètes (the Poets' Park at Auteuil in the 16th arrondissement, strewn with plaques of poetry, to which Sybille said they went regularly) or to other spots such as the Cluny and Rodin Museums, or they might just stay put. The family then returned to Ottawa, where my mother saw them several times. After that, she would see Sybille every few years, usually in Paris but also once in Brussels, to which Sibylle's husband had been posted.

In 1971, at the Paris home of Claudette and Jean Fouchard, my mother made the acquaintance of Muriel Lamothe, a young French-Canadian married to a Haitian, Willy Lamothe. The two women took to each other immediately and, as Muriel said to me, "Figuratively speaking, we never left each other's side after that." During Muriel's initial stay, they had several dinners together and walked a lot, visiting the Louvre and the Marais, among other landmarks. They would catch

up in Haiti each year, and Muriel became my mother's clos-
est friend in Paris after she and her second husband Frantz
Merceron moved there in 1986. They saw each other very
often, and in later years, Muriel did many thoughtful and
kind things, which included phoning my mother every morn-
ing for a brief chat and having her to Sunday family din-
ners. My mother watched Muriel's two daughters by Willy
grow up to become accomplished and successful women—
Sabrina, a public relations executive now living in Montreal,
and Vanessa, a copyright attorney in Paris.

Robert Nadal, who was known as Ti Robert to distinguish
him from his father (the brother of Joseph Nadal, Marie
Lavaud, and Alice Villard), encountered my mother at a din-
ner at Marie-Alice Gatbois' in 1973. But it was not until four
years later, when he came to live in a small apartment a few
blocks from my parents,' that they spent time together. He
would stroll over to visit unannounced, and my mother would
invite him for lunch or dinner quite often (where, he told me,
"each guest was more interesting than the other"). He and
his brother Olivier had had a tough childhood, and I think my
mother was for a while an anchor for him. "What fascinated
me about your mother," Robert said in an e-mail, "is that
she was ahead of her time in almost everything, such as
religious searching, educational and pedagogic innovation,
marrying your father at a time when it was not well seen in
the U.S. She was more than open-minded about things and
was connected to so many things, people, experiences. She

did not restrict herself to a country, a culture, a religion, nor a color or class; she just seemed to blend with the whole universe. She was always positive and never sad, and never tolerated mediocrity. I found her always loving and caring, welcoming new things while cherishing the good things of the past (such as her love for classical music)."

Noha Akiki made my mother's acquaintance in 1977 when she was transferred from her native Lebanon to the General Services division of UNESCO. (She had met my father during a trip he made in late 1963 to Beirut to see the Director of the Regional Office of the Arab States, for whom Noha worked.) She and my mother saw each other often at each other's home and outside the home as well, and Noha was very helpful to my mother when she was organizing and dispatching copies of my father's papers to various institutions. My mother also got to know Noha's older sister Soumaya, who had trained at the American Hospital in Paris in 1972 before moving to Canada; her younger sister Souha, who came to Paris in 1984 to continue her studies; and their mother Najla, who joined her daughters five years later.

Jacqueline and Carlos Pereira were introduced to my mother by Muriel in 1978. She is French; he was American; and they were living in Haiti at the time. (In fact, Jacqueline had lived in Haiti since the age of one month.) When, in the 1980s, my mother was working on my father's papers, Carlos lent her a very helpful hand in gathering material for her in Port-au-Prince and getting it shipped to New York and elsewhere. He also drove her out to Damien so she could consult the files there. My mother would see the Pereiras during her trips to Haiti and during their yearly visits to Paris. Jacqueline told me the following in an e-mail: "Your mother had great qualities. Carlos and I liked her very much and we admired her. She never stopped being interesting and inter-ested in things. Your mother had lots of true friends, and your parents shared a great love."

The Pereiras' daughter Melissa, the youngest of their four children, came to live in Paris in 1983, a year after gradu-ating from Middlebury College in the States. She had met my parents in Port-au-Prince and now became very close to my mother, coming over for dinner every week or two and going to a lot of theater and art exhibits together. Melissa said she saw her first play in Paris with her, Pirandello's To Each His Own Truth. *During Melissa's first year in town, my mother loaned her the apartment while she was away. There was a time when Melissa was traveling to Moscow once a month on business and would bring back caviar, which my mother loved. She told me that she regarded my mother like a grandmother.*

Rosario Etayo (whose formal name is Maria del Rosario Etayo Valencia), a Colombian national who had come to Paris to make a better life for herself, said she first saw my mother walking in the lobby of our building (as a change of scenery from walking in the apartment) doing rehabilitation exercises for her mending leg. This was in June 1981, when Rosario was working for a couple living on the top floor. Shortly thereaf-ter, the husband introduced her to my mother, who he knew was looking for a housekeeper and also knew that she spoke Spanish. During the next twenty-two years, Rosario was wonderful to my mother: loyal, helpful, resourceful, and car-ing. The two were both Capricorns, and Rosario brought my mother a bouquet of flowers on each of her birthdays. "I had a great deal of affection for your mother," Rosario told me in an e-mail. That same year, 1981, the newly elected president of France, François Mitterrand, made good on a campaign promise to legalize the status of foreigners who'd entered the country through 1980, provided they had proof. Rosario told me that although she qualified, she had no one to help her and so sought my mother's advice on how to proceed to stake her claim. Fond of Rosario, sensitive to issues of resi-dency and citizenship, and ready for a righteous challenge, my mother did something doubly unheard of in France: she phoned each of Rosario's other employers (in France you do not call somebody cold; a third-party introduction is always required) and pressed each to prepare a formal statement concerning Rosario's employment with them. The employ-ers must have been so dismayed at being approached by a stranger and being told what to do that they all said yes! "Thanks to your mother," Rosario continued, "within months I was able to obtain my first papers granting me the right to work, was registered with social security (your mother was the first to sign me up), and received my first carte de séjour *(residency identification card) valid for five years, which allowed me to go back to Colombia to visit family for the first time since my arrival in France."* In 1988, Rosario *became the* gardienne *(the current name for the old-time* concierge) *of an apartment building in the 8th arrondisse-ment in exchange for a salary and a tiny studio* (loge) *free of charge. This allowed her to cut back on her houseclean-ing jobs (although my mother was one of the clients she kept). By 2000, Rosario had put enough money aside to buy a small three-and-a-half room apartment in the 13th arrondissement, which she proceeded to rent out. She finally retired in 2011 and moved with François, her French beau of many years, to a town outside Lyon, so that he could start a new business. (In an aside, Rosario added that "when your mother became aware of François' existence, she wanted to meet him so she could get to know him. She asked me if he would want to come to tea, which François accepted, and your mother came away with a favorable impression of him." Being protective of Rosario, if my mother had come to any other conclusion, she wouldn't have been shy about letting it be known.)*

* * *

But old friends and relations also were passing on. In addition to Ralph Bunche, Marie Lavaud, and Harriet

Pomerance, my parents lost Mary and Joseph Bendler, Bob Benjamin, Phil Blume, Doris and Charles Bock, Madeleine Bouchereau-Sylvain, Valério Canez, Suzanne Comhaire-Sylvain, Vashti Cook, Oncle Jehan Dartigue, Simone Dupuy, Caroline Farber, Frances Guille, David Hammond, Hank Jaffe, President Lescot, Pierre Liautaud, Didine Maximilien, Phyllis Haas Picard, Alice Villard, our cousin Agnes Voigt, Andrée and Dody Wiener, and Uncle Lowell Wyville.

And then it was my father's turn. In early June 1983, suffering from what my parents thought was acute appendicitis, my father was taken for surgery to the Ambroise Paré Hospital. The doctors discovered, however, that he had advanced colon cancer, said it was too late to operate, and sewed him back up. He spent some time there before coming home to die, which he did at 4 am on July 9. His last words, to my mother, were in Creole, "M pa kapab" ("I can't any longer"). They had celebrated their fifty-third wedding anniversary only four months before.

Chapter Thirteen

Paris, Part III (1983-2003)

Don't die at home is my advice to anyone living in Paris (and possibly in any part of France). At least that was the case in 1983. I never asked for the twisted logic of the law, but a body had to remain in situ for several days before it could be removed by an undertaker. My mother was not usually given to making a fuss, but there are times when one must insist. She said she was not about to sleep only a few feet from a corpse, nor even in the next room, and made such a scene that the mortuary folks were cowed and did what she asked.

After the embalmer and body left, Rosario came to help clean up the bedroom. Others were also immediately supportive, inviting her over or out for dinner, or bringing in food—Alice Daifuku, Noha Akiki, Pat Fuller (who was in Paris at the time), Marie-Alice Gatbois, Ida Subaran, Claude-Hervé Liautaud, Claudette Fouchard, her daughter Claudinette, Liliane Moravia, and Lina Assad (who was visiting from Haiti). Paulette Brandt also happened to be in town. She took my mother to dinner and, on another day, to Chartres as a distraction. She accompanied her to Père Lachaise for a small memorial service for my father, attended also by Lily Vieux, the Pougets, and my cousin Marie-José, who had kindly come in from Lille.

My mother began to attend to the myriad details of set-tling an estate, then took a break by going to Zurich and Vienna, where she showed me Reithofferplatz and we visited a Reithoffer hardware store, one of a chain. (There were no Reithoffers on the premises, assuming any were still alive, so we were unable to explore the possibility of a family con-nection, unlikely as that was.) In August, she traveled to London for a week, saw her nursery-school parents Rae and Fred Gronich and six plays, and did a lot of sightseeing.

In October, she flew to Haiti to bury my father. Doing so earlier would have been very tough on her; "it might have done me in," she wrote, because of the terrible sum-mer heat. Consequently, the body had been refrigerated and then later placed aboard the same Air France flight she took. (She could have saved herself a lot of trouble, for six months later she found among my father's papers a note in his hand-writing saying he didn't care where or how his remains were disposed of. It was only then that she remembered the conversation he'd had with her, but obviously the point was now moot.)

In Port-au-Prince, the closed casket was displayed in a receiving room (belonging to the funeral home Pax Villa) across the street from Sacré-Coeur, where the church service would be held. Family and friends gathered, and we then moved to the church, where more friends joined us. There were some two hundred in all, including Sister Joan from St. Vincent de Paul and a number of Salesian nuns and students, come to support my mother. No sooner were we seated than a bell rang, inviting us to stand for the arrival of a second coffin. We regained our seats, but moments later the bell sounded again; we stood, and a third casket was installed. We had just sat down when another bell rang; we got up, and a fourth coffin was deposited in front of the altar. My mother and I found these proceedings very odd (in fact, she broke into silent laughter); but since we were unfamiliar with local custom and since the service was in theory under-way, there was nothing to be said or done.

At the ceremony's conclusion, we rode to the cemetery, where my father was laid to rest in the family vault alongside his parents, his two maternal aunts, his sister Thérèse, and his brother Jehan. (Tante Renée would join them in mid-July 1985. In 1973, she'd had a radical mastectomy and in 1984 would suffer a stroke. With great reluctance on the family's part, she was moved to a nursing home because she'd become very difficult. My mother visited her often during her

1984 stay in Haiti and also the following year. Tante Renée's death brought to an end that generation of Dartigues.)

After a month in Haiti, my mother embarked on another of her whirlwind tours of family and friends in the States and beyond—to Punta Gorda to see her sister Betty; Sarasota, where Margaretta and Fred Kroll were now living; New York for a few days with Jeanne Barron; Cleveland to catch up with her siblings John, Art, and Sue; Oberlin for Eleanor and George Simpson; Ottawa for five days with Sibylle Brandt and her family; Chicago to stay with Mildred Grant and her brother and sister-in-law Ben and Trudy Meeker; to me in Los Angeles for her first visit to the city, where she met my close friends, the Einbinder sisters Amy and Bette, and saw Ashley Boone and his sisters Cheryl and Velma, as well as Claude-Hervé Liautaud, who was now living in Diamond Bar (a half-hour's drive from L.A.); Los Gatos (near San José) to see Marion Pearce; back to New York; out to Great Neck for Jean Benjamin, Alice and Jacques Lippetz, Sophie and Paul Alpert, and Frances and Lester Velie; Roslyn for Annette (Metis) and Des Gallagher; Mineola for Marie Bourand, who seemed to be traveling a great deal between the U.S. and France; back to Great Neck for Lena and Helge Five; into New York for a few more days with Jeanne Barron; return to Paris for two days; off to Brussels to spend Christmas with Pat and Hal Fuller; and finally back to Paris, where on December 30 Rosario came with a bouquet of flowers for my mother's 75th birthday. My mother spent New Year's Eve and

Day alone, thus ending a stressful six months on a quiet, reflective note.

* * *

My mother had long felt that all the effort my father had expended in Haiti to improve the lot of so many of his countrymen in the areas of education, agriculture, and labor, and the work he had done in various parts of Africa, especially in the Congo, had been underappreciated. And in the case of Haiti, there'd been a barrage of almost daily severe criticism in certain circles, especially journalistic, in the 1940s that he'd had to endure. My mother seemed to have a plan in mind: getting a book written and published on my father's career and placing his papers with various institutions, thus laying the groundwork, she hoped, for belated recognition and further discussion of his thoughts and achievements.

Haiti was very largely an agrarian society; 90% percent of the population were peasants. The success of a rural economy, my father believed, must rest firmly on a complementary education that fully integrated agriculture and other aspects of rural life with the three Rs. As he wrote in his 1938 monograph, Conditions rurales en Haïti (Rural Conditions in Haiti), there needed to be a "comprehensive plan...involving hygiene, agricultural extension, irrigation, the organization and consolidation of the agrarian system, *rural credit and direct aid to peasants." At the same time, he added, "there has never been an example of a contempo-rary movement of national reconstruction that is not based on the education of the population at large." My father con-tended that grades one through six formed the basis for a country's entire educational system and beyond, since they afforded the opportunity for a common future of nationhood, citizenship, a commonality of customs, ideas, and ideals to be formed.*

But public education in Haiti, rural and urban alike, had been woefully neglected for over a century, ever since the country's independence in 1804. (The farm-schools were the one exception. They had been successfully introduced in the 1920s by the Technical Service of the American Occupation, modeled on those of the Tuskegee Institute in Alabama.) The neglect seemed principally due to two factors. Education had traditionally been a dumping ground for political patronage, allowing incompetence to run rampant as teaching positions were handed out to the unqualified. Many had no skills; many just wanted a guaranteed paycheck for life. Some never set foot in a classroom, while others paid the equally unqualified to substitute for them. Schools were in disrepair; classroom materials, extremely limited.

The other factor was the attitude of Haiti's small upper class. To use current terminology, most of the 1% didn't think about the other 99%, let alone about their needing an education. They did not see the influence schooling could have on improving the social and economic conditions of the 99%.

Both in his fifteen years in rural education (ultimately rising to the position of Director) and in tackling urban education in his four-and-a-half years as Minister of Education, Agriculture and Labor, my father's first step was to banish politics from the Department of Education. Only those who passed a fair, competitive examination open to all would be certified as teachers, while those who failed were dismissed. Personnel would be recruited on an as-needed basis, not to repay a favor. Additionally, he sought to find grants and fellowships for study abroad (usually in the States and very often at his alma mater, Columbia's Teachers College) for those who showed the most promise for advancement in their chosen fields—teachers, school inspectors, supervisors, educational planners, and statisticians. It was essential, he thought, to create a cadre of civil-service experts who could carry on the work of the Department year in and year out, regardless of who was minister. He instituted summer courses to further expose teachers to new methods of education, to sharpen their skills, to learn what they might have missed before. He also dispatched into the field two kinds of touring missions: one to make and fix school furniture, and another to provide help to teachers and further training if required. He wanted to instill an "esprit de corps," especially among those who might be isolated, and he organized regional meetings to make those individuals feel that someone cared about them.

My father insisted on discipline and a seriousness of purpose. Like Hercule Poirot, he believed in order and method. He arranged for surveys to be made so that the Department would have a complete understanding of the problems it faced and how best to allocate the meager government funding it had. He closed schools that couldn't be salvaged and repaired others that could be. He was the first to introduce secondary education for girls and provided living accommodations for them. He raised salaries, though certainly not lavishly because of his budgetary limitations, and promoted those who merited it. Many of the staff were devoted to him and felt he really contributed to the modernization of the school system.

Urban education presented additional challenges because it involved not only primary and secondary levels, but vocational schools (for such skills as masonry, cabinetry, plumbing) and the graduate schools of such disciplines as medicine and law. He hoped to establish a University of Haiti and toward this end squirreled away a bit of money each month to buy land for a campus.

At the primary level, he introduced physical education and experimented in teaching Creole and teaching in Creole. At the secondary level, he made Greek and Latin optional and English and Spanish mandatory, as well as the histories of Latin America and the United States, and the economic history of Latin America, so that a greater understanding of its neighbors, large and small, would allow Haiti to move forward more effectively.

And there was more, much, much more that he did, not only in the field of education, but in labor and agriculture as well, but this gives the reader an idea of what he did accomplish and what he was capable of accomplishing. Foreigners came to visit, study, and learn, including a group from Yale whose members, when they heard what his budget was, exclaimed, "How can you have done so much with so little money?"

However, there were quite a few in the Haitian upper class who were horrified at what they considered assaults on their cherished educational system, which was slavishly modeled on the French. Modernizing a substantial part of Haitian society, my father believed, would benefit the country as a whole. But this was barbaric, uncivilized, too American, cried his detractors, who were blindly wedded to a tradition that my father labeled as foreign and artificial to the Haitian purpose. He wanted, for example, to do away with the standard textbooks brought from France (not only to Haiti, but to France's possessions globally) that intoned, "Our ancestors the Gauls had blond hair and blue eyes!" Elsewhere, the books spoke of France's mountains and rivers rather than of Haiti's. (This is the reason he and his good friend André Liautaud wrote Géographie Locale, *published in 1931 and re-issued several more times.) He wished to create an authentic, original Haitian culture that might incor-porate what was best in the world and would, at the same time, allow Haiti to step into the new scientific era that he saw as the future.*

My father applied these same principles and all he had learned in Haiti (and at the UN and in his first years at UNESCO) to the chaos that was the Congo in 1960, and to the other assignments he subsequently carried out and the programs he organized in various parts of Africa, including the first-ever conference for African Ministers and Directors of Education from Tropical Africa, held in Addis Ababa (1960); the Regional Group for Educational Planning (later known as the Regional Bureau of Educational Development in Africa), in Dakar (1963-65); the first-ever training courses for African teachers, in Cairo (1964); and the university-level, teacher-training school, the Ecole Normale Supérieure, in Bujumbura, Burundi (1966-68). The international agencies would not have been able to find anyone else as well quali-fied and experienced a technician in the problems of and solutions for education in developing countries.

* * *

The idea of a book about my father was not new. My mother had suggested to him that he embark on such a project upon his retirement from UNESCO in 1963. But his subsequent eight years in and out of Africa on various missions kept him from making a start. With his complete retirement in 1971, the subject arose again, but by now his health had begun to undermine his energy and focus. I remember him telling me a year or two later that he found he couldn't concentrate and that his memory had been affected. (I listened sympathetically but did not fully understand until 1996, when I, too, underwent prostate-cancer surgery and subsequently felt my mind and memory going, which of course was very alarming since I was still working. Fortunately, I latched on to gingko biloba in liquid form, and it proved a lifesaver. [I know there have been studies showing that the stuff doesn't work. In my case, that was true of the tablets, but the drops were highly effective.]) The result was that the book project lay dormant.

My mother's initial intention after my father's death was to find someone who would write the book, while she herself would locate all of my father's papers (and other correspondence referring to him) in Paris (both from his home files and at UNESCO), in Port-au-Prince (at the Bibliothèque Nationale [the National Library] and at Saint-Louis de Gonzague, a secondary school with an excellent library), in New York (in the UN Archives), and in Washington, D.C. (at the National Archives); familiarize herself with the material; and make lists so that she could guide the writer and aid him/her in whatever way she could.

In mid-September, she met with Markku Järvinen, UNESCO'S Chief of Archives, who would be supportive throughout the life of her project. (He and his wife Anja, who were from Finland, became close friends of my mother's.) She began what evolved into several years of research there, which she supplemented with the correspondence and other files my father had kept at home and with interviews she later conducted with some of his former colleagues.

During the month she spent in Haiti after my father's funeral, she started going through the reams of documents from his career in Haiti that she had stored for safekeeping at the Bibliothèque Nationale in the 1950s. (At first, she faltered, unable to work, feeling still, understandably, the effects of the funeral; then she rallied and plunged in.)

My mother started the new year 1984 in her usual forge-ahead fashion. She went through the home files and separated out all my father's letters. She spent much of the next two months at the UNESCO Archives.

In late March, she again traveled to Haiti, and in her four weeks there (during which, having sold the house in Pétionville, she stayed principally at Fatboy's but also spent a few days at the Pereiras'), she delved further into my father's papers at the Bibliothèque Nationale, placing the material in special protective folders/classifiers that she bought at Stecher's, Fatboy's giant stationery store. My mother also retraced her steps through many of the towns she'd visited with my father in 1932—Saint-Marc, Chatard, Gonaïves, Limbé, Plaisance, and Cape Haitian—which would serve her well for the book she herself would eventually write about my father and for the account of the first part of her own life.

She also was introduced to a writer with whom she made a contract to produce a book about my father's career in Haiti. Resolving this aspect of her plan was a great relief to her, and the writer could commence his work immediately in the Bibliothèque Nationale files that she'd been organizing.

Her next stop, in May, was the United Nations Archives in New York. She'd been advised there were files of my father's that could be consulted on the premises, although locating them would be time-consuming. However, as she wrote in 1992 to her friend Patricia Tsien, "I worked for several days in the Archives, where I had access only to certain interoffice documents, and I gleaned what I could from the little I was permitted to see." (Mrs. Tsien had, remarkably, held onto this and others of my mother's letters for all these years; her daughter Ying-Ying Yuan recently came across them and very thoughtfully asked if I'd like to have them.)

Upon her return to Paris, she began buying books on the UN's role in the Congo as background for that period of my father's career. Over the next two years, she worked both at home and at the UNESCO Archives, combing through books and documents and making extensive notes and lists. She also contacted a number of my father's former coworkers (most from his days in the Congo) to arrange interviews with them: Francis Bartels, René Ochs, Dragolub Najman, Wilhelm Van Vliet, Michel Doo-Kingué, Robert Hennion,

Antonio Chiappano, Wiendrati Alibazah, and, later, Ricardo Diez-Hochleitner and Pio Carlo Terenzio (whom she flew to Geneva to see). She corresponded with Malcolm Adiseshiah, former UNESCO Deputy Director-General, who was now back in India. When the Nadals invited her to spend two weeks with them in Plascassier, she brought a stack of her paper-work along.

In May 1986, she flew to Montreal to meet with several members of the Centre de Recherches Caraïbes (Center for Caribbean Research), who were also affiliated at the time with the University of Montreal. Dr. Carolyn Fick, a historian and now a professor at Concordia University in Montreal, told me that she believes it was Jean Fouchard who had alerted my mother to the Center. Carolyn kindly put my mother up "in her lovely apartment," *noted my mother, who also met Charles Pierre-Jacques, Frantz Voltaire, and several other Haitians. They* "seemed interested" *in seeing something done on my father, my mother later wrote on her calendar, although, as Carolyn explained, there would have to be a grant application made for funding and the project could take a number of years.*

My mother returned to Paris hopeful and "worked most of the [rest of the] year on Maurice's career." *In February 1987, Charles Pierre-Jacques submitted an application to the University of Montreal for a project titled* Education et Modernité: le cas d'Haïti à travers l'oeuvre de Maurice Dartigue (Ministre de l'Instruction publique en Haïti, 1941–45, et Chef *de la mission spéciale de l'UNESCO au Congo, 1960–61) (or, Education and Modernism: The Case of Haiti as Seen through the Work of Maurice Dartigue [Minister of Education in Haiti, 1941–45, and Chief of the UNESCO Special Mission to the Congo, 1960–61]). A few months later, my mother, who was once more in Haiti, arranged interviews for Martine Pierre-Louis, a research assistant whom Pierre-Jacques had dispatched to talk to people who had known my father and to judge and make note of what files of his were available in the Bibliothèque Nationale. Toward the end of April, Pierre-Jacques and Carolyn Fick formulated a sixty-page report to supplement the February application.*

However, in that same year, my mother was dealt two major setbacks. In March, during her trip to Haiti, she saw that the writer she'd hired three years earlier "had done very little, [so I] told him to stop. I have lost my money. [At least] he did revive Maurice's name in newspapers" (*through a number of articles that appeared in* Le Nouvelliste *in Port-au-Prince). The book contract, which I came upon only recently, called for a deposit on her part and provided no penalties for nondelivery. I don't know whether she brought the project to a halt because she sensed it would go nowhere or because she felt the Caribbean Center might be able to move forward. Or possibly both.*

Some six months later, she was informed by Carolyn Fick and Charles Pierre-Jacques that the University of Montreal had yanked its support from the Caribbean Center, and it would thus be phased out. This was, of course, a huge disappointment to her.

Fortunately, Pierre-Jacques was keen to see the book become reality and pursued the project through a different Montreal institution, the Centre International de Documentation et d'Information Haïtienne, Caribéenne et Afro-Canadienne, or CIDIHCA (International Center of Haitian, Caribbean, and Afro-Canadian Documentation and Information), which was a library as well as a publishing house. Frantz Voltaire, who'd also been involved with the previously mentioned center, was CIDIHCA's Director and in May 1989 drew up a budget and agreement that would require a one-third contribution from my mother and equal shares from CIDIHCA and the Canadian federal government's Secretary of State for Multiculturalism. Pierre-Jacques would be the writer. He would have full access to all the material my mother had recently donated to CIDIHCA and would travel to New York for research at Teachers College and to Paris to root around the UNESCO Archives and conduct interviews with some of my father's former colleagues.

As a contingency, I suspect, my mother decided to produce a book of her own. All the while she had been tracking down and organizing my father's papers, she had taken copious notes and little by little had converted them into an English-language manuscript.

Mr. Järvinen wrote in an e-mail that "I have memories of discussions with your mother when she expressed doubts *about her ability to carry out the work. We took up the idea of finding in France somebody interested, a younger researcher who, under the guidance of a French professor, could do the work. I remember that she wrote to one professor explaining her plan, but she received no answer. We also looked at different directories at UNESCO to locate institutions in the world specializing in Caribbean or Haitian affairs."*

At first, she focused her book on my father's career at the UN and at UNESCO (probably, I think, because she hoped to still find someone who would address the Haitian portion of my father's career), and then she made up her mind to include a section on Haiti after all. In 1988, she gave a copy of the completed manuscript titled The Contribution of Maurice Dartigue to Education in Haiti, the United Nations and UNESCO *to the UNESCO Archives, the Schomburg Center for Research in Black Culture (a division of the New York Public Library), the Milbank Memorial Library (now known as the Gottesman Libraries) of Teachers College at Columbia University, and the Bibliothèque Nationale and Saint-Louis de Gonzague in Haiti.*

Then, after seeing a story in L'Express *(a French Time-like weekly news magazine) about the self-publisher Editions "J'Etais Une Fois" ("I Once Was..." Publishers), she contacted its head, Simone Wallich, and entered into an agreement. Wallich worked with my mother, making various suggestions and assisting her with her French.*

The result a few years later, in 1992, was Un Haïtien exceptionnel Maurice Dartigue. *It appeared in select Paris bookstores and at UNESCO, and my mother gave a dozen copies to Charles Pierre-Jacques (who was in Paris at the time on a research mission) to take back to Frantz Voltaire and CIDIHCA in Montreal, while sending fifty copies to Port-au-Prince to be sold in the bookstore of the Maison Henri Deschamps, a publishing house founded in 1898. She also asked if Deschamps would be interested in producing a Haitian edition. The company wrote to say that if the political situation in Haiti were different and if the book had not just come out in France, there might be reason to consider it. However, should things change and if the French publisher would be willing to lend them the photographic plates, then it would be something to keep in mind.*

Subsequently, she contracted with an American self-publisher in New York, Vantage Press, for an English-language version, which she herself translated from the French and revised. It saw the light of day in 1994 as An Outstanding Haitian, Maurice Dartigue, *and Vantage arranged for it to be sold at various bookstores, including Barnes & Noble in Manhattan.*

The books received a few notices—positive ones—in UN and UNESCO publications. One was by Patricia K. Tsien, the only daughter of V.K. Wellington Koo, the renowned Chinese statesman, diplomat, and Hague judge. Mrs. Tsien had been a former UN Trusteeship Department colleague of my father's, and her review in 1992 of the French version (in which she described the book as "fascinating" and "moving") now brought the two women together as good friends.

Copies of both books were donated to the Library of Congress in Washington, D.C.; the United Nations' Dag Hammarskjold Library, the Schomburg Center, and the Gottesman Libraries at Teachers College, in New York; the College of Wooster, my mother's alma mater, in Wooster, Ohio; the CIDIHCA in Montreal; and the UNESCO Archives in Paris. Just the French-language book went to the franco-phone division of the Bibliothèque Sainte-Geneviève in Paris, as well as to the Bibliothèque Nationale and the library of Saint-Louis de Gonzague in Port-au-Prince. To complete the circle, a copy of the English-language book was sent in fall 2012 to the American Library in Paris, a short walk from my mother's former apartment.

Thus, between the ages of 83 and 85, my mother had produced not one but two books—a signal achievement of which she could be very proud. They were actually stagger-ing the reams of documents she had pored through and then distilled; it had required tremendous patience and stamina.

Although sales were never stratospheric, Vantage Press was sufficiently pleased to ask in 1996 for a renewal of the contract. However, three years later, the publisher informed my mother that it needed to clear out its warehouse to make room for newer product. She decided the remaining cop-ies would be divided up in the following way: twenty each to her in Paris; to the Libreri Mapou (a Haitian bookstore) in Miami; to the Haitian writer Max Manigat in Queens (the New York City borough with a sizeable Haitian population), *who might have placed some locally and transported the rest to Haiti; and to Carolyn Fick in Montreal to give to Frantz Voltaire, who recently told me that he distributed the majority in Haiti, held on to three at CIDIHCA, and sent one to the Dominican Republic and two to Cuba, where there are large Haitian communities. The remaining 165 copies came to me for mailing, with a cover letter, to the libraries of American black colleges and universities and to a select number of white schools with black-studies programs. (I don't know how the remaindered French version was handled; perhaps the print run had been smaller and had therefore been naturally exhausted because my mother had only a few copies in her possession at the end.)*

She hoped for and patiently awaited the completion of Charles Pierre-Jacques' undertaking. Finally in 2002, at age 91, she received a copy of D'Haïti à l'Afrique, Itinéraire de Maurice Dartigue, Un Educateur Visionnaire *(From Haiti to Africa, Itinerary of Maurice Dartigue, a Visionary Educator), which was complimentary to my father, and its publication made my mother very, very happy.*

Her perseverance, her tenacity, had paid off. What had been despairing to her in the late 1980s—after thinking she might see two projects underway (the Haitian writer's and that of the Center for Caribbean Research) and then only one (the Center's) and then none at all—had been turned around and had ultimately led to three fully realized tomes (her two and Pierre-Jacques' one). (It reminded me of what a good friend of mine, Mark Reina, would occasionally say in our Warner Bros. days, "Turn a no into a maybe and a maybe into a yes.")

* * *

The first part of my mother's plan had been to see a book produced on my father's career. The second was to place copies of his papers in a number of libraries and archives. As early as 1984, she had met with librarians of various institutions to ask whether they would be interested in receiving the material as a donation so it could be made available to researchers upon request. They assented, and in the late 1980s stacks of photocopies went out, followed a bit later by shipments of microfiche of the Bibliothèque Nationale (BN) files. (Soon she would become nervous about the future of my father's papers at the BN—material dating from 1927 to 1946, plus certain other material belonging to her father-in-law (Jean Baptiste Dartigue) covering the period 1903 to 1920. Would it be properly looked after, or would it be neglected? So after getting the documents microfiched locally, Carlos Pereira further helped my mother by getting the original BN files packed up and sent to the Schomburg in New York.) The last of the deliveries—which included my father's original home files—was made in 2001. The recipients of some or all of these originals or duplicates were the Schomburg Center, Teachers College, the CIDIHCA in Montreal, the Library of Congress (four hundred pages of correspondence on SHADA, a highly controversial project in its day), and the UNESCO Archives (correspondence from 1956–1971), while Saint-Louis de Gonzague received a mix of primarily my father's monographs, reports, and speeches.

As I've said, my mother's ultimate goal in all of this was to prompt others to talk about my father's ideas and accomplishments and have an understanding and appreciation of the man himself. Already a bit of this had been realized with a handful of newspaper articles published in Haiti following my father's death, one or two in Le Septentrion *and the rest in* Le Nouvelliste, *praising his work and reforms. In 1996, a Canadian publication,* Dire *(funded by the University of Montreal), published Ian-Pierre Scott's* "Un Réformateur parmi les réactionnaires" *(A Reformer among Reactionaries), an excerpt or distillation of a master's thesis he presented that same year at the University of Montreal titled* L'Éducation en Haïti: la pensée et l'oeuvre de Maurice Dartigue 1941– 1945 *(Education in Haiti: The Thought and Work of Maurice Dartigue 1941–1945). In 1998, another master's thesis was prepared, this time at Teachers College, by Rahel L. Gottlieb, called* A Lesson in Educational Borrowing: Jean Joseph Maurice Dartigue, Teachers College Alumnus, Haitian Minister of Education and UNESCO Education Chief. *In 2002, as I've mentioned, Charles Pierre-Jacques' book appeared (with Ian-Pierre Scott listed as a collaborator). By then a professor at the University of Sherbrooke (in the province of Quebec), Pierre-Jacques promoted his book in interviews and appearances in Montreal and in the Miami area. CIDIHCA has a copy of the book in its files, as do the Schomburg Center and Teachers College, among others.*

Around this time, my mother received a letter and then a phone call from Chantalle Francesca Verna, then a Haitian doctoral candidate at Michigan State University, who had been vouched for by Carolyn Fick. Chantalle had developed a strong interest in the subject of Haitian-American relations, and a mentor, historian Irma Watkins-Owens, had pointed her in the direction of the Schomburg in New York, where the late André Elizée, an archivist at the library, introduced her to my father's papers and my mother's book. Chantalle now wanted very much to meet with my mother to talk about my father's work in Haiti, which would provide her with additional material for her dissertation exploring the relationship between Haiti and the U.S. between 1934 and 1956. Although nothing immediately came of this letter and phone call (my mother was no longer traveling, and Chantalle's plans to come to France did not materialize), Chantalle would in time make significant contributions to my mother's goal.

In the spring of 2003, Haitian historian and author Marcel B. Auguste organized a half-day conference at the University of Quebec in Montreal to honor my father, who would have celebrated his 100th birthday that year. Joining in were Charles Pierre-Jacques, Creutzer Mathurin (a sociologist and principal adviser to the Haitian Ministry of Education), and CIDIHCA's Frantz Voltaire (who in 1990 had proposed to my mother the idea of holding a Maurice Dartigue Day similar to this). Although my mother couldn't attend, she did send a message of thanks for "this homage to a Haitian, Maurice Dartigue, who in his soul and his conscience served well the interests of his country."

Much earlier, in 1984, she had written to Teachers College (TC) to see if there would be interest in estab-lishing a scholarship in my father's name that would go to a Haitian student writing on education and Haiti who would pledge to return to Haiti after graduation to do something worthwhile there in the field of education. As discussions progressed, the political situation in Haiti became more and more unstable, and consequently TC urged that the expectations for the scholarship be revised. The upshot was that in 1994 a doctoral candi-date, Jean Y. Plaisir, active in the New York-area Haitian community, was recommended by a TC faculty mem-ber to receive The Maurice Dartigue Scholarship in the amount of $5,000.

In 1989, my mother made a contribution to the restora-tion of International House's auditorium, site of many dif-ferent activities, most notably the Sunday Suppers my par-ents had attended back in 1930–1931. In acknowledgment of the donation, a bronze plaque was installed "In memory of Maurice Dartigue."

Thus there had been a progression of steps, some more meaningful than others, but steps nonetheless towards my mother's goal.

* * *

In the mid-Seventies, while in Port-au-Prince, my mother had visited Max Mangonès and admired his extensive collection of Haitian books, one of which dated back to 1536! Over time, she herself acquired, by ones and twos, books having to do with Haiti. She spent many an hour on the prowl at Strand's in Manhattan and the bouquinistes (secondhand bookstalls) in Paris, as well as in traditional bookstores in those two cities and in London. In 1984, she donated from her collection eighty-six books in French, sixteen in English, and three in Spanish to the francophone section of the Bibliothèque Sainte-Geneviève, at the Pantheon in Paris. Three years later, she gave them nineteen more, including my father's monograph, Conditions rurales en Haïti,; dispatched additional English-language books to the Schomburg; and sold thirty others to her friend Muriel Merceron, who wanted to start a collection of her own. After her death, a last batch went to the Schomburg, while I kept a few to supplement what I had.

* * *

Sometime around 1984, my mother joined UNESCO Community Service (UCS), which had been founded twelve years earlier as a group similar to the United Nations Women's Guild she had belonged to in Great Neck and New York. It consisted of volunteers, largely spouses of members of UNESCO's staff, NGOs (nongovernmental organizations recognized by UNESCO), and permanent delegations. As its name indicated, it performed services for the UNESCO community, primarily for wives coming from all over the world to a foreign environment, most for the first time, obliged to deal with a lot of new issues, including a different language, different customs, and a different currency. UCS sought to be a welcoming committee, offering information about such important matters as housing, transportation, and schools. It was also a place where people could meet one another. In other words, it served as an invaluable support system.

Its president at the time was my mother's good friend Raymonde MBow, wife of UNESCO's then-Director-General, and the organization went about its mission quite effectively. But in October 1987, there was a changing of the guard with M. MBow's departure and the arrival of a new Director-General (D-G), Federico Mayor, of Spain. Several months later, on February 22, 1988, M. Mayor issued a memorandum announcing UCS' dissolution, with its functions to be absorbed by existing UNESCO departments.

This came as a complete shock to the membership. Outwardly, it could be said that the D-G was responding to *a mandate to reduce UNESCO's overall costs by any means necessary. However, other factors were likely at play, including bureaucratic politics, especially since the savings (an annual subsidy of $4,800, the telephone bill, a secretary's salary, and office space) were truly minimal.*

It was customary for the presidency of UCS to be bestowed upon the D-G's wife. However, it was a considerable responsibility and not every individual was cut out for it. At a membership meeting, Austin Atherley had recommended the position be made honorary to avoid such a potential problem, but a majority felt this might be deemed insulting to the new officeholder.

When the D-G's letter was received, three UCS members—Austin Atherley, Shari Rajah, and Jeannette Verhoog—met with the new UCS president, Maria Angeles Mayor, and detailed the depth of the organization's work, how invaluable it was to newcomers as it was to all members, and how serious its loss would be. As a newcomer herself, Mme Mayor was unaware of all this and, seemingly moved, offered to speak to her husband to dissuade him. Unsurprisingly, nothing came of that.

In accordance with UCS' statutes, a General Assembly of all its members needed to be convoked and without delay. This was scheduled for less than five weeks later, on March 27. Like the Old Girls returning to their alma mater to do battle in defense of their school in the wonderful 1954 British film comedy The Belles of St. Trinian's, *the membership rallied, and at this point, my mother joined Austin and Shari to help lead the charge and became the person designated to sign the memoranda going to the D-G. My mother felt she was probably the least vulnerable of members since she wasn't a UNESCO employee, did not have a husband who was, and her pension (as surviving spouse) was paid directly by the United Nations in New York.*

A committee meeting with the D-G was requested and held on March 14 to discuss the gravity of the situation and a hoped-for reversal of position. Subsequently, in a memorandum to the UCS membership, my mother reported that at their get-together with the D-G, M. Mayor "went so far as to assure us that UCS will continue its activities, will dispose of a space for its administration and meetings, keep its own funds which it will handle itself *(the group's "kitty" of about $80,000 was no doubt coveted by some at UNESCO)*, and, lastly, make new and simpler statutes which will permit UCS not to be under the direct authority of the D-G." *Now addressing the D-G himself in that same memo, my mother wrote*: "These reassuring words and the guarantee which you have given to insert other points in the agenda show that you have not all together envisaged the dissolution of UCS."

The greatest challenge was, of course, time because the group now had only two weeks in which to revise its statutes for presentation to the General Assembly for its approval. The D-G had advised the special committee to meet with the

UNESCO Legal Advisor to discuss the revisions, but when they sat down with him on March 21, the person in question claimed he couldn't help because he had not been at their March 14 meeting with the D-G and had never received instructions to work with the group on this project. Was this the slow-moving wheels of the UNESCO bureaucracy, or an intentional monkey wrench? But the women were undaunted and, with the considerable behind-the-scenes help of Rosita Armerding (the daughter of Togo's Sylvanus Olympio), miraculously produced, within a week, a draft of simplified statutes.

On March 27, when M. and Mme Mayor walked into UCS' General Assembly meeting, they seemed shocked to see the size of the attendance. It was likely they had anticipated a handful of people; instead there were 90! It appeared that the D-G had not counted on the membership's commitment to the organization and its mission. (At one point in the D-G's address to the gathering, my mother, who didn't believe in beating around the bush, slammed her hand down on a table top and fearlessly shouted, "That's a lie!," which naturally stunned the entire room.) The membership went on to approve the group's new statutes and to disapprove dissolution by a vote of sixty-six to twenty-three, with one abstention.

However, three days later, the D-G issued a new memorandum that disregarded the UCS vote and ordered the organization's demise. This, too, was a shock in light of the

March 14 meeting, but there it was. However, although UCS lost its battle, what seemed to have emerged was a compromise that both sides could interpret as winning the war. While the D-G was able to declare UCS officially dead, the group was immediately reborn as the UNESCO Community Association (UCA), through the exhaustive efforts of, again, Rosita Armerding in dealing with all the legal work and the actual setting up of the new organization. UCA received office and meeting space in UNESCO's Bonvin building and carried on its work as usual. Volunteers continued to man the reception desk (my mother, for example, spent three hours there one afternoon a week). Her many years with UCS/UCA (she was a member till the very end of her life) gave her satisfaction in having helped innumerable women and their families adjust to Paris. In early 1999, UCA celebrated her 90th birthday and threw another party for her the following year. (She was its oldest member.)

In typical fashion, she made a whole new set of friends: Rosita Armerding (from Togo), Austin Atherley (Barbados), Pamela Barabas (UK, married to a Hungarian), Nieves Claxton (Malta), Shari Rajah (India), Uma Rao (India), Letitia Thompson (Sierra Leone), and later Lindsay Mathews (USA), and saw them socially—especially Shari, with whom she lunched almost weekly at one point.

In addition to her UCA office work, my mother, starting in 1992, held English conversation classes. (Was she reminded of the English classes she had given in Haiti sixty years earlier?) At first, the group assembled only once a month at UNESCO, but later it became a weekly gathering for three hours at her home. The class was advertised in the UNESCO newsletter, and her "students," usually a half-dozen at a time, came from all over the world. She got to know some of them well, socializing with them outside of class.

It was also during this period that she gave separate English lessons to Virginie Lavaud, the daughter of Ségolène and Gérald Lavaud (and the granddaughter of Marie and Franck Lavaud). Virginie had never completed her schooling, and during the course of the English lessons, my mother encouraged her to resume her studies, which she proceeded to do and ultimately received her baccalaureate and then her master's, although my mother didn't live to see these achievements.

My mother had known Ségolène for years but didn't become friendly with her until the mid-1980s. Now and then she would have her over for lunch or dinner along with her cousin (by marriage) Marie-José Nadal (who was by then divorced and spending more and more time in Paris). Born in the Moselle region in northeastern France, Ségolène had had a diverse and, in some ways, fascinating career: working in high fashion (as a model for Christian Dior and later as a ready-to-wear manager for both Ted Lapidus and Madame Grès), in communications (as Information Officer for the U.S Air Force Protocol Office), home decorations for adults and children, and advertising (as an agent for forty-to-fifty illustrators). Some years after retiring, she returned to school for her own satisfaction and pleasure: at 70, she earned a DAEU (Diplôme d'Accès aux Etudes Universitaires, or Diploma of Access to University Studies), a special degree for adults in place of a baccalaureate; at 75, a master's, producing a brilliant thesis (memoir, in French) *on the Haitianization of the written, painted, and metal arts; and at 80, a doctorate in modern letters.*

* * *

In 1990, my mother began a great friendship with Richard Allen. She had wanted to hire someone to type up the manuscript of her book and asked Noha Akiki if she knew of anyone at UNESCO. Noha inquired in the typing pool, and Sandy Allen, a Filipina, was recommended. Sandy was married to a young African-American who was a singer and later also taught business English to French clients. Subsequently, when my mother signed up for an in-home emergency-response service, Richard kindly agreed to be on call in case of a mishap and in fact did have to come several times late at night when she had fallen. In the mid-1990s, my mother would have dinner with Richard and Sandy every few weeks. Later, along with Noha and Melissa Pereira, they formed what Noha dubbed "la bande d'Esther," Esther's gang, who went to dinner together, usually to a Chinese restaurant and often to her favorite, Empire Céleste, in the Latin Quarter.

In 1997, Sibylle Brandt's younger daughter Bianca, now aged 20, came to Paris for about three months and saw a lot of my mother, whom, she told me, she "loved very much. We would go to the movies, go eat, walk around such areas as the Place des Vosges." (They also went to the Egyptian Collection at the Louvre, my mother noted on her calendar.) "She would talk about movies, about getting old, about life. I learned so much from her. I recall her ordering a dish without tomatoes, and when I asked her why, she said the acidity hurt her. She told me to eat all I want in my youth because when you get old, your body grows old, too, and some things you just can't digest. I always think of her now when I eat tomatoes. I remember her wearing a man's watch, your dad's watch, and I have adopted wearing men's watches, too. I recall that when she wanted to remember something, she would switch the watch onto her opposite wrist; she said it felt odd and reminded her she had something to do. I do this now, and it's a great way to remember! I liked being with her so much; we liked being around each other. I feel we had a special bond that went beyond age and culture."

My mother was thus fortunate in having a host of friends of all ages in Paris and in continuing to make friends to substitute for (but never to replace) the chums and relations who were inevitably disappearing, including Sophie and Paul Alpert, Mary Blume Asch, Tamara Baussan, Clifford Brandt, Mercer

Cook, Mildred Meeker Grant Coutts, Gladys Cumming, Tante Renée Dartigue, Martine de Lavernette, Joseph Farber, Lena and Helge Five, Jean Fouchard, Eleanor and Milton Gould, Margaret Guille, Mme Herbinière-Lebert, Amy Hostler, Polly and Allan Hulsizer, Helen Jaffe, Viola and Sidney Kantrowitz, Kathy and Rudy Kessler, Peggy and Bill Krauss, Margaretta and Fred Kroll, Jesse Kuh, Blanka and Fred Landau, Franck Lavaud, Ghyslaine Liautaud, Jacques Lippetz, Alix Mathon, Suzanne and Ed Mathon, Maître Misard, Louise and Broadus Mitchell, Liliane Moravia, Jacqueline Nadal, Liliane and Joseph Nadal, Lee Pomerance, Pierre Pouget, Georgette and Pierre Rouzier, Ruda Schulhof, Becky and Morris Schwartz, Amélie Séjourné, Nathalie and Eddie Shavitz, Eleanor and George Simpson, Yvonne Sylvain, Letitia Thompson, Frances Velie, Auguste Viatte, Sallie Washington, and Yolande Wiener.

Aunt Betty's sudden death in April 1993 came as very unhappy news for both my mother and me. Betty had suffered from a number of major health problems, including diabetes, high blood pressure, and stroke. Since she and my mother had been very close, I worried how the news would affect the latter when I phoned. My mother was sad, of course, but seemed to take it in stride. I decided to check back a few hours later, but there was no answer. Around 9 pm (Paris time), still no answer. At 10 pm, still no answer, at which point I phoned Marie-Alice Gatbois to see if she'd heard from her or if my mother had gone there. Not so, I learned. Finally, at 11 pm, she picked up the phone. She'd gone out for a very long walk through the streets of Paris to absorb the news and deal with her great sadness.

* * *

On October 26, 1992, the American Consulate in Paris handed my mother a new Certificate of Naturalization. It was one of the happiest days of her life: restoration of her American citizenship. It was something she had dreamed of for more than fifty-four years, ever since it had been taken from her on February 2, 1938.

She was the first in her family, she said, to have become a naturalized American, on August 9, 1930, seven months after turning 21 and two months after graduating from Wooster College. She'd made the mistake, she admitted, of not visiting the Immigration and Naturalization Service in New York before shipping out to join my father in Haiti in 1931. However, "immediately upon arriving in Haiti," she wrote, she went to the American Consulate to ask what she would need to do to retain her precious citizenship. She was told that all that would be required was registering with the consulate once a year and returning to the U.S. every two. She did the annual registering but was less diligent about the travel: she went back to the U.S. in 1932, but her next two trips weren't until 1935 and 1939. However, by the latter date, her fate had already been sealed, because in 1938 she was informed by the consulate that her naturalization had been revoked. She was "stunned and shocked," *for there had been no prior warning. My mother suspected her marriage and therefore race had been a factor, for, she wrote in a letter to me in 1964,* "at the time [*mid-1930s*] there were people at the Consulate who were openly against mixed marriages and sometimes let it be known that Consulate [workers] were not to mix with Haitians except in business. Several very nice people were sent out of Haiti because they had made Haitian friends." *(One is reminded of the calls Marion Pearce made to my mother. On the other hand, there were the examples of David Hammond and Bill Krauss, who circulated openly and comfortably in Haitian society. Did their positions as vice-consuls insulate them?)*

The consulate had been instructed to have my mother sign a consent form and waiver (indicating that she would not sue) and to have her return her original Certificate of Naturalization. Incensed and "in protest," *she refused to do either, which appeared to create a certain awkwardness and embarrassment in American government circles, in both Port-au-Prince and Washington (in the State and Labor Departments), for officials were obliged to admit their inability to carry out a seemingly simple request, thereby acknowledging that an individual could and did thwart their wishes. (The State Department oversaw embassies, legations, and consulates, while the Immigration and Naturalization Service was housed under the Labor Department.)*

Suddenly stateless, my mother immediately acquired Haitian citizenship, which her marriage to my father gave her the right to do. Thus when she traveled to the U.S. in 1939, 1942, and 1946, it was on a Haitian passport. Shortly after we settled in Great Neck in May 1947, my mother consulted Dorothy King, a well-known New York immigration attorney, who kindly offered free of charge to look in the Federal files in Philadelphia during an upcoming trip she was making on behalf of another client. Ms. King found my mother's file in the morgue and subsequently told her that she certainly had a case, that she hadn't had her day in court. But—and it was a big but—it would be a very costly process. My parents had just enough money for food and rent, so clearly a legal fight was out of the question. Nor did my mother feel the social climate (vis-à-vis mixed marriages) would be favorable. She was naturally demoralized. (Ms. King had been involved in the Harry Bridges case, in which an Australian who'd become a naturalized American and a potent force in the American labor union movement was relentlessly pursued by the U.S. government on various charges, including fraud in obtaining his citizenship (he'd not revealed his communist affiliation), until he won his case before the U.S. Supreme Court in 1953.)

In 1964, Kate Schneider, a naturalized American who had been stripped of her citizenship after she'd gone to live with her husband (a German national) in Germany, had it reinstated, again after fighting all the way to the Supreme

Court. My mother was thrilled, hoping this case might open the door for her own victory. She asked Bob Benjamin if someone in his law office (Philips, Nizer, Benjamin, Krim & Ballon, of which Bob was still a partner while holding his position at United Artists) might be able to look into this for her. Jacob Usadi made inquiries of the firm's considerable connections in Washington but was obliged to report a disappointing answer. The State Department could not help because it had been a Justice Department matter, and Mrs. Schneider had sued under the Immigration and Nationality Act of 1952, whereas my mother's status had been deemed a violation of a 1906 act. Mr. Usadi's feelings were the same as Ms. King's: there was a case to be made, but at considerable cost. So once again my mother was dejected.

In 1985, two years after my father's death, my mother and I talked about me (as blood kin) sponsoring her as an immigrant so that she could be eligible for a Green Card, allowing her to enter and leave the United States as often as she liked while continuing to live abroad within the limits imposed on a Green Card holder. Jack Golan, a neighbor and an immigration attorney, handled her application which was approved forthwith, and she received a card.

Never one to give up, as you have been able to gather, six years later she met with a very nice American consul in Paris who listened to my mother's account and submitted it to Washington. The plea was once again denied, but in her letter, the consul offered extremely useful advice: my mother could sue in District Court in Ohio (where the original order to vacate her naturalization had been made). When I heard this, I encouraged my mother to ask Uncle John for his help. John had long been, among other things, CEO of the Geauga County Association of Realtors (for forty-eight years!) and heavily involved in local politics, knowing everyone there was to know. (In April 1959, when Senator John Kennedy was in Ohio some nine months before announcing for the presidency, Uncle John, who was Chairman of the Geauga County Democratic Party, received a call from his counterpart in Cuyahoga County [Cleveland is its county seat], asking, "Would you like to have Kennedy in Geauga for three hours?" "You bet I would!" was John's answer. It was the middle of the annual county Maple Festival, and Kennedy, said John, "was all over the place. He really worked the crowd well." There is a photo of the two Johns and Jacqueline Kennedy in a fiery-red Cadillac convertible amidst a street parade, brass band and all.)

Uncle John took up the standard for his sister and contacted attorney Paul Chalko, the American-born son of Lithuanian immigrants, who, John felt, might have sympathy for my mother's situation. Chalko's first step was to look for my mother's file in Cleveland. The folder was there but the court records were gone. Among the remaining papers was a note saying that she was married to a Negro (in the parlance of those earlier days). (This reminded my mother of what a year earlier, in the National Archives, she'd found in old State Department correspondence files concerning my father: a memorandum dated May 1941 indicating that he was married to a white woman and suggesting that consequently he might be supportive of American interests. And so my mother's long-standing hunch may have been right, that race had played a factor in bringing her to the court's attention in 1937 and that the trail led back to the American Consulate in Port-au-Prince. White America's obsession with color!)

Coming up empty-handed in Cleveland, Chalko then wrote to Uncle John's congressman in Washington, asking if he would make a request of the Department of Justice for my mother's file. This time Chalko was successful and was now able to see exactly what the original case had been all about, allowing him to formulate his brief on her behalf. The law Congress had passed in 1906 stipulated that a newly naturalized American could not leave the United States for a period of five years and could not take up permanent residence in a foreign country. However, because the U.S. had since relaxed itself in such matters and because successful suits (like the Bridges and Schneider cases) had set strong precedents, Chalko asked that the Court find Section 15 of the 1906 Act to be discriminatory and stated that there had been a violation of my mother's due process under the Constitution's Fifth Amendment. He requested that the Court thus void the 1938 nullification of her 1930 naturalization, for the government, he contended, had failed to give notice of its intention to strip my mother of her citizenship and so had failed to give her the opportunity to rebut, to bring forward witnesses—in other words, to have her day in court. A judge of the Ohio District Court agreed and ordered my mother's citizenship reinstated.

* * *

Pat and Hal Fuller, the American couple my mother had met in Burundi, were now settled in Virginia, where they attended church, Hal Fuller wrote, at "the Unitarian Universalist Congregation of Fairfax [County], which had a partnership relation with a Unitarian church in a small village in Transylvania. When your mother learned of this, she shared with us the fact that she was born in a district not very far from our partner church... and because of the connection she contributed very generously to a health clinic that we were financing in the village where our partner church was located." In the summer of 1993, the Fullers went to the area and later sent my mother photos (which she kept) of Sibiu (previously Hermannstadt), the larger town some ten miles from Ocna-Sibiului, the Romanian name given to my mother's Vizakna.

* * *

My mother first read T.E. Lawrence's Seven Pillars of Wisdom *in 1963, and she became such a fan that she must have reread the book more than a dozen times over the next forty years. (After completing a French biography of Saudi Arabian king Ibn Saud, she noted that it was a* "good thing Lawrence wrote up his side of the story or the French would have left him out in their telling of it.") *She consumed as much as she could get her hands on by and about him, including Lawrence's own* The Mint, Oriental Assembly, *and* Revolt in the Desert *(an abridged version of* Seven Pillars*), as well as* The Secret Lives of Lawrence, *both* Letters of T.E. Lawrence *and* The Letters of T.E. Lawrence *(Vyvyan Richards' and Charles Edmonds' separate books, respectively),* The Desert & The Stars, Lawrence of Arabia *(B.H. Liddell Hart's and Alistair Maclean's separate books with the same title),* Lawrence The Rebel, Richard Aldington and Lawrence of Arabia, T.E. Lawrence in Arabia and After, *and* T.E. Lawrence by His Friends. *She usually found the works in secondhand shops, where she also came upon Gertrude Bell's* Amurath to Amurath *and* The Letters of Gertrude Bell, *both having to do with the so-called female Lawrence of Arabia, who had had a significant hand in setting up and helping to govern the nascent state of modern Iraq. For a woman of her time (1868–1926), Bell wielded extraordinary power, was invaluable to the British government, and was one of the few agents of the monarchy the Arabs remembered fondly.*

In the 1990s, my mother became passionate about the Delaney Sisters and Colin Powell. She read and reread and talked about the two women's account of their lives, Having Our Say. *She was also very impressed with Powell and would return from time to time to his book,* My American Journey.

In 1999, at the age of 90, she decided to revisit Proust's massive A la recherche du temps perdu *(In Search of Lost Time), which she hadn't taken up in nearly thirty years. Back then she'd been with my father and the Krausses on a visit to Proust country, specifically Illiers, the market town in north central France that Proust had immortalized (calling it Combray in his text). She had walked around, stopped in the church and in Aunt Léonie's house, and bought madeleines (which the novel's narrator munches on, triggering an involuntary memory). However, my mother found that* "the house is mediocre; the town, small; and only the imagination and nostalgia [for] Proust have given the town, the house and the surroundings significance." *In 1971, she had gone with Maître Misard to a Proust exhibit (which she described as* "very well done"), *and a few years later, she bought* M. Proust, *written by his housekeeper, which she found* "fascinating."

* * *

My mother had been having serious problems with her knees for many years. They hurt more and more, and the deterioration of the right one was causing that leg to go out at an angle. Knee-replacement surgery was recommended for both, which created a certain anxiety, understandably. (How did the doctors know the operation would work? Might she be in excruciating pain for the rest of her life if it failed? What if she could no longer walk?) She spoke to several who had had the operation, and the advice she got was to have the surgery and to do it with Dr. Jean-Pierre Roux at the Clinique Geoffroy-Saint-Hilaire in the 5th arrondissement. Coincidentally, her sister Sue, eleven years her junior, was also planning to have the same operation, but on both knees at once. My mother didn't think this was the best approach for herself, and so in the fall of 1994, at the age of 85, with her two books behind her, she underwent surgery on her left knee (which meant that the steel rods inserted after the 1981 motorcycle accident also had to be dealt with).

Her recovery at the clinic and at home (a physical therapist came almost every day for five weeks) went exceedingly well, and she was ready, she felt, for the right knee six months later. However, this time things did not go smoothly. Almost immediately after the operation, Dr. Roux left on a ten-day holiday, and it quickly developed that the right knee wouldn't bend. My mother was furious, and when the doctor returned, she told him so, saying she had felt abandoned. Two days later, she was placed under anesthesia, and the doctor succeeded in adjusting the knee. However, the pain during the mandatory post-op exercises was very strong;

but she gritted her teeth and persisted. After three weeks, she was taken to a rehabilitation center in the suburb of Courbevoie, where Muriel Merceron, whose office was close by, would visit her on her lunch break. Rosario Etayo also very kindly came several times a week to be with her and to help her. Finally, my mother was allowed to go home. It had been a difficult and wearing experience. She was told to be careful how she got up from a chair, how she sat down, not to fully bend her knees, and never to kneel. These prostheses gave her a new lease on life, as did the cataract operations she had (one eye in 1990; the other, six years later), which reopened a world of vivid color. (I remember her remarking how the yellow in a Van Gogh painting had come alive again for her after years of her seeing the color as gray.)

In 1996, at the age of 87, she was diagnosed with a ductal carcinoma in situ, a very early breast cancer, which can be cured with localized surgery (a lumpectomy) and radiation. After the surgery, she spent a year having weekly outpatient radiation at the Hôpital Sainte-Périne, on the outskirts of the 16th arrondissement, which was not easy for her to reach, requiring two buses, after which she still had a number of blocks to walk. She dutifully went each week, of course, and at the end of the twelve months, was declared cancer free. (However, to prevent recurrence of such growths, she was prescribed a daily dose of a medication.)

* * *

Despite her increasing knee issues over the years, my mother still got to her art exhibits (including Gauguin, Picasso, Van Gogh, Titian, Caravaggio, Fragonard, Bonnard, Renoir, Dali) and had not hesitated to travel. She'd gone to Lille to see her niece/my cousin Marie-José receive her doctorate with a mention of "très bien" (the equivalent of magna cum laude); to Bayeux for the famed tapestry show-ing the lead-up to the Norman conquest of England; to Belle Ile, off the coast of Brittany, to be with Alice Daifuku and her companion Victor Kadani, a former RAF fighter; to Carnac, elsewhere in Brittany, for the Stonehenge-like giant stones dating from 3000 BCE (and possibily 4500 BCE); to Monet's house in Giverny with Tamara Baussan; and to Bad Ragaz, a spa town in Switzerland, to meet up with Blanka and Fred Landau. She took two UNESCO-sponsored group trips, to the Carcassonne/Toulouse area of France and to Holland and Belgium.

Since 1972, she had been going to Haiti almost every year (she missed in 1986, the year Jean-Claude Duvalier was overthrown) and sometimes twice a year, but she ceased doing so after 1989 (at age 80). I wonder if she'd had a pre-monition that 1989 would be her final year in Haiti, for that May she arranged with Lina Assad, who with her husband owned the hotel Villa Créole, to give a tea there for some two dozen lady friends as a way of reciprocating for their invita-tions over the years and as a way of seeing them that year, since during this trip she'd been particularly busy working at the Bibliothèque Nationale. (In fact, Marie-José, who was now back in Port-au-Prince after her years in France, kindly spent several days helping her.) The reason she stopped going to Haiti was probably the unpredictable political situation on the heels of the 1990 election of the priest Jean-Bertrand Aristide to the presidency. Though deposed just a year later and succeeded by a military junta, he returned for another two years (1994–1996) and yet again in 2001 (while acting as a behind-the-scenes "regent" in the intervening years). Throughout these regimes, things remained combustible, and it made little sense for her to find herself in harm's way.

* * *

She kept making her annual trip to the U.S. through 1999, always spending time in New York and in Ohio to see friends and family. In Cleveland, she made a point of visiting her cousin Bill Reithoffer (David's father) from 1987 on, after he suffered a debilitating stroke. In Wooster, she attended her fifty-fifth and sixtieth college reunions, seeing Margaret Guille on both occasions.

In 1985, during her second visit to Los Angeles, my mother had briefly considered retiring to Ojai, California, where Margaretta and Fred Kroll and Peggy and Bill Krauss were now living. But she decided she wasn't yet ready. In

1992, during her last visit to these parts, she looked at retirement communities in Los Angeles and Orange counties. Again she passed on the idea but some years later confided to her friend Nieves Claxton that she thought she'd made a terrible mistake by not moving to California. I think it's natural for elderly parents to want to be geographically close to their child/children. I personally thought my mother would be happier in Paris, surrounded by the people and things she knew, whereas here, despite her facility at making friends, she might have felt alien, since she would have few if any points of reference to the American day-to-day life of the previous thirty-five years. But obviously the decision was hers to make. In retrospect, what I should have proposed was her living in a retirement community in the Los Angeles area for six months, at the end of which she could decide whether she would prefer continuing on the West Coast or returning to Paris. Yet another suggestion could have been maintaining two residences.

During that last stay in L.A., she met my dear friend and Warner Bros. colleague Marilyn Nelson (with whom we had dinner at the Dragon Regency, an excellent restaurant which sadly no longer exists, in Monterey Park [an L.A. suburb]), and saw Ashley Boone and my mother's former Paris nursery-school pupil, Daphne Gronich, who'd become an attorney with 20th Century-Fox.

But after 1999, she was obliged to stop traveling. The pains that had been plaguing her for years in her back, shoulders, and right hip had become too acute for her to tolerate air-port waits, long plane rides, jostling ground transportation, and uncomfortable beds. She had consulted a number of specialists over the years, but there was no cure and no real improvement despite acupuncture, pills, and injections of one kind or another. She was now on morphine tablets, which sometimes worked and at other times didn't. The pain could be excruciating, but she rarely voiced a complaint.

* * *

My mother had never wanted to have a hired hand in the house. She wasn't keen on someone hanging around all day; she worried she'd have to talk to them and feed them. But in the fall of 2001, she reached a compromise with her-self and asked Odile Blondy, the social services contact at UNESCO, to recommend someone to come for several hours three afternoons a week to accompany her on short walks and to do odd neighborhood errands or home chores such as mending. Daniele Bargat was a very nice French woman who came for a while until an accident sidelined her. She was fol-lowed, serendipitously, by a very pretty young Bangladeshi of 27, Taskin Saadat, who was trilingual (her native Bangla, excellent English, and very good French) and whose father was ambassador to France and UNESCO. She was no longer in school, was currently unemployed, and therefore insisted on coming six afternoons a week, although my mother felt Taskin should have weekends to herself. She was very good with my mother and came to regard her like a grandmother.

My mother had others in her support system as well. Rosario Etayo came twice a week: late afternoon Mondays to do the hand-washing and to clean the bathroom and kitchen, and Thursday afternoons to do the general house-cleaning and grocery shopping (for those items like fresh fruit, eggs, yogurt, and cheese that were, understandably, unavailable from the frozen-food company Picard, with which she placed a monthly order for home delivery). The Monday visit always began with the two women having a demitasse of coffee together and a nice chat. The building's "gardienne," Mme Rodriguez (from Spain), stopped in several times a day except Sunday: in midmorning, she would open the heavy metal shutters, get my mother's thigh-high compression stockings and shoes on her (since my mother was not allowed to bend her artificial knees more than a certain degree), and air and then make up her bed; around 6 pm, she popped in to close the shutters; and between 8 and 8:30 pm, she returned to wash the day's dishes, turn down the bed, and remove my mother's stockings. (On Sundays, the shutters remained closed and my mother stockingless.) Around 9:30 pm, Maria Fereira (from Portugal), who lived a few blocks away, would come help my mother with her shower and dry her off. A physical therapist was scheduled for twice a week to work gently on her back, shoulders, and legs, and when needed, her general practitioner (whose office was in the neighborhood) would drop by around 8 pm. (Yes, doctors in France still made house calls!) Fortunately, all these expenses, with the exception of Rosario's, were reimbursed 80% by UNESCO through their generous medical insurance plan, while the remaining 20% was covered by a supplementary insurance policy.

* * *

My mother was in the habit of noting on her calendar each anniversary of my father's death. Twenty years to the day, she was puttering about her bedroom late at night, something she was accustomed to doing, when her left leg went numb. She was in the middle of the room with nothing close at hand to grasp or lean on. She was at a loss as to how to deal with this predicament. She then decided to try to move and in so doing fell, hitting her head either on the dresser or on the carpeted floor. She cried out to the emergency-response folks, and soon Richard Allen was there to pick her up and put her to bed.

I learned all this the next day, a Thursday, on my regular thrice-weekly call to her. I suggested she see a doctor; she declined, saying she was OK, except for a bit of a headache. I phoned on Friday, and she said she still felt all right and had taken her afternoon walk with Taskin, although she was perhaps a bit achy and the headache had gotten worse. On Saturday, July 12, I was later told, she had been out to lunch with Melissa Pereira and Sandy and Richard Allen and in the afternoon had done her customary "constitutional" with Taskin, whom she'd then "dismissed" at 5 pm as usual. Mme Rodriguez came in at 6:30 to close the shutters, and they exchanged a few pleasantries. At 8 pm, Mme Rodriguez returned and found my mother in a coma. Not immediately locating a phone number for the fire station, she ran the fifteen yards or so to the local stationhouse. Unable to revive my mother, the firemen arranged for an ambulance to transport her to the new Georges Pompidou hospital some fifteen minutes away. Mme Rodriguez then had an upstairs neighbor call me. By the time I phoned the hospital's emergency room, my mother had died, of a subdural hematoma caused by her fall.

Chapter Fourteen

For the rest of that day and for the next few, I was on automatic pilot. I made calls to let some people know what had happened. Just as my mother's fall on my father's twentieth anniversary had been one of those odd coincidences, so was the fact that as my mother was being brought to the hospital's emergency room, Muriel Merceron, her best friend in Paris, was upstairs in Intensive Care, having suffered a heart attack the day before. Neither woman knew (or had known) of the other's situation. And, of course, once I told Muriel's husband the news, he rightly opted not to tell his wife for several days for fear of the shock it might cause her. But he did pass word along to someone in Haiti and they on to others, because by the time I phoned Paulette Brandt, she had already heard. The Haitian grapevine at its most efficient.

Richard Allen was picking up a friend at Paris' Charles de Gaulle airport on June 16, the day of my own arrival, and he kindly offered to wait a half-hour longer for me. This was very much a blessing since it provided a comfortable transition to an empty apartment, the first time in forty-seven years that my mother had not been at home when I appeared on the doorstep.

My first priority was to locate a spot for a memorial service, and fortunately, the American Church, just a few blocks away, was accustomed to renting out the nave, as well as a large adjoining room for post-service refreshments. While I spread the word to my mother's friends, Ségolène Lavaud kindly took care of buying food and beverages, which she and her daughter Virginie set out.

Some fifty people attended the service on July 22, including a sizeable contingent from UCA (UNESCO Community Association). I spoke, as did the president of UCA Suzanne Malherbe, followed by Muriel Merceron's husband Frantz. The closed casket stood at the front of the church, with a throw of yellow flowers (my mother's favorite floral color) over it, and was then taken to a mortuary for cremation. This was frankly not an easy decision for me to make, but given the dangerous time Haiti was experiencing, it was the most practical, since I wanted to have my mother and father together in the family vault in Port-au-Prince. I stored the urn in the apartment until my return to Paris in October, at which point, the French funeral home Robelot dealt with the bureaucratic snail's pace and minutiae of getting all the consular (Haitian) approvals for shipping the ashes by air. (The urn, for example, had to be bolted shut, to foil any attempt at placing a gun, say, or a bomb inside it—that's how jumpy the situation in Haiti was at the time.)

When I called Fatboy to let her know my plan for the urn, she asked that a small memorial service be held in Port-au-Prince so she could say goodbye to my mother, whom she had known for seventy-one years. "Your mother was also the last link to my parents; now there's no one left who knew them," she had said to me in July. (Her sister Nicole had died in the 1940s.)

The urn was finally cleared for departure, the Haitian funeral home Pax Villa took possession of it upon arrival (as they had my father's casket twenty years earlier), and my cousin Jehan Henri very kindly organized the small service (complete with more yellow flowers), although he had to wait for a lull in the shootings, which were almost daily occur-rences in Port-au-Prince, before it could actually be held. After the service, he and his older brother Robert thought-fully accompanied the urn to the cemetery and watched while it was placed in the vault. (I had wrestled with going to Haiti but finally chose not to; it would have been a mistake to be caught in the midst of flying bullets.)

I spent a month in Paris after the American Church service to begin settling my mother's affairs. Ségolène was wonder-fully kind, having me over for dinner very often, which gave me a lift at the end of a day of sifting and calling and meet-ing. It had been my intention to hold on to the apartment, *but after a five-week break back in Los Angeles, I realized that doing so made little sense. It was too old to be rented out as is and would have taken approximately $100,000 to properly renovate. (The electrical wiring, for instance, was very fragile, dating, as it did, from 1930. The bathroom and kitchen needed to be completely redone.) If I kept it for my own use for just one month out of the year, I would be spending a considerable sum in monthly maintenance, plus the frequent special assessments for the endless stream of building problems and their repair.*

The French generally don't care for ground-floor units, and the building's outside manager told me the Board would never allow me to sell to a doctor, dentist, or lawyer for professional offices. Therefore, I was extremely lucky when the couple who owned the studio apartment across the hall, which they used as a pied-à-terre, *expressed strong interest in buying. The wife came into town from Fontainebleau for several days out of the week, wanted something larger than her present studio, and preferred to remain in the building. We arrived at an equitable price (at a time when Paris real estate was flying high).*

Thus I spent the next four weeks dismantling forty-seven years of my parents' acquisitions and my memories. I set aside certain things I would have shipped back to Los Angeles for myself, including the Haitian paintings, the 1950s mono-grammed silverware from Macy's, various books, Haitian table linens and mahogany serving pieces, the Luneville and faux Limoges dinnerware, the Baccarat crystal, two carpets, Haitian knickknacks, and the collapsible three-shelf bookcase my mother had found in the rented house in Pacot in 1932.

I offered my mother's friends the opportunity of having one or more keepsakes. Taskin Saadat asked for the sewing kit (my mother had taught her several stitches); Melissa Pereira, for a small angel in glass and metal that she'd brought back from Moscow; and Muriel Merceron, who was an excellent cook, for my mother's cookbook and the "industrial-strength" manual meat grinder (the kind you secure to the edge of a kitchen table like a vise). Nieves Claxton selected a few books and several decorated pillboxes to add to her own collection; Pamela Barabas, a pair of small mahogany bookends in the shape of horses' heads, one of which she placed in her Paris apartment and the other in her co-op on Spain's Costa del Sol (about six miles from where my parents had had theirs in Torremolinos). Noha Akiki, Rosario Etayo, Ségolène Lavaud, and Ida Subaran chose pieces from among her furnishings. My mother's English-language books were donated to the American Library in Paris; those in French, to the library of Paris 7, the university Ségolène and Virginie Lavaud were attending. The rest of her possessions went to Abbé Pierre, an advocate for the homeless whose charity my mother had supported in a modest way.

The sale of the apartment was finalized in January 2004, with Ségolène kindly representing me (so I wouldn't have to make a trip in the dead of winter). It marked the end of our family's living in Paris after nearly fifty years.

* * *

But it was not the end of my mother's dream to gener-ate interest in my father's work. In 2005, Chantalle Verna's doctoral dissertation, Haiti's Second Independence and the Promise of Pan-American Cooperation, *was submitted and accepted. It contained a section about my father, which two years later evolved into a ten-page article titled "Maurice Dartigue, Educational Reform and Intellectual Cooperation with the United States as a Strategy for Haitian National Development 1934–1946" that appeared in the* Journal of Haitian Studies, *a publication of the Haitian Studies Association produced at the University of California at Santa Barbara.*

Now an Associate Professor of History and International Relations at Florida International University in Miami, Dr. Verna will have Cornell University Press publish a forthcom-ing book with the working title Haiti and the Uses of America: Rapprochement Culturel with the United States, 1930–1950 *that will contain material about my father.*

Following that, her plan is for a book, with coauthor Regine Ostine Jackson, about Haitians who worked outside of Haiti, which will include mention of my father's years at

UNESCO and in Africa. Its very tentative working title is Diaspora and Development: Haitian Migration to Congo and Beyond, 1958–1971.

As such, Chantalle has become the leading torch-bearer in disseminating information about my father, for which my mother would have been very, very grateful. And Chantalle is even thinking of including my mother's observations (as they appear in this book's Chapter Six) of the aftermath of Dominican dictator Trujillo's 1937 massacre of Haitians, as part of a work-in-progress she is co-editing for Haiti Reader, *to be published by Duke University Press.*

In 2011, Chantalle introduced me to the Digital Library of the Caribbean (dLOC), an internet undertaking jointly administered by Florida International University and the University of Florida, both in Miami. Its director, Brooke Wooldridge, has had the French and English versions of my mother's book about my father—Un Haïtien exceptionnel Maurice Dartigue *and* An Outstanding Haitian, Maurice Dartigue—*digitized, and they can be found at dLOC.com (where one then enters the name Maurice Dartigue). Furthermore, Brooke and the Gottesman Libraries of Teachers College (TC) have come to an agreement that will provide the dLOC with access to materials my mother donated to TC in the Eighties so that a selection can be added to the dLOC site. (Other than the microfiche,TC digitized its complete Maurice Dartigue Collection, as well as the eight articles appearing in Haitian newspapers on the heels of her 1935 speech on women's* education in Haiti, the seven early education articles she wrote between 1958 and 1970, and the pieces that ran in the three editions of the Association France-Haïti's Bulletin.)

The libraries of Teachers College and the College of Wooster, as well as the American Library in Paris and CIDIHCA in Montreal, have agreed to receive a copy of the present book, and it will be offered, too, to the Schomburg, dLOC, and Saint-Louis de Gonzague in Haiti. Copies will also be going to the handful of people who were so helpful to David Reithoffer during his trip to Transylvania. This would, I think, especially please my mother, because it brings her life full circle, back to where it all began.

This book is presently available in paperback at the publisher's own website, CreateSpace.com/3893479, and at Amazon.com (including its outlets in England, France, Germany, Italy, and Spain). Later this year, I plan to have a website that displays images of some of my parents' published works, as well as short bios, CVs, and a selection of photographs, accessible through www.dartigue.com, www. estherdartigue.com, and www.mauricedartigue.com.

* * *

The twelve months beginning December 2002 through November 2003 took their toll on the Reithoffers. Rose Reithoffer Hawley died in December 2002, at 92. Katherine

Reithoffer Knesper died in August 2003, at 97, a month after my mother, at 94. Thus the three sisters born in Hungary all passed away within eight months of each other, in ascending order. And then Sue Reithoffer Rose suddenly died in November 2003, at 84. It meant that the surviving brothers Art and John lost all four sisters within the space of a year. And then in March 2010, Art passed away, at 95.

* * *

When, in 1931, my mother disembarked in Haiti, she was leaving behind a world she'd known for nearly twenty years and entering one about which she knew nothing. But she did so without a moment's hesitation or hint of reluctance. She glided easily, fluidly into Haitian life. She fully embraced this new land, to such a degree that years later, Jacqueline Pereira recounted, "Max Sam, a former professor of mine in Port-au-Prince, was enormously complimentary about your mother. He told me one day, 'Mme Dartigue est sincèrement plus haïtienne que les haïtiens' ('Mrs. Dartigue is sincerely more Haitian than the Haitians')."

Too, when she boarded ship in New York, she was, economically and socially speaking, low man on the totem pole. Five days later, she was still poor but was catapulted to near the top of the social stratum, for my father had an excellent name, which counted for a great deal.

For any number of reasons, my father was fortunate in his choice of life partner. He had found someone with no airs or pretensions, an easy mixer regardless of the level of society, up for challenges, and accustomed to being thrifty. My mother was a great believer in my father and in his work, always supportive and fiercely loyal. Plus, she was madly in love with him, and he with her.

My mother was proud of the three countries of which she was a citizen at one time or another—Hungary, the United States, and Haiti—and although she was officially only one thing at any given time, she carried strong feelings about the other two within her. As for France, where she spent forty-seven years of her life, more than anywhere else, (though none of it as a citizen), she'd said in the Errant Page that she enjoyed living in Paris. However, she wasn't a complete fan, for the French tended to keep people at arm's distance and the bureaucracy was generally insane.

Over the course of her years, she attempted eight languages—Hungarian, English, French, German, Creole, Spanish, Italian and probably a bit of Kirundi (the official language of Burundi)—and succeeded with four-and-a-half, finally settling in at three-and-a-half. (The half was Spanish, and for a while the fourth was Hungarian until it faded away, probably in her thirties.)

She wasn't kidding when, in the first chapter of this book, she said that she'd never gotten over Romania's annexation of Transylvania. In the late 1990s, at a follow-up medical appointment, she encountered two interns with her doctor. She said to one, "I know where you're from; you're Chinese. But," turning to the second, "I can't tell about you." "I'm from Romania," he said. "Ah, well, I hate you," she blurted, then smiled and explained about the two million Hungarians in 1920. The doctor and his interns were, however, stunned in the face of such bluntness.

But she was just naturally frank—"That's one of the things I liked about her," both Ghislaine Rouzier Ruas and Jacqueline Perreira told me separately. (Jacqueline was an exception [probably the result of her being raised outside of France], because most French are unused to plainspokenness which they consider rude and to which there is usually a noticeable recoil.) But when my mother spoke, it was never to hurt anyone; it was an unconscious desire to get to the core, to the truth of something.

She loved Christmas, Easter, and Thanksgiving, celebrating them each year without fail. She always put up a tree, for many years a fresh one, but later a good fake (that Noha Akiki had encouraged her to buy from Auchan, one of France's answers to Walmart, and that Noha transported by car to the apartment). My mother decorated her trees with lights, balls, and tinsel we'd brought with us from the States, some of it dating back to 1946 (and that I would occasionally replace). There was also a copy each of [The] Night Before Christmas *and* The Children's Story of Jesus, *in large format and illustrated, as well as a book of carols with music* and lyrics, all of them placed under the tree (with a bit of Scotch tape added from time to time). (The three publications were from the very early to mid-1940s.) My mother loved hearing carols, and if she couldn't find them on the BBC (radio), she would sing from the book. At Easter, she colored at least a dozen eggs and then gave them to friends. Sometimes Melissa Perreira would join in the coloring. (Both Christmas and Easter no doubt took her back to her earliest days, in Hungary.) At Thanksgiving, there was always a dinner with many of the traditional trimmings (usually on the weekend, since the French, understandably, didn't celebrate the holiday). In the early years of our living in Paris, turkeys were hard to come by, and I think she relied on a thoughtful American mother in her nursery school to get one for her at the Army PX. In later years, some of the French grocery stores stocked them.

A mini-tradition developed in the 1990s. Eliane Laraque received every Christmas a crock of real foie gras. She would bring it over to the house, where we each had a piece. At the end of dinner, she'd take another slice home and leave the rest with us. My mother and I were very happy at this annual windfall.

Beginning with our arrival in Paris, good food and my mother became fast soul mates. It's not to say that every restaurant meal she had was a triumph, but those that were good were delicious. There were, for instance, the visits to Saulieu, a twelve-course meal in Strasbourg that I recall, and the heavy cream scooped onto a plate of wild strawberries, generously sugared from a shaker, at Sous l'Olivier, just off the Champs-Elysées. (Unfortunately, it no longer exists.) In later years, she developed a passion for both soft-shell crab Chinese-style and hot pastrami sandwiches, and since in the Eighties and Nineties she tended to go to New York when the former were in season, she would feast on them a number of times during her stay and never failed to go to the Carnegie Deli at least once for the latter.

She was curious about unfamiliar foods and could thus be adventurous in what she ordered or sampled. At a Chinese Embassy reception in the 1960s, she spotted "one-hundred-year-old eggs" (as they are variously called). She'd always heard about them and had been determined one day to have one. Here was her chance, which she seized, took a bite—and couldn't wait to rid herself of it and the rest. She had to admit that she had finally met her Waterloo.

She was indefatigable and moved at a clip. Jean Benjamin, who had plenty of energy herself, shook her head in dismay as my mother outpaced anyone she was walking with. Was she in an unconscious competition to see who could get somewhere first, or could she just not control her speed? To me there's little doubt that it was the latter—and it probably propelled her through life—since one of her favorite verbs was to race. In describing what she might have done during a day, she might say that she had raced to get theater tickets, or raced to the pharmacy, or raced over to an exhibit.

She rarely described herself as walking (unless she were just taking a stroll); the slowest she ever seemed to be was trotting off somewhere.

Although she had briefly belonged to the Women's League of Social Action in Haiti in 1935, my mother wasn't a feminist in the classic movement sense, but she certainly was in a universal sense. She believed in women's and girls' rights, starting with her own. When she left home at age 11, she was regaining her right not to be exploited at home (with those dreadful chores, that, yes, someone needed to do but not a young child!) and her right not to be beaten. She was also exercising her right to pursue an education and to determine her own future.

Her concern for women's rights continued throughout her life. In 1999, at the age of 90, she wrote to her friend Patricia Tsien about the plight of divorced spouses of UN employees. These were women who'd stood by their husbands for years while the latter worked at the UN (or UNESCO or wherever), were suddenly divorced, and at the husband's death received no survivor benefits. "We feel these women," my mother said, "have a right [to a pension] that the UN has neglected," and asked Mrs. Tsien for her help as an honorary board member of AFICS, the UN organization in New York representing the interests of former workers and retirees. Two years earlier, another of my mother's friends, Austin Atherley, in her capacity as president of UCA (UNESCO Community Association), had addressed a letter to the UN

Joint Staff Pensions Board in New York to lend UCA's support to this matter, and along with Shari Rajah, Rosita Armerding and my mother, also lobbied the UNESCO Staff Unions, the Retired Persons Association, and the Personnel Department. They got lots of promises, Austin told me in a recent e-mail, but never any action. (Unbelievably, it would take another fourteen years before the blockheadedness of the UN would understand the importance and necessity for change.)

In a similar situation, my mother invested many, many hours, both in Paris and Port-au-Prince, in securing for her friend Serge Defly the monthly pension to which he was enti-tled from the Haitian government (but which the government seemed reluctant to part with, until my mother intervened). As Ti Robert Nadal said to me in an e-mail years later, "Your mother fought for what she thought was right and good."

She did what she did because she was also generous and caring, willing to be of help if she could. An early memory of mine from Haiti is her patiently holding and occasionally stroking a friend who was suffering— we now know (but no one at the time did)—from post-partum depression. The friend spent hours crying and crying, unable to stop, while my mother sought to soothe her. In Paris in the 1970s, she occasionally had tea with an older neighbor from the floor above, who some years later fell ill and was bedridden. My mother took to spending time with her, until the inevitable. One day, she met an American woman in a Paris café who was staying in a very cheap hotel that lacked bathing facilities.

My mother invited her over to take a shower and gave her lunch. I doubt that she ever heard from the woman again, but that wasn't the point. If she received a call from someone just arrived in town, she might well ask them to drop by for lunch or dinner. She agreed to see friends of friends as a way of their having a contact in Paris, and invariably she had them over for a meal. Occasionally, my mother and the other person hit it off well. Case in point was Dellie (Sydelle) Bloom, a very close friend of Jean Benjamin's, whom my mother found "very interesting" and would see when she visited with Jean during her subsequent trips to the States.

My mother always worked in some capacity—whether paid or unpaid—from foraging for firewood as a child to keeping my father's flame alive until the end of her life. It was all work, a lot of it hard work, and she rarely had any down time in all of her nearly ninety-five years. But then, she would have never wanted to be idle; she was well aware that she would have been bored silly doing nothing. For my mother was a doer; she had that can-do quality normally associated with Americans (but that exists the world over). It was something I believe both Mlle Vincent in Haiti and Mme Herbinière-Lebert in Paris recognized in her and that drew them to her. (Of course they were both doers themselves.) If something had to get done, no task was too menial since my mother had probably done 'em all, from scrubbing floors to boiling diapers. She had years of organizing and cooking experience behind her that served her well at Thorland, during my father's ministry, and in home entertaining wherever she and my father were. In preparing for an official cocktail gathering in Haiti in the 1940s, for example, my mother could be found trimming tea sandwiches. Was it to save my father money, or did she feel she could do a better job than the assembled help, or did the job need doing and no one else was free? Some guests tsk-tsked behind their hands on seeing or hearing about what she was up to, but she didn't care. Exactly what was the problem if she hacked off crusts? All she asked was that people stay out of her way so she could get the task done and move on to the next because inevitably there was always a next.

Over time, she watched hours and hours of concerts, opera, and ballet on France's classical-music TV channels. The only appointment-TV she cared about happened twice a year: the New Year's Day performance of the Vienna Philharmonic Orchestra, direct from the Austrian capital, and the tennis matches of the French Open, broadcast from the Roland Garros stadium on the edge of Paris.

One of the first questions she invariably posed in meeting someone new was "Where did you go to school?" It wasn't out of nosiness or snobbery; it was that education was so important to her that she couldn't wait to know.

In fact, she was the furthest thing from a snob, although occasionally someone might mistakenly think of her in that way. Because she'd lived outside the U.S. for more than two-thirds of her life, she had little reference to the American everyday; but since she was bright, gregarious, and inquisitive and enjoyed being in a conversation, she was likely to invoke what she knew: her day-to-day life in Paris, experiences connected to Haiti and UN/UNESCO, teaching, her travels, reading, and her interest in so many other subjects.

She did not care at all for flattery and disliked it when people were overly solicitous. She at times displayed a no-nonsense quality that might be intimidating to some. But she also loved to laugh, and around the house she might suddenly burst into short spurts of song.

It was Sylvia Washington Bâ who first made me realize how unintentionally amusing and occasionally eccentric my mother could be. Before that, I may have cringed or failed to see the humor; but after the revelation, Sylvia and I would have a good laugh—not at my mother, but at the situation, which often involved the French who served as unwitting foils to her straightforward approach. That in turn opened my eyes to what she'd done with her life, and it led to an appreciation and admiration. She was really a very interesting person to be around and a very interesting character, in the best sense of the word.

When she left home at the age of 11, she'd had time to establish a solid connection with her siblings born in Hungary (although in time the ties would weaken and break). Of the American generation, however, Art was five, Betty two, Sue just a year old, and Johnny would not come along for another four years. Yet in the latter part of her life especially, until the pains in her back and shoulders prevented her from travel, she tried hard to maintain a bond between herself and her younger brothers and sisters. She and Betty, for instance, although separated by geography for most of their lives, were extremely close.

Did the little girl who set out in 1920, armed only with her intelligence, determination, and fearlessness, know where the road would lead and how much ground she would cover— that there would be, for example, a fifteen-year adventure in a place called Haiti, where she would comfortably rub elbows with peasants and presidents, poets and politicians? And that there would be a lifetime romance with a tall, dark, handsome man she would meet along the way? Hardly! She only knew that she wanted an education and that going it alone was the way she had to do it.

One gets a sense of this determination when one con-siders how she pursued getting the books about my father done: she just persisted, refusing to give up. It helped, too, that she possessed what Jacqueline Pereira said was "an iron will."

Her story is like that of the little engine that could. It serves as an example of and inspiration for what a young person can do who has the motivation and grit to overcome surmountable obstacles through inner resources, luck, and sometimes outside help, and to just forge ahead, an apt expression of how my mother dealt with what she encoun-tered in life.